"What this book does is see through the superficial question of 'What path are you following?' to reveal the crucial one which is 'What is the purpose of your spiritual practice?' David Cooper seems clear that we practice in order to reconnect with the kindness and compassion which is our essential nature."

Sylvia Boorstein, co-founder of Spirit Rock Meditation Center

"*Entering the Sacred Mountain* can help you find a map for your own vision quest. It points to the higher possibilities that allow East and West to live in one heart in the sacred Presence."

Zalman M. Schachter-Shalomi, *Aleph Alliance for Jewish Renewal*

"*Entering the Sacred Mountain* is an excellent resource for spiritual seekers. The author's exciting odyssey proves that each person can tailor retreats and spiritual practices to the specific nature of his or her own soul."

Values & Visions

"Cooper takes the bold step of allowing the practice of Buddhist Insight Meditation to blend with his practice of Judaism in a manner that enriches both traditions and moves the reader to a greater insight into their shared silence."

Rami M. Shapiro, *Parabola*

ENTERING

THE

SACRED

MOUNTAIN

EXPLORING THE MYSTICAL
PRACTICES OF JUDAISM,
BUDDHISM, AND SUFISM

❧

RABBI DAVID A. COOPER

BELL TOWER

NEW YORK

Published by Bell Tower, an imprint of Harmony Books, a division of
Crown Publishers, Inc., 201 East 50th Street, New York, New York 10022.
Member of the Crown Publishing Group
Originally published by Bell Tower in 1994

Random House, Inc. New York, Toronto, London, Sydney, Auckland

Bell Tower and colophon are trademarks of Crown Publishers, Inc.

Manufactured in the United States of America

Library of Congress Cataloging-in-Publication Data
Cooper, David A., 1939–
Entering the sacred mountain : exploring the mystical practices of
Judaism, Buddhism, and Sufism / by David A. Cooper
1. Cooper, David A., 1939– 2. Mysticism. 3. Religious biography—
United States. I. Title.
BL73.C654A3 1994 93-34025
291.4'22' 092—dc20 CIP [B]

ISBN 0-517-88464-X

10 9 8 7 6 5 4 3 2 1

First Paperback Edition 1995

CONTENTS

సౌ

INTRODUCTION

My earlier works, *Silence, Simplicity, and Solitude* and *The Heart of Stillness*, are guides to help people discover their inner voice through the process of spiritual retreat. Many readers of these books have asked about my personal journey, and I have found that the telling of my own background has often provided vital insight for others.

People study the world's wisdom traditions for inspiration and guidance, but often these teachings are lofty or inaccessible, implying the necessity for superhuman efforts. However, as we gain more direct individual experience with wisdom teachings that have been transmitted over many centuries, ordinary people like you and me give each other permission and encouragement to explore our own inner realms—and the results are extraordinary. We are able to have similar experiences to those described by spiritual seekers for thousands of years. The more we have our own experiences, the more we validate the potential for human beings across the planet. We are all mystics on one level or another—and now we are discovering that our capability for individual spiritual growth may be limitless.

One of our main tasks as we enter into the domain of mystics and illuminated beings is to learn how to discern the difference between extravagance and honest reporting, poetic license and faithful rendition, fiction and truth. This is not an easy job, because whereas the material world lends itself to physics, chemistry, biology, and other sciences that have methods to observe and test things, the mystical plane is metaphysical, subjective, and unverifiable. So we are left to wonder: Did this person really experience such profound states of mind, and if so was he or she a special being with a gift for attaining something beyond the reach of mortals, or is this level of awareness something available to all of us?

The best we can do is appraise our own experiences honestly and share these with each other in the hope that our collective knowledge will open the gates to these mysterious realms. My own discovery has been that almost all limits of spiritual inquiry are self-imposed; we need only be aware of the experience of someone with whom we can identify to break out of these imaginary limits into a world of indescribable potential.

I once sailed my small sloop from the Virgin Islands to Newport, Rhode Island, stopping at Bermuda. It was my first ocean-sailing experience, and I was the skipper. When we arrived at Bermuda, my engine began spouting water in all directions, and I knew we were in serious trouble. The boat sat at the dock for many days while I pondered how I was going to deal with this crisis. I needed a working engine to continue the voyage, but I had only forty dollars in my pocket, and this was already allocated for other, necessary supplies.

I had never had any technical training. When I purchased this boat in St. Thomas, my mechanical education could be summed up in my ability to change the oil. I had learned about engines as I began to maintain my boat, but solving this problem seemed beyond my capabilities. One day a stranger came on board, diagnosed what was wrong, and then looked at me and said the magic words: "You can do it." In those brief moments I felt myself change from an inept, bumbling, all-thumbs dimwit to a self-confident, methodical, skillful mechanic. I tore apart the entire engine, replaced the damaged freeze plug—a fifty-cent item—and then reassembled everything in its proper working condition. The simplest lessons in life are the most profound: "You can do it." Almost twenty years after this event, I continue to carry that damaged freeze plug on my key chain as a constant reminder.

The idea that "You can do it" is at the core of many changes that have taken place during the last two centuries, and particularly in the last thirty years. Our current trend toward democratization not only is happening in government, politics, business, and social values; it also is a noticeable phenomenon in the world of spiritual inquiry.

Sharing my personal account in a way that will encourage others is the incentive for this book. Fortunately, I have kept journals during dozens of retreats—short retreats of a few days, and longer sessions that lasted between forty and a hundred days. These notes consolidate the best instruction offered by a wide variety of teachers and include guidance regarding the enlightening process gleaned from hundreds of books. I do not wish to imply that retreats of forty to a hundred days are necessary for spiritual work—most people do not have the time for this—but that whatever spiritual practice one undertakes, the potential for attaining new levels of awareness is probably greater than most people imagine.

Many spiritual teachings have endured for centuries because of their intrinsic truth—a truth that penetrates to the essence of the soul. These teachings touch us deeply when we encounter them in our normal frame of mind; but when we spend extended periods on silent retreat—or when we engage in other serious spiritual exercises—we often enter different states of consciousness, and then these truths have the power to shatter and transform lives.

This book, then, is designed to communicate my retreat experiences over a twelve-year period and to show how dramatically they affected my wife and me as our spiritual lives deepened. Each chapter describes part or all of a retreat. Each retreat is like a voyage into unexplored terrain, and each has its own personality. Retreats often take us on strange adventures, filled with visions and fantasies, bizarre dreams and impassioned mind states.

I have been selective in excerpting from these diaries. Frankly, the choices were difficult to make. I was concerned that the reader might think a selection was pretentious or petty. Moreover, as distinctive mind states develop during intense inner work, there are both extraordinary visions of light and episodes on the edge of madness.

The major question was whether I should offer an ideal model for spiritual adventurers, or reveal the many twists and turns along the way, the self-deluded thinking, wild flashes of insight, and exotic voyages into mysterious worlds. With some trepidation I have opted for the latter. It exposes—and, I hope, will help readers avoid—many possible pitfalls. Throughout this book, the extracts from my journals—edited for clarity—are shown in italics.

I do not wish to give the impression that I have attained something unique, that I have been blessed with an unusual talent, or that I am graced with profound awareness. None of these things is true. I have spoken with a significant number of committed meditators who have had equally interesting incidents in their ongoing spiritual explorations.

Many inexperienced people are under the impression that the wonderful visions evoked by deep meditation are a goal of the process. It turns out, however, as readers will discover, that most of the visualizations and connections with other realms that I had during the initial stages of my spiritual work were actually diversions from the development of deeper awareness.

As was noted in my earlier books, some people are fortunate enough to have a personal teacher. But most of us must rely on our inner voice to urge us along and help us avoid dangerous sidetracks and dead ends. My own guide has been a marvelous navigator. I am often slow to get the message, but I have come to appreciate the presence of this guide—and recognize it in every person I meet.

Our inner guide works in obscure ways; most of the time we are oblivious to it. Throughout history, human beings have posed the question, Do things happen at random, or is there an unseen hand that prods and continuously tests us? Mystics do not ask this question; they believe that nothing is random and everything fits together in an astonishing structure of enormous intricacy. It is not necessary to see how each piece fits, but rather to appreciate the nature of the process. Indeed, the essence of the spiritual path is to find meaning in the most minute details of life.

There is a long history of spiritual biographies, but this book attempts to be quite different. Others tend to follow a traditional religion and are loyal to its teachings or doctrines. This book meanders through a number of paths—Sufi, Jewish, Buddhist—yet it maintains a universal perspective throughout. Many other biographical accounts are about the lives of monks, nuns, saints, or gurus. This book is about a couple of average people who at a certain point in their lives are "called," and they walk away from security and comfort into an unknown world—for reasons that are not easily articulated. Finally, other stories are usually about one person's journey, while this journal is about two people traveling a spiritual path arm in arm.

This book is a treasure map, but not like any you have seen before. Most people believe that the object of a treasure hunt is to find a chest of gold. The mystical approach, however, is that the search itself is the treasure. Each step is its own reward, continuously reinforcing and expanding our awareness, rapidly bringing us to new levels. Here is an affirmation of the potential of this process, and an invitation to begin an exploration of the treasure fields of your own mind. This journey into the interior of the sacred mountain of spiritual inquiry is the most exciting and rewarding adventure you will ever take.

Lord, who shall abide in your tent?
Who shall dwell in your sacred mountain?
He that walks in simplicity, acts justly,
and speaks the truth in his heart.

Psalm 15:1-2

SUFISM

AND

JUDAISM

1

> *"Whoever walks four cubits [six feet] in the land of Israel is
> assured of a place in the world to come."*
> Talmud, *Ketubot* 111a.

The passenger boat *Birgena,* flying a Greek flag, steamed into Haifa
harbor on a balmy September day in 1981. Shoshana and I
watched from the deck in silence as we slipped past the breakwater.
The port buildings and loading cranes along the piers had an aura
of bland grayness, but the Carmel hills in the background were
lovely and welcoming, greeting us with rounded, maternal tenderness. When the boat docked, we went to our tiny cabin, looked at
each other, and simultaneously burst into tears.

Earlier in the year, we had been married. Shoshana had changed
her name from Susan at the time of her conversion to Judaism, just
before the wedding. One of our friends, who was a rug merchant,
decorated a large, dilapidated barn near our home in Virginia with a
lavish display of Oriental rugs, and the community joined us in Sufi
dancing and singing at the beginning of the ceremony to invoke be-
neficent and friendly spirits. Rabbi Zalman Schachter-Shalomi was
present to perform the religious rites, having traveled to our tiny
town of Batesville from his home in Philadelphia.

In a traditional Jewish wedding, the bride circles the groom
seven times when she first joins him under the *chuppah* (the wedding canopy). I had written a brief guide for wedding guests, ex-
plaining how during this ritual, souls unite on seven levels of
creation, but Shoshana and I were still unprepared for the impact
of the experience. Later, at midnight, as we sat by the fireplace in
our honeymoon suite, enjoying fresh fruit and wedding cake, we

discovered that both of us had felt a mysterious union at that moment of circling under the *chuppah*—in fact, Shoshana had almost
fainted from the power of the experience. Although we had already
been together for six years, a new level had been reached: Something unfathomable happens in the soul realms when people join
in matrimony.

After the wedding, we spent four months attending to important
business matters, and then we departed on a delayed honeymoon.
The first month of this honeymoon was spent in Europe, but our
primary goal was a two-month visit to Israel to explore the possibility of making it our home.

After the boat docked, passengers waited in long lines, talking
excitedly among themselves, while passport and customs officials
sauntered to their makeshift desks. Each of them carried a coffee
cup and cigarette as if trained in the ritual of nonchalance, calcu-
lated to increase the tension and anxiety of the excited passengers.
We remained in anticipation, herded into sweaty holding areas,
while the officers sipped from their cups and slowly, methodically
arranged instruments of bureaucratic torture—thick computer lists,
documents, ink pads, and rubber stamps.

After an hour and a half it was our turn to creep into this maze. I
discerned the first hint of trouble when one of the officers double-
checked a dog-eared computer printout, looked up at me curiously,
and took my passport to one of his seniors standing behind the long
row of tables now cluttered with disheveled stacks of paper.

They directed us to a large couch in the back of the cabin, and
proceeded to grill us together and separately for two hours. Had
we ever been to Israel before? Where were we born? Is there anyone here who could vouch for us? Where were we before we came
here? Did we speak Hebrew? Where were we in 1979? Were we
certain that we were not recently in Israel? And thus it continued
from one interrogator to another. The Haifa police showed up,
lending an even more ominous tone to the process. They scruti-
nized us, added new questions to the list, and then went to make
international telephone calls and run more data through a computer. We waited.

The entire line of passengers cleared passport control and customs. We sat alone in the large cabin, accompanied by people in
various shades of uniform blue and gray. Another hour went by
before a police officer explained to us that someone with my name

was wanted for a crime that had been committed in the Negev a couple of years earlier. The officials had to be convinced that I was not that person. They had finished their investigation, and we were now free to go—sorry for the delay.

Sunset and sunrise in the Holy Land penetrate the soul. Phantoms and angels dance on the edge of shadows, casting a reflection of other worlds, causing everything in sight to shimmer in surrealistic patterns of color and shade. Even the darkest alcoves seem to emanate an ephemeral glow.

Recently I learned a Jewish mystical teaching that the first appearance of the Torah, when Moses was on Mount Sinai, was an all-encompassing white fire, a blinding light, which represented the mind of God, so to speak. Black fire appeared in this white fire, forming the four letters of the tetragrammaton, the unpronounceable name of God. Moses looked at the four letters and could make nothing out of them. Suddenly, tens of thousands of letters streamed forth, swirling into an unending line of black fire on white fire. Still Moses did not comprehend.

The letters became joined into words, with spaces separating them; but even this Moses could not understand. Finally, after many organizations and reorganizations of words into different patterns, Moses recognized the opening line of the Torah, which is usually translated: "In the beginning God created heaven and earth." This was finally the human edition of the Torah, written at a level that we could comprehend.

Dark letters hide light; behind each letter is a multitude of mysteries. The sages say that everything we see in the universe is like a dark fire that conceals a white fire within—every molecule or atom is like a letter of a word spoken by the Divine. Thus even shadows, or the darkest night, are permeated with light—if we could but see. It is not the kind of light we know from the sun. It is a primeval form, the first light of Creation, with which Adam could see to the ends of the universe.

The sages also believed that Jerusalem was endowed with a super-abundance of this mysterious elementary light. Perhaps geologists or meteorologists would have another explanation, but whatever it is, most people agree there is a special ambience in Jerusalem. An emanation pours forth, especially noticeable in the light of dusk or dawn, and an awesome yet perfectly serene power pervades the entire city—its

*presence caresses something within, and there is a sense of dwelling in
the interior chambers of holiness. The ancient rabbis taught: "He who
has not seen Jerusalem in her splendour has never seen a desirable city
in his life."[1] They also said: "Ten [portions] of beauty descended to the
world: nine were taken by Jerusalem and one by the rest of the world."[2]*

We went directly from the port of Haifa to Jerusalem, to connect
with one of our few contacts in Israel—a casual acquaintance developed at a weekend retreat in Pennsylvania a year earlier. When
he and his family heard that we would be coming for an extended
visit, they arranged for us to sublease an apartment but insisted we
be their guests for the first week—which happened to be the week
of Rosh Hashanah, the Jewish New Year.

This was our introduction to the life-style of a Jewish family
involved in serious traditional practice. We arrived at their home
Friday afternoon, a few hours before sundown brought in the Sabbath. In a gentle but firm manner, we received a few simple direc-
tives concerning the Sabbath restrictions, which turned out to be
an abbreviated outline of a complex body of laws and customs that
require years of study to perfect.

The family accompanied us to a small building not far from their
home where people assembled every Friday evening at sundown to
welcome the Sabbath. In the West, most Jewish congregations
meet in synagogues; in Jerusalem, although many synagogues are
active, hundreds of small prayer houses fill the city, many of which
are reminiscent of gathering places in the "old country" known as
shtibls. The *shtibl* was used for prayer and study, but it was also the
social center and communication hub of the community.

The modest *shtibl* our friends frequented was at the end of a narrow, winding street. As we walked past the diminutive, ramshackle
homes and crumbling stone walls, my sense of time began to distort.
This neighborhood had probably not changed in generations—perhaps it had even looked this way at the turn of the century. The most
powerful time shock occurred when we arrived at the unpretentious
shtibl—as we passed over the threshold, like Alice through the looking glass, we entered eighteenth-century Poland.

The men wore black satin caftans that reached below the knees.
They had *shtreimels,* thick, wide hats, trimmed around the circum-
ference with luxurious fur. Although they were dressed in black,
their cheeks and eyes glowed in the soft light, and the entire room

reflected a mood of contained but obvious joy. All of the men had beards of various dimensions, from meager outcroppings on teenagers to bushy expanses on wrinkled faces; some beards reached down far enough to rest on rotund bellies.

The women sat in a back room, separated from the men by lace curtains. At one point, I glanced between a split in the curtains and noticed a number of women gathered around Shoshana. She had covered her hair with a scarf, wore a long-sleeved blouse, and looked as though she had been doing this for years. The women laughed and chatted in a mixture of languages, hardly any of which Shoshana understood. Later, she told me that she felt welcomed and completely at home despite the enormous cultural differences.

There were only about two dozen men in the congregation. Each of them, including the young boys and a man who needed assistance to walk, came over to shake my hand, many with the greeting "*Sholem aleichem*" ("Peace unto you"). I had learned earlier the response "*Aleichem sholem*" ("And unto you, peace"), and some took this as an invitation to begin a conversation in Hebrew or Yiddish, but they soon realized the futility of this exercise. Despite the language barrier, however, it was clear that Shoshana and I were being invited to meals for the upcoming week.

There are three festive meals every Sabbath, and two every holiday. As Rosh Hashanah is a two-day holiday, when we counted the Sabbath meals at either end of the week, there were going to be ten major meal gatherings during the next eight days. We enjoyed a number of these festive occasions with our hosts, but a half dozen were spent with families we met for the first time at the dining table. A number of these families had roots in Israel that reached back to immigrants who had arrived seven to ten generations earlier. Very few of the adults spoke English, but often a student was at the table to translate.

Almost all the families lived in tiny, sparsely furnished apartments. Invariably, the heart-center of each home was the dining table, beautifully arranged. The meals were lavish, but the menus were similar: gefilte fish, chicken noodle soup, roast chicken, noodle or potato *kugel* (casserole), and usually *cholent*—a thick meat-and-bean stew. The sages teach that everyone receives an extra soul on holy days, including the Sabbath. Whenever anyone mildly protested about the amount of food he or she had been served, the housewives—smiling with the gentle concern of Jewish mothers—

invariably said that the added food was to be certain each person's extra soul would be properly nourished.

Later we learned that all of our host families were poor. Typically, they spend their entire food budget on Sabbath meals—the rest of the week is for leftovers. When holidays appear, such as Rosh Hashanah, they have a separate budget, which builds from an exceptionally frugal life-style. I noticed that guests were often given the meaty portions of the chickens, while the family received necks and wings.

The discussion at these tables revolved around the Torah, the Sabbath, or the meaning of current holy days. The political scene in Israel was never mentioned. The economic situation, with inflation in those days running over one hundred percent a year, was not discussed. These homes had no television sets, and movies were not considered healthy experiences. If anyone spoke about sports, he or she would be considered an ignoramus. There was hardly any discussion of other people in the community, for even the most innocuous comments were considered to be gossip. And there were only cryptic references to major world events, which, for the most part, were not considered interesting subjects. Yet conversation at these meals was never dull; moreover, the mental and spiritual nourishment was as satisfying as the food itself.

But it was the children who impressed us the most. They not only often led the boisterous singing that was an integral part of many wonderful meals, they were bright, respectful, and bubbling over with questions and answers that had been learned during the previous week of religious study. Many of the meals we attended had discussions of considerable depth about the meaning of the biblical events and commandments. Participants between ages five and eighty-five spoke with and questioned each other as study partners rather than playing out parent- or grandparent-child roles. Those roles were clearly defined, however, and in any activity except discussing Torah, there was no question as to the seat of authority.

The desert creeps into the city in the early morning hours. A soft, warm breeze begins soon after the muezzin sound the Arabic call to morning prayer from loudspeakers atop tall parapets. The heralding voices echo from the many mountains surrounding the city, blending into a strange cacophony that seems in perfect harmony. We learn in science that the approaching warmth of the sun is the cause of the morning wind, but for me the wind in Jerusalem is vitalized through this call to God and inspired by God's answer. Dawn is an eternal mystery provoking the soul.

During Rosh Hashanah, I experienced the haunting sound of the ram's horn—the shofar—trumpeting from all parts of the city. It is a call directly to the All-Knowing, they say, replicating the cry Sarah uttered when she had a vision that her son Isaac was about to be slaughtered by his father, Abraham. It is also taught that the sound of the shofar confuses the heavenly prosecutor whose job it is to see that we are paid in kind for all of our misdeeds. Rosh Hashanah is one of the rare times, like a bubble in the ocean of cosmic justice, when the flow of cause and effect can be interrupted and our life-path redirected, as if a switch is thrown and we forever follow a different track.

One other time in my life I heard a sound like the shofar. I was sailing out of St. Thomas harbor in the spring of 1975 on my thirty-five-foot teak sloop Tawi, *embarking on a blue-water initiation, to navigate northward to Bermuda and then on to Maine, sailing far out to sea, at times a thousand miles from the closest land. A friend who skippered the large, beautiful schooner* Te Amo *stood on his poop deck like the ancient mariner, and blew long, wailing groans on a conch shell, inviting the gods of wind and sea to accompany us safely to our next port. I used to belittle rituals like these; but strangely the sound vibrated within me during the weeks of the voyage, and especially when we were in danger of foundering in a Gulf Stream storm.*

Our lives in Jerusalem's religious community seem to lure us into a different plane of existence. Issues that used to matter have no meaning; questions that previously never arose now become dominant preoccupations. God seems to be on everybody's mind. Each thought and action is cause for reflection; the lunar calendar attunes us to a cosmic harmony of kabbalistic significance. The week's focal point is the Sabbath—the remaining days seem almost inconsequential, even though they are filled by a constant flow of new ideas through the study of Torah, Talmud, and hasidic teachings. This community is complete unto itself, and there is little interest in joining the rest of the world—too much would have to be surrendered.

Israel is a land filled with worship. Each day has five designated times for Islamic prayer and three for Jewish prayer—plus, for Jews, an additional prayer offered by mystics at midnight. As the Christian community is a small minority, its presence is not as obvious, but church bells announce prayers at different hours throughout the day, and are especially noticeable during the holy seasons. Many Muslims carry a small prayer rug; it is common to see men interrupt their daily activities to fall on their knees and bow in the direction of Mecca. Every morning thousands of religious Jews can be seen hurrying to prayer gatherings, carrying or wearing *tefillin* (phylacteries)[3] and *tallitot* (prayer shawls). Midday and evening, the men again pray, this time without all the paraphernalia. Friday evenings and Saturday mornings large numbers of men and women assemble at the Western Wall to honor the Sabbath. In addition to the weekly Sabbath, almost every month in the Hebrew calendar has at least one holy day or a special day of fasting.

After a week of festive meals and intense socialization with those who had instantly adopted us, we moved to the apartment that our newfound friends had subleased for us in a part of the new city of Jerusalem called Bayit VeGan (house and garden). Jerusalem is composed of many distinctive neighborhoods, each with its own ethnic and religious spirit. This section of the city had been chosen for us because its population was composed mainly of English-speaking people who had immigrated to Israel for religious reasons. At the time, we did not know that the neighborhood was clearly recognized by residents of the city as an observant religious community; the streets throughout were barricaded against traffic every Sabbath for the entire day. We did not know what we were getting into.

Within days we had met dozens of neighbors. Once again we were greeted with the hospitality that had overwhelmed us the first week—we rarely made a new acquaintance without being invited to a meal. Our social calendar for the next two months was soon full.

The truth is that notwithstanding the marvelous generosity, or perhaps as a result of it, we were exhausted. Moreover, the constant diet of chicken and thick, meaty *cholent* was much too rich for people like us—we were primarily vegetarian before our arrival in Israel. Yet, although this graciousness, abundance, and kindness overpowered us, like a family party that never came to an end, the tidal wave of warmth and openheartedness swept us away, and we fell hopelessly in love with this way of life and all that it promised. This was clearly what we were looking for: a spiritual family that would shelter us in times of need, and nourish not only our bodies, but our souls.

A community like this lives in the spirit of the old *shtetl*, which is a Yiddish word for Jewish towns in what used to be the Soviet Union and Poland, but also in other parts of Europe. *Shtetls* existed from the sixteenth through the twentieth centuries, ending in the flames of the Holocaust. I did not realize this experience in Bayit VeGan was the world of the *shtetl* until I read a paragraph in the *Encyclopedia Judaica:*

> **Life in the *Shtetl*.** *Yidishkeyt* ("Jewishness") and *menshlikhkeyt* ("humanness") were the two major values of the *shtetl* community around which life centered. Both the sacred and the profane were integrated in this way of life. The traditional ideals of piety, learning and scholarship, communal justice, and charity, were fused in the warm and intimate life-style of the *shtetl*. Thus the *Yidishkeyt* and the *menshlikhkeyt* of the *shtetl* were expressed in innumerable activities, all of which were geared toward the goal of living the life of a good Jew and were manifested in the synagogue and at home, in the holiness of Sabbath and the humdrum existence of the market, in the structure of the community, and in the organization of the family.[4]

It happened that we arrived in Israel in the most festive month of the year. The ten days that begin with Rosh Hashanah and culminate in the High Holy Day of Yom Kippur are called the Days of Awe. The weeklong festival called Sukkot, known as the Feast of Booths, begins a few days after Yom Kippur. Sukkot ends in a celebration called Shemini Atzeret, and then the whole process is crowned on the day of Simchat Torah, when people of all ages dance in the streets with the holy scrolls in their arms. Thus there are three weeks of holidays and Sabbaths, a continuing commemoration with a broad emotional array, from the introspective reverence of the Days of Awe to the joy of the Sabbath, to the cheerful, multicolor harvest festival of Sukkot.

The richness of this process was beyond all expectations. I had never before prayed in a congregation, much less experienced the long hours of sitting and standing required for the holiday liturgy. The Rosh Hashanah services lasted over five hours, and Yom Kippur was an all-day event with the prayer book, except for an hour's break in the afternoon. There was no slow adjustment to this prayer discipline, no separate room for beginners—it was an instant immersion. Had I not been an experienced retreatant, disciplined in long days of spiritual practice, this immersion might have driven me away. But I was able to adapt quickly to the arduous discipline—only the form of the practice changed.

As this was limited to a two-month experience, we easily surrendered to the daily routine of the modern *shtetl*. Our dress became modest, we learned more of the intricacies of Sabbath restrictions, we studied the laws and customs of religious practice, and we quickly blended into the weave of this simple life.

Last week, a well-known local rabbi told a story that continues to haunt me—he said that it was true. About twenty years ago, he met a doctor in the Soviet Union who for many years had secretly traveled long distances around the nation to perform circumcisions at no cost. In those days, there was an unwritten law against such religious practice, and he risked serious consequences.

This doctor had always wanted to emigrate to Israel from the Soviet Union, but his wife did not want to go—and so she did everything in her power to prevent him from leaving. Whenever the arguments became heated, she would ultimately pull out her trump card: She would threaten to reveal his secret practice of ritual circumcision to the authorities. He knew she would not hesitate to carry out this threat. It would mean spending the rest of his life in Siberia.

The doctor longed to go to the Holy Land. But as time passed, he knew that the realization of his dream was highly unlikely. He was tormented by this obsession; it seemed the most important matter in his life. Finally, he made a decision.

One day the rabbi who told this story received a request to visit this doctor at his office. When the rabbi arrived, the doctor asked him to promise to take something back to Israel when he departed the following week. This was not an unusual request, as many people smuggled out manuscripts, or jewels and gold, in preparation for the future. The rabbi agreed and then was asked to wait a short while.

The doctor came out of his office fifteen minutes later. He held a small box in his newly bandaged hand. He had amputated the top joint of his little finger—and that was what was in the box. The rabbi was shocked beyond belief as the doctor explained that he knew he would never get out of the Soviet Union alive, but he wanted a part of himself to be in Israel right now, so that he could find peace in his soul.

The rabbi did as he was asked and buried the little box somewhere

*on the Mount of Olives, where it is said that the resurrection of righ-
teous souls will take place in the messianic era.*[5]

Before we returned home at the end of that first trip to Israel,
Shoshana and I decided to make *aliyah,* which literally means "going up," to immigrate and become Israeli citizens. It was not as
much a choice as a sense of spiritual imperative. The language was
strange, the people were not like-minded, the religious practice
was difficult, the land was stark, and the sociopolitical structure was
replete with petty bureaucracy, but it was not as much a physical
home we were seeking as a dwelling place for our famished souls.

Our decision was not rational. We had a beautiful home in Virginia surrounded by hundreds of acres of spectacular forest. I had
a lucrative business that was entering a new phase of growth; the
possibilities for fame and fortune seemed limitless. Shoshana was
an established professional in nursing, moving up the tenure track
as an assistant professor at the University of Virginia. We had just
cleared our debts and were positioned to begin a long-term in-
vestment program toward a comfortable retirement. Things could
not have been rosier in the context of the Great American Dream.

But we had been infected by a virus that started an irreversible
condition called "the quest for truth." It had happened four years
earlier, when we attended a retreat at a community in upstate New
York called the Abode of the Message. This was an important turning point, which I will soon describe; but at the time, Pir Vilayat
Khan, the leader of the community, said something to me that has
always remained as a gentle eddy in the currents of my daily
thoughts. During an event called *tawwajeh* by the Sufis, which the
Hindus call *darshan*—sometimes translated as the "holy sight" of a
spiritual teacher who is able to see into soul realms—Pir Vilayat said
to me: "I see that you have been bitten by the dervish." When he
said this, an image immediately formed in my imagination: a desert
nomad stood silently, leaning on a long, knobby staff; his eyes
pierced through my mind like ruby daggers, igniting a spark long
dormant—and a flame blazed, which continues to flare even now.

Dervishes are Islamic ascetics who often appear to be madmen
in rags or loincloths, but when they speak—if one listens carefully—the words cut through all illusions and pretense. Dervishes
are peculiar; they do not think in the same way as the rest of humankind. Their wisdom is odd, illogical, almost absurd. Often, a

person will be confronted by a dervish and will walk away confused. The message is never clear; it may come as a riddle or an enigmatic phrase. Sometimes it acts like a bolt of lightning, and the person is instantly and permanently changed. At other times, it is like glowing phosphorus, slowly burning into the center of the being. In the middle of a busy market place, the dervish whispers in our ear, and although we may initially discard these words as nonsense, they linger in our thoughts, becoming a rhythmic repetition, until they have embedded themselves in our biomolecular structure, and we are transformed.

The dervish then is the mystic's mystic, the teacher of teachers, the embodiment of truth where the outward form is irrelevant but the inner essence is crystalline, flawless, and harder than diamonds. I later realized that Pir Vilayat's inner dervish was speaking to mine, and in that communion, my life was changed and the spiritual quest became my dominant preoccupation.

While we were in Israel, we experienced so much light and joy that all alternatives evaporated. When we returned home, however, life seemed more complicated. Days would pass, sometimes weeks, when the task of daily maintenance all but obliterated thoughts of returning to Israel. After a while, it all seemed very far away. But the dervish's glowing coal of phosphorus continued to descend, getting closer and closer to the essence, burning away the thick veils of confusion, and ultimately the force of it broke through.

It was the spark of the dervish in each of our hearts that caused us to cry the day our boat arrived in Haifa. It was an impenetrable mystery that brought us to Israel. Try as we might, we could not explain it. I often wonder, "What finally inspired us to tear up our roots?" and my thoughts return time and again to my first solitary retreat, four years before we were married.

2

Flies, bees, strange winged creatures buzz and drone in harmony with my constant mantra, AUM. In the warm, moist heat of the midday sun, I wander a few hundred yards up the trail from my small cabin to a plateau where tall grass bends and ripples like a huge string section of nature's symphonic orchestra. As I stand on a rock with my arms spread wide, I call out in full voice, rich in overtones and nasal harmonics: "Ahhh . . . ooo . . . mmm." Everything whirls about in perfect symmetry with this sound, and the wind rustles leaves near and far in gentle whispering counterpoint. The Great Conductor marks the rhythm each and every moment; the world would disappear in an instant if a single beat were missed.

The flora on this mountain is luxuriant. Wildflowers shimmer in the thin air. Their bright colors pierce the woods with such intensity, they beckon like the sirens' call. Mushrooms push lustily through the ground alongside thick, green moss that invites a fingertip caress. Life here is vital and fecund to compensate for the short reproductive season.

From this height, over nine thousand feet above sea level, weather fronts can be sighted a hundred miles away. Thunderclouds, larger than cities, move ponderously across the valley below. A thousand shades of gray swirl into each other, mixing in a huge cauldron like a witch's brew. Bolts of lightning rip the sky silently in the distance, too far off for sound to travel. When the clouds come closer, thunder prevails, and the sisters of bedlam, chaos, and pandemonium shriek in the wind.

But in my simple hut, home base during a weeklong hermitage, I am snug, warm, and dry. My bed is a foam mat two inches thick. A rough-hewn stand is my table for eating and writing. The only seat above the floor is built into the wall, where a window opens upon a breathtaking view. A couple of well-used cushions are my meditation companions. A small, cast-iron, potbelly stove provides warmth, and a one-burner kerosene heater is used for cooking.

The mountain winters here are long. A narrow storage shed alongside the hut is amply supplied with wood. It is a nesting haven for many creatures, the noisiest of whom are the mice. They scurry across the cabin floor in the middle of the night, squeaking; they seem to be having a good time. Many people would hate this place. However, my idea of heaven is to spend a whole winter here in seclusion.

The High Hermitage of Lama Mountain is perched just below a ridge of the San Cristobal range, overlooking a spacious portion of northern New Mexico. The broad valley below extends to other mountains in the south, west, and north. A person on retreat can sit at the window seat and watch the endlessly changing spectacle of wind *devas* (spirits) propelling weather fronts like chess pieces. Except for the time spent in meditation and walks in the forest, I was drawn to the window throughout my weeklong hermitage. I sat there dozens of hours, untroubled, constantly enthralled. I expected that isolation in the lonely hut would prove boring, especially in contrast to my active life-style. Yet I was perfectly content to be altogether passive, endlessly watching clouds, day after day.

The first two nights were spent in wakefulness—strange sounds and nervous energy filled the dark. I was an alien in a frightening land; beasts and danger filled my imagination. In the wilderness, an extraordinary world awakens at night; it creeps, slides, runs, or waits motionless for its prey. Those first couple of nights I heard the snap of every twig as nocturnal prowlers lurked not far from the hut. Inside it was quieter, but still the shadows moved. I was scared.

It is remarkable, however, how quickly I succumbed to a fresh rhythm. After three days the little critters became my friends. Spiders and mice, beetles and ants, crickets and moths, all were welcome companions. I also found that the eerie night sounds no longer disturbed my sleep. An occasional visitor to my bed was an annoyance, but I did not jump in terror, as I had the first few nights.

Even the bees and wasps that flew through the open door during the day, and to whose stings I am exceptionally allergic, became more intriguing and less threatening. If I had been accidentally stung and had had a bad reaction, I would probably have died there. But I lost my fear sometime midweek when I realized that death always buzzes a few inches from my neck, whether in the wilderness or in the midst of a crowd. This awareness of death constantly by my side produced an interesting reaction: I became utterly calm.

An ant today had a ball of pollen attached to one leg. God is all, everything, and everywhere, "they" say. So the ant touched the flower as part of God's everywhereness. Then it wandered, not in a happenstance manner, but each move blending in tune with a cosmic melody, until I glanced its way, as was meant to be, and started thinking about the everythingness and everywhereness of God.

The flies twist and buzz in a confused frenzy of activity. Yet could it be that each turn, every stop and go is part of the mystical dance? If I brush one away, if I don't, is it all the same? A fly smashes into a window, reels back stunned, falls in a daze. This too? A lesson for the fly, for me, or what? Either we believe it is all an accident, or there is a creative force. Einstein said he did not believe God throws dice. So there is nothing less godly about a stunned and confused fly than one in perfect harmony, functioning as a fly should. Moreover, whether we, as human beings, are in a state of emotional balance or we are bewildered and flustered, we are still an expression of the Divine. When we are "enlightened," we glow with God's light; but it is no different when we are dense hulks of neurosis and anxiety— we still radiate the same light for those who know how to see.

An interesting pastime during the week was watching the many creatures that gathered inside the window. I left the door open during the days so the mountain breezes would keep the room fresh. Flies entered and, after an exploration of many circuits around the interior of the cabin, would usually complete their tour at the panorama window, skittering up and down, trying to get to the other side. After the first few days of being irritated by them, I became fascinated. I observed that they buzzed incessantly at the window throughout the day, seeking freedom, while the door was always open on the opposite side of the room—if they had but turned in the other direction. This seemed the perfect metaphor for the spiritual quest. I was beginning to open the gates of inner vision, a path followed by thousands of others. I was not really certain how to proceed, but there was an important message at this window.

Whatever it was that I was seeking, it was not going to be something attained in a straightforward manner. The door was behind me, the path to freedom required an entirely new perspective. Even with eyes that see in a thousand directions at once, even with precise instinctual abilities, a fly does not have the unknown inner substance that allows it to transcend to a new world of consciousness. Human beings do have this quality. This is one of the meanings of the idea that we are created in the image of God.

We are led to believe that a part of each of us is godly or godlike. Surely we must ask ourselves, What about the other parts? Indeed, all of us is God, not just a little part. Our shortcomings, triviality, meanness, anger, sadness, all of it. Not just joy, happiness, and ecstasy, but the dark side too. God is illusion as well as reality. It does not matter which side of the mirror we view—both sides and the mirror itself are God. In the words of Ramana Maharshi (twentieth-century Hindu saint/guru):

> *If everything is God, are you not included in that everything? . . . To see God is to be God. . . . He alone is.*[6]

The last few days I have been sitting in silence, wondering over and over: What pushes us on one path or another toward the realization of expanded awareness? What do we really want? Is it to short-circuit the cycle of reincarnation? To get into heaven? An ego trip? Is it to escape from the pain and suffering of the world? Or is it something else; something that really has no goal but is an aspect of the human condition, planted in our essential nature, and we have no choice but to attempt to uncover it?

The High Hermitage is famous. The best-known spiritual guides in America during the sixties and seventies have dwelled on this mountain. Luminaries such as Ram Dass, Pir Vilayat Khan, Brother

David Steindl-Rast, and Rabbi Zalman Schachter-Shalomi have spent periods of seclusion here.

The guardian and caretaker of the hermitage is the community called Lama Foundation, located a few hundred yards down the mountain slope. The mountain itself is called Lama, meaning "mud," and a local spring of fresh water coming from it has sacred qualities, according to local Native Americans who know its history. A well-worn path cuts across the mountain, passing not many meters from the High Hermitage, traversing the San Cristobal range. For dozens of generations this footpath has been known as the Peace Trail, because many hundreds of years ago an unwritten treaty between hostile tribes agreed that no acts of war would be tolerated along this path. Thus, the mountain itself, and particularly the spring below, was known as a sanctuary, and the local Pueblo Indians still believe that the sacred spirits in this area are wondrous healers. Indeed, many people will attest even now that their experience on this mountain has transformed their lives.

The founders of Lama climbed the mountain in the late sixties and built a large dome, which remains the dominant feature at the heart of the community. The most famous personality associated with the original group is Ram Dass, who departed to India in the sixties as Richard Alpert—Harvard psychologist; investigator of psychotropic drugs, including LSD; colleague of Timothy Leary—and returned with a new name and the teachings of his guru, Neem Karoli Baba. Ram Dass came up this mountain, and in a yellow school bus he wrote a book that was to profoundly influence an entire generation: *Be Here Now*. The yellow school bus still sits in the woods, its dilapidated condition reminding us that here and now things are constantly changing.

My partner, Susan, and I had driven to Lama from Boston, where I had just finished a course in acupuncture. We had rigged up an old green van as a camper, and had given it the name *Hoku* before departing. *Hoku* is a well-known acupuncture point located in the fleshy part of the hand between the thumb and forefinger. It is used for many symptoms, and we felt that *Hoku,* the camping van, would be used for many journeys to alleviate our affliction of spiritual malnourishment.

I had begun the study of acupuncture because of my interest in healing and well-being. My studies quickly revealed the power of the spiritual side of healing, the unknown surge of life within us that transcends medicine, the force that is the wellspring from which miraculous recoveries occur that continue to astound modern science. This study exposed me to many different forms of alternative healing, and awakened a spiritual thirst that was now the impetus carrying us to new discoveries. We had decided to spend the summer vacation cruising in our van, visiting a number of communities that represented various spiritual traditions.

Our first stop out of Boston was the Sufi community at the Abode of the Message in New Lebanon, New York, where a weeklong meditation retreat was being offered. Prior to that summer, Susan and I had been slowly awakening to the world of the New Age, as it was called, but mainly we had been secure, middle-class citizens, in an environment of academia, business, and politics. So this retreat at the Abode was a new beginning for us.

The community's spiritual guide was Pir Vilayat Khan, the leader of the Sufi Order of the West. Sufis are Islamic mystics who have been important teachers and poets for a thousand years. There are many lineages of Sufism; most of those existing in other parts of the world require devotion to the teachings of Muhammad. The Sufi Order of the West, however, is eclectic and not bound to Islamic law. Its emphasis is on meditation and devotional prayer.

On the fourth day of the retreat, Pir Vilayat offered a guided meditation that culminated in the playing of a lovely piece of music called Pachelbel's Canon. I was touched. Something welled up within me, a consciousness that was both familiar and unknown, and a stream of tears rolled down my cheeks. I sobbed for over an hour. Everyone else had left the tent, but I could not move. This was a new experience for me—an affirmation, a welcoming, and an enormous release—opening an inner "knowing" that there was more to life than the daily routine of survival.

I accepted initiation into the Sufi Order of the West the next day. It was another moment of magic, late in the afternoon, as I walked up a hillside path, the setting sun dappling leaves the entire way. Pir Vilayat stood at the top of the path in a long, flowing, white robe. The forest murmured in anticipation of the approaching nightfall. The soft dusk light reflecting through Pir's white beard and hair cast an aura, like a halo, around his head. "This is too much," my ever-present cynic whispered. "Nothing could be this perfect." But it was. Simple perfection.

Walking down the hill after this initiation, I looked up at the sky through misty eyes, and taking a deep breath while stretching back my shoulders, I felt a phenomenal crack in my chest around the solar plexus. I did not realize what had happened until later that evening when I reached down and felt the presence of new cartilage in the center of my chest where the two lower ribs meet. I would never have known about this if it had not been for my work in acupuncture.

Students of acupuncture practice on each other's bodies, locating with precision hundreds of "points" where needles are inserted to treat various conditions. Throughout the course, neither I nor my fellow students could find on me a small sword-shaped cartilage just below the sternum, called the xiphoid process. Everyone else had a normal anatomy in this respect, a clearly delineated bump appeared exactly where it was supposed to be. We assumed that mine was simply too small to be noticeable—anomalies of this sort are not unusual. Just after this Sufi initiation, however, I realized that the cartilage actually had been pulled back into my chest by muscle tension, locked tight as a result of an unknown constriction. Now when I reached down and gently massaged the sore area around the newborn prominence, it felt as big as a marble and moved freely. At the time, I took this to be an esoteric message— the first step on the path of liberation—an indication of spiritual and physical release.

Years later I read about Ramakrishna, who spent one period of his life imitating Hanuman, king of the monkeys in the epic poem the Ramayana. Hanuman is regarded as an ideal devotee because of the way he worshipped his lord. Ramakrishna wished to experience this sense of perfect devotion, so, as was his way, he became absorbed in a complete imitation of Hanuman, the divine monkey. He said:

> I had to eat like him [Hanuman] and do every action as he would have done it. I didn't do this of my own accord; it happened of itself. I tied my *dhoti* around my waist to make it look like a tail, and I moved about in jumps. I ate nothing but fruit and roots. . . . My eyes got a restless look, like the eyes of a monkey. And the most marvelous thing was—the lower end of my spine lengthened, nearly an inch![7]

At the time of my initiation, I had no clear idea of what I was doing; I was drawn by something outside my consciousness. As

Ramakrishna said, "It happened of itself." The words of William Blake ring as if they were the power of prophecy encircling every human being, whispering in our ears:

> I rest not upon my great task to open the eternal worlds, to open the immortal Eyes of Man inwards into the Worlds of Thought: into Eternity ever expanding in the Bosom of God, the Human Imagination.[8]

That meditation experience on the fourth day of the retreat had given me my first personal glimpse into unexplored depths, opening something long buried and constrained. As a result, I surrendered to the idea of spiritual initiation, which a week earlier would have been unthinkable, and this in some way had overcome a psychic obstruction. It remains a mystery to me why this breakthrough was expressed by the appearance of the previously hidden xiphoid process. Yet to this day, when I touch the middle of my chest and feel the freed cartilage, a warm glow radiates from the center of my body.

The day after I realized this fresh, gentle presence of spiritual awareness, Susan decided to take her Sufi initiation. She had not been as transfixed by the meditations as I, but when she experienced my glow, she wanted a direct taste herself. Neither of us felt as though we had joined an association, and we only minimally identified ourselves as "Sufis," but we knew the initiation was important for other, unknown reasons; it was a key ingredient for the process of alchemical transformation into the "higher" realms.

We continued in *Hoku* across the country to California to visit family, and then set out for Lama Mountain to participate in a ten-day yoga retreat. During that retreat, I heard for the first time about the High Hermitage, and inquired about its availability. There had been a late cancellation for the week just following the yoga retreat, so I signed up.

I felt uncomfortable and guilty pulling out a blade of grass today. The critic within me sneers at my sanctimoniousness, this pseudopride. But there is another feeling buried in my gut. A curious world is opening. A moth goes too close to the flame of my kerosene lamp and sizzles in a flash. What is that new feeling I experience as the moth is transformed into a burst of light?

The planet Venus is remarkable in the early morning. She touches me. Why have I not seen her before? What has clouded my eyes? The woods too are so alive; beings of some other plane sit motionless, just off the trail. In the more dense, damp sections, I can feel them; I can see them. Hallucinations? I think not. Life becomes muddled in our survival dance—the stillness of this retreat lets the distractions settle; a fresh clarity evolves.

Everything seems to have its own spirit. Plants, insects, rocks, even the firewood. This hut also has a spirit, a different kind, one that has been nourished by the thoughts of previous hermits. This hut-spirit tends the local mice and chipmunks. It sets tasks for the human beings who spend their time here. I was moved to repair the table, fix a window, and mend other odds and ends. This spirit also has a splendid sense of humor; I like it very much.

I did not know how to plan my spiritual practice for this retreat. I chanted the AUM and also a mantra that was given to me during my initiation. I used meditations that Pir Vilayat taught during the week at Sufi camp. And I repeated prayers composed by Pir's father, Hazrat Inayat Khan, who was the prime mover to introduce the Sufi message to the West in the early part of the twentieth century. This message was that all paths lead "Toward the One." The prayer that I enjoyed the most was called *Khatum:*[9]

O Thou who are the Perfection of Love,
  Harmony and Beauty,
  The Lord of heaven and earth,
Open our hearts, that we may hear thy voice,
  which constantly cometh from within.
Disclose to us thy Divine Light,
  which is hidden in our souls,
  that we may know and understand life better.
Most merciful and compassionate God,
  give us thy great goodness;
  teach us thy loving forgiveness;
  raise us above the distinctions and differences
  which divide men;
Send us the peace of thy Divine Spirit,
  and unite us all in thy Perfect Being.
Amen

I had no idea of what to expect at the High Hermitage. I had never thought of doing a retreat by myself before arriving at Lama, but the moment I heard of a secluded hut waiting at the mountaintop, the thought of it radiated in me like a beacon from my long-forgotten home. I became obsessed; nothing could dampen my urge to have this experience.

The first day, I had to haul my food and water up the mountain. The food took one trip up the winding, steep path; the water took three trips. The first climb was only twenty minutes long, but as altitude sickness began to get the better of me, each additional climb took longer than the previous one. I found myself getting nauseated on the second trip up, but my will and enthusiasm cloaked illness so that I was able to finish the provisioning before I collapsed. The rest of the afternoon was spent retching up my breakfast as if I had just been through a violent ocean passage. The next day was spent mostly at the outhouse.

Upon reflection, my physical reaction early in the week was symbolic of a cleansing to prepare me for another level of consciousness. Despite the discomfort of the first days, my physical release, dealing with an outhouse, the absence of all conveniences, and acclimating to the natural surroundings, the situation felt just right to me—I never thought of leaving early. I imagine many other people might have regretted the commitment to solitude or the primitive conditions; they might have quit before the week was out. But something about the hermitage experience is in distinct harmony with my inner being despite the discomforts.

This retreat revealed a major attribute that needed to be cultivated if I was to move forward in my spiritual work. It had to do with learning how to be aware of each moment. In a little book by Krishnamurti called *Think on These Things,* the subject of awareness is discussed:

> Do you know what is happening in the world? What is happening in the world is a projection of what is happening inside each one of us; what we are, the world is. Most of us are in turmoil, we are acquisitive, possessive, we are jealous and condemn people; and that is exactly what is happening in the world, only more dramatically, ruthlessly. . . . And it is only when you spend some time every day earnestly thinking about these matters that there is a possibility of bringing about a total revolution and creating a new world. And I assure you, a new world has to be created.[10]

Moment-to-moment awareness is not simply a prerequisite for spiritual development, it is essential for overcoming the disease that affects the world. Ultimate revolution is not something that takes place through violence and destruction; it results from a transformation in our inner process.

But learning how to "be here now" is not so easy. We rarely escape from our constant forgetfulness. We cannot simply decide to be present and aware of our thoughts—a practice is needed. The Russian philosopher, G.I. Gurdjieff, suggests a practice called self-remembering. It is done by "stopping" thoughts. He says:

> Try to stop your thoughts but, at the same time, do not forget your aim—that you do it in order to remember yourself. . . . What prevents self-remembering? This constant turning of thoughts. Stop this turning, and perhaps you will have a taste of it. . . . You *can* stop thoughts, but you must not be disappointed if at first you cannot. Stopping thoughts is a very difficult thing. You cannot say to yourself "I will stop thoughts," and they stop. You have to use effort all the time.[11]

A number of years ago I had a cuckoo clock in my house. It made a cuckoo sound every fifteen minutes. After the first couple of days, I hardly noticed it. One day I heard the cuckoo sound and realized it was the first time I had been aware of the clock for an entire week. Pondering this, adding up the amount of time I had been in the room but oblivious of the clock, I arrived at the stark realization that I was consciously aware of my environment less than two percent of the time. That cuckoo may have been a steady reminder in my subconscious mind, just as we are continuously prompted by the environment, but my consciousness was in its own domain ninety-eight percent of the time.

I began to pay attention to the cuckoo, and consequently heard it more often. I noticed that when I was sensitized to the clock, I was also more aware of what was happening around my house. Paying attention to the cuckoo brought me to a higher level of general awareness. This is what Gurdjieff is talking about. By "stopping," we catch our thoughts midstream, and we also raise our overall awareness level. This continues to self-generate until we attain a new consciousness that has its own built-in stopping mechanism. This is a cornerstone for heightened awareness.

The clouds on the horizon turned crimson this evening, brilliant hues of red, orange, and yellow. Tomorrow I will carry my things down the mountain. I have thought about the week past. No dazzling flashes of fresh awareness, but a clear, solid cohesion of contemplative thought. This has been a marvelous experience, sitting quietly, moving in complete harmony. Perhaps the best part was the ability to set my own rhythms. There was no time demon pressing on me. I never felt that time was being wasted, nor did I feel that I had to achieve anything.

I would not mind staying longer, but I know another hermit is coming up soon. Some day I may be able to return here. I hope that between now and then I will be able to practice self-remembrance and that there will be greater stillness in my busy mind.

3

GLENDALE, VIRGINIA: JULY 1978.
EIGHT-DAY RETREAT IN A RENTED
HOUSE ON A DAIRY FARM;
NO NEIGHBORS IN SIGHT.

In the morning mirror I gaze upon a stranger I have known all my life. He returns my look, not much changed over the years but for an occasional worry-line here and there. How could he and I live in the same body all this time and still not know one another?

I'm the one who has the dreams; he's the one who makes the moves. I know the longing, feel attuned to muffled nuances of other worlds, and perhaps I am even graced with a grain of divine awareness; he does the eating, coping, and surviving. I am lonely, driven to end the agony of separation from my source; he lives in an illusion, whipped by an endless rush of emotions, false struggles, and fantasy.

After our summer excursion and my retreat in the High Hermitage, we returned to the East Coast and rented an old plantation house in Orange County, Virginia. On my last day in the hut on Lama Mountain, I had put a pinhole in a map at Charlottesville, Virginia, because we had heard that a group of Sufis from California were relocating near this city. It seemed to be a good choice for us as well, not too far from Washington, D.C., where I had to go occasionally for my work, and a day's journey to the dunes of the Outer Banks near Cape Hatteras, which we loved. We searched around Charlottesville, and found a dairy farmer who was renting a dilapidated home in the middle of a large pasture a half mile up a private dirt road, fenced on all sides by forest.

Two massive columns marked the front entrance of the house.

The wooden veneer covering them had fallen away, revealing dry rot within. To one side of the house, abandoned slave quarters were cluttered with rubble and sad memories. Next to the moldy slave shanties was a caved-in spring house, bone dry inside; shredded remnants of a harness hung from a rafter. An antiquated windmill behind the main house stood as another sentinel of decay; rusted iron framework and frozen gears appeared through jagged openings in the walls. The wind, once the windmill's friend, now ripped it to pieces.

The plantation house was not large, yet its grandness was inescapable. Each of its five rooms was lofty and wide; two had immense fireplaces. It did not feel as much like a cotton plantation as a manor for country gentry. Perhaps the master of the house had been a merchant. Although the house once had servants, and probably slaves, it had a quiet, gentle atmosphere. The ghosts were friendly.

Not so the groundhogs and gophers who broke through the garden fence for tender shoots of my prized corn. Rather than enjoy the local vegetation, they converged on our little plot from hundreds of acres around. Our new golden retriever puppy, Moses, was no match for the wise, tough, little beasts who made a shambles of the spring garden—my first in many years.

In the summer I took a weeklong retreat. My room upstairs was a perfect sanctuary: warm, noiseless, secure. We were isolated; friends never dropped by without calling. My window overlooked the main pasture where cows grazed. Our agreement with the landlord was that we would feed the cows once a day. All we needed to do was go to the midpasture shed and put corn feed in a trough. In exchange we lived in the mansion house for a reasonable rent, and as a bonus we received all the raw milk we could drink or churn into butter. My karma yoga (mindful service) on retreat was to take care of the feeding each day—it was a special kind of meditation.

Actually, it was something of a joke for a person like me, who had spent most of his life as an urban dweller. Cosmic humor. Young cows associate any two-legged creature with food. Unlike older cows, who stand and gaze, the young ones will follow any leader. What begins as an amble soon becomes a rush, and a single ambitious cow can turn the herd into a stampede. These cute overgrown calves each weighed five hundred pounds or more, so when they were rapidly bearing down in bovine single-mindedness to get the food, a terrified person's wisest move was to drop the grain bucket and get out of the way.

My strategy was to sneak out the back door when the herd was across the pasture. I crouched low and ran the long way around, Moses at my heels. War games. I cut through the side door of the shed, got the bucket, and filled the feeding trough. Once the work was done, I rang the bell, and my heart leapt when I saw the huge brown eyes of the herd's leader rapidly approaching. I took Moses in my arms and stepped back out of the crush, happy that I had outwitted those cows once again. These were the small pleasures of country life for a city slicker.

The solitude and peace has been exquisite. God's ever-presence has become my obsession—everything and every thought reflects divinity. A growing awareness swells within; I feel it just below my level of consciousness, like a simmering kettle whose lid must be raised carefully to avoid being scalded by the steam.

Frequently, as I sit in the dark stillness of inner observation, a globe of clarity enters a hidden mental nook, casting a beam of new ideas. So much is concealed in these chambers. A glimpse in one flashing moment reveals myriad doors with rusty padlocks and sagging hinges. I feel the excitement of anticipation; there is so much to learn, but I know that opening the doors does not entirely depend upon me.

The dairy farm was located a little over one hundred miles from Washington, D.C. Once a week I went there to maintain my contacts as a political consultant. Many years had passed since I worked for the Democratic National Committee at the Watergate. I left there just as the scandal was growing around Richard Nixon's Committee to Re-elect the President. They had hired some sleazy characters to break into our offices to find any evidence of scandal they could use in the election. They had bugged some of our telephones; I am not certain if mine was tapped, but the office next to mine—ten feet away—was. The fellow who worked in that office ultimately collected a tidy sum as compensation for invasion of privacy.

My consulting firm did very well. We handled a large number of congressional clients, polling their constituents. It was a good business, but I had not developed it to its potential because I did not want to live full-time in Washington, D.C.—I had too many other interests. Indeed, some of my friends wondered how I could live the schizophrenic life of country cowpoke and meditator on some days and be a high-powered Washington consultant on others. Somehow it worked.

In my late teens I had gained an insight that had proven enormously rewarding throughout the rest of my life. It was this: The most valuable commodity in the world is *time*. Other people work for material benefits; I worked to buy time. Things are of little consequence to me, except for life's necessities, while time is always precious. Thus my life's pattern had been to work intensely for periods of one to three years, and then to give myself as much time as my savings would allow. This rhythm afforded me a wide variety of experiences, and an earnest exploration into the inner being. The result had been the ripening of an ever-growing faith that became the foundation of my spiritual development.

Every thought is a voyage in a different universe. Memories whirl, endless loops on a tape wearing thin. One moment I watch the deer at the edge of the woods, the next I am in a familiar haunt in Paris, Crete, Amsterdam, Seville, or Lausanne. What is the journey? Whose myth is this? Why all of the wandering? I have worked in San Francisco, New York, and Washington, D.C. Travels have taken me to Europe, Asia, Central America, and into the Amazon backcountry. I have sailed my small sloop, Tawi, *throughout the Virgin Islands and north to Bermuda and Maine. Many faces appear, but solitude is the theme. In the thickest crowd or the middle of the ocean, it is still the same me—separate, alone.*

Now I begin a new journey—an excursion inward—I do not have a map. I notice that there are signs posted, but I need to learn a new language. It is strange here, yet I am not at all lonely. Nothing is missing; this world is measureless, complete. Still, I wonder, "What is possible on the inward journey—and where does it lead?"

After we settled into the routine of living in the country and caring for the herd of large calves, we began to seek out the community of Sufis who had moved to the area from California. Many of them visited our home, and we formed friendships. In a short time, we were invited to join five other families in the purchase of four hundred acres of hillside forest in a small community named Batesville, about a half hour south of Charlottesville.

The teacher for many of these folks was Samuel Lewis, known affectionately as Sufi Sam,[12] who was on the San Francisco scene in the mid-to-late sixties—the period of the flower children. He created a new form of spiritual expression—special songs and dances of praise—for the hippies who flocked to San Francisco in search of truth. His students also learned the practice of *dhikr*,[13] a way of chanting mantras that quickly leads to altered states of consciousness.

Our new friends taught us these spiritual practices, and thus, on my retreat I did a great deal of *dhikr* along with other specialized mantras. I arose at 3:30 A.M., and although my mantras were outwardly silent in the early morning hours, they roared in my head. The predawn stillness in the house invoked an otherworldly quality, neither dreamland nor wakeful reality. During these hours I lived in a field of shadow gardens where wispy shapes wrapped themselves around thought skeletons, adding fantasy flesh to ephemeral notions. These projections were sometimes seductive, soothing, and gentle; at other times they molded themselves to my negative energy and frightened me with images of destruction and death.

After Susan left for work and the daylight invited a more familiar consciousness, I chanted out loud, creating yet another universe so as not to be lulled into a habitual, open-eyed sleep. How many sleepwalkers stumble through life, having learned social routines to fake interest, but in truth their minds dwell in separate realities?

A pin-drop of light pierces the horizon, and a soft gray hue slowly engulfs the dimming stars like tears mixed with mascara spilling over sequins on a black satin blouse. The ancients determined the arrival of dawn as the moment a person could distinguish which of two threads was white, which dark. Some cultures said that dawn was the time one could clearly recognize a friend a short distance away. People over millennia have used a subjective demarcation to know when it was officially dawn because in many traditions the approach of the new day is a proper time of prayer. But I have been sitting in my own prayer for hours while it was still night and the question arises: When is it time not to pray?

Dawning continues. In truth there is no beginning or end point. The dark blends into morning, which becomes noon-ing, afternoon-ing, even-ing, night-ing, midnight-ing, and so the cycle turns. We may know when we have arrived at a particular part of the day, but the in-between times are impossible to label one way or the other. I am aware of my breath entering and departing the body. However, when does it change from an inhalation to an exhalation? No matter how closely I observe, the precise moment the incoming breath ends or the outgoing breath begins remains completely unattainable.

There is really no way to measure anything accurately; indeed, exactitude is theoretical. The best we can do is approximate—but something unknown is always a residual. The most accurate measuring stick cannot get closer than its own molecules or those of the thing being measured. We want life to be predictable, but we can only make educated guesses.

True awareness grows when we fully realize our inability to be exact, which is most clear when we contemplate any transition. Zenith and nadir, yin and yang, alpha and omega, birth and death, dawn and dusk, all the extremes and limits where an ending is concurrently a beginning offer us insight into the cosmic design. Indeed, we discover that an instant does not exist and our sense of reality evaporates as we dive into the pool of time in search of discrete moments only to find a fluidity that has no beginning and no end. When we escape illusion of movement by focusing on the constant, infinite nature that exists "between moments," so to speak, the continuous presence of the Divine becomes overwhelming.

Words always fail in this type of contemplation. The letters of the words dance in suggestion, but never suffice to fully explain. Understanding arises only through experience. In a moment of bliss, the words are seen by the sharp eyes of an eagle, carrying us to sublime heights of perfection. The next day, these same words may turn into pale shells that are fit only for hermit crabs.

I repeat a mantra in my morning practice. At times, there is just the mantra and I am but a voice; all else is transparent. Most of the time, however, there is a "me" making sound, a mind constantly thinking, a body that hurts. It is uncomfortable, boring, and it seems like a waste of time. But I trust that it is not a waste. I cannot say what it is, but I must continue. This is the path of the Great Quest, and somehow Faith compels me to follow Her.

Faith for me transcends belief systems. The most common association in the West is faith in God; in the East, there is faith in *samsara*, the wheel of life, the ceaseless process of becoming. People immersed in science have faith in rationality; those in religion have faith that there is an ultimate truth, political observers and economists have faith—however transitory—in theories of maximum benefit to humankind.

My faith is not like any of these—it is much more mystical. Each of the above is an important component, and is vital in the cosmic order. But each will fail at certain times, and the devotee of that system will be completely lost.

Mystical faith is paradoxical. It is based on the assumption that there is always something bigger, grander, more profound than our capacity to think or imagine. If we can envision anything, it is by definition less than infinite. If we believe something is impossible, faith disagrees. Two things can be in the same place at the same time. Indeed, space and time are a function of limited perception; faith dwells in the timeless realm of infinity.

In truth, the nature of reason is filled with contradiction and paradox. For example, one perspective may focus on the pain in the world, the suffering, ignorance, and mutual destruction; another may center on the ideal order, absolute perfection, and flawless harmony of all creation. When faced with incompatible thoughts such as these, we have only one choice: to let go. When irrefutable ideas conflict and there is nothing to hold on to, our minds boggle, our senses become numb. This is that. It is not that. It is not not that.

Steeped in rationality, the twentieth-century mind tends to flee from absurdity or paradox. It seeks a safe haven in logic, for without some guiding principle there is a feeling of utter emptiness, a chasm of futility. There *must* be something we can grasp, or the whole creation is senseless. Indeed, it is this conviction that has led to so much angst and despair in our times.

Mystical faith transcends belief, recognizes absolute limits for the intellect, and abides in realms where nothing of substance exists and paradox reigns. Yet it is grounded in a certainty that everything and every action is precisely as it must be, flowing out of events, leading to others, whether guided or not, an awesome unfolding that we are privileged to witness, simultaneously onstage and in the audience. We are not in control, yet our actions influence everything that follows them. We cannot conceive of a reason to exist, yet we are sustained, somehow, in each breath—knowing that at any moment this could end.

Whereas the *knowledge* of "nothingness" may lead ultimately to a sense of no purpose and despair, *mystical faith* regarding nothingness opens the floodgates of delight, wonder, and affirmation in the very experience of our own existence. How does this happen? It is the result of the strength we gain from such faith to give us the courage to "let go" of our encumbering thought processes and step out of the constriction of our contemporary myths; it empowers us to follow the call that seems to beckon from the horizon of our possibilities, but really comes from the inner core of our souls.

The anonymous author of the Christian work *The Cloud of Unknowing* wrote in the fourteenth century:

> How wonderfully is a man's love transformed by the interior experience of this nothingness and this nowhere. . . . At times the sight is as terrible as a glimpse of hell and he is tempted to despair. . . . He who patiently abides in this darkness will be comforted . . . and finally there will come a moment when he experiences such peace and repose in that darkness that he thinks surely it must be God himself.
>
> However much a man may know about every created spiritual thing, his intellect will never be able to comprehend the uncreated spiritual truth which is God. But there is a negative knowledge which does understand God. It proceeds by asserting everything it knows: this is not God, until finally he comes to a point where knowledge is exhausted. This is the approach of St. Denis, who said, "The most divine knowledge of God is that which is known by not-knowing."[14]

Knowing by not-knowing is at the heart of all spiritual inquiry. Almost two thousand years ago, Plotinus (third century) said: "The One is in nothing at all, and therefore in this sense 'nowhere.'" Also: "The One is present only to those who are prepared for it. . . . The One is as it wakes itself to be: the wakening is beyond being, beyond essence, and beyond conscious life."[15]

Thus I sat quietly in my retreat room watching the cows sauntering among the grass and weeds, occasionally meandering in my own thoughts of how to outwit the wily groundhogs, but all the while trying to empty, quiet, and calm the mind with nothing in particular as a goal. This ongoing process of inner clearing is always supported by an underlying spiritual gravity called *faith*.

The truth is that the Great Quest takes so many forms, it is deceptive. When we look within ourselves, we find a yearning to be in touch with the Divine, to know who we are, what we are, and why we are here—this yearning lies within the very fiber of life itself. Every aspect of creation is drawn to that which vitalizes it. All movement, each breath and heartbeat within us, is an expression of this ongoing and eternal process where the One becomes Many, and the Many become One.

Whenever I am able to stop my mind and be here, between beginning and end, at the elusive turning point that does not exist except in paradox, I disappear into the Oneness. Even though it may last for only an instant, it affirms the truth of the Great Quest and gives me the strength to go on.

Last night's dream presence: a figure appeared dressed in a long grayish, thick robe—rough woven raw wool—with a cowl covering under which there was no face, but a frightful darkness that I felt would consume anything that entered. No other features like hands or feet were visible; it stood before me silent and ominous. But I knew it could speak.

"Will I ever attain realization?" I asked.

It answered, "There is nothing to attain."

"Then what am I doing here?"

"What are you doing anywhere?"

I complained that these answers were too vague. It asked me if I wanted truth or ignorance. I said that, of course, I wanted truth. It said nothing. After some moments of waiting, I asked how I could recognize my spiritual level. It said nothing. I said, "I thought you were going to give me the truth."

It answered, "The truth is hidden in the question—the only truth in your question is silence."

I asked it to explain this. It responded, "Look to the core of each question, and you will find the answer. A question that comes from the heart of wanting reveals its answer in silence."

I did not understand. I asked, "Help me understand your explanation—what do I need for understanding?"

It said, "Patience. Tolerance. Perseverance."

The image began to fade, and I felt myself coming out of the dream. I cried out to it, "Will you be here when I need you?" Its receding voice said, "I am always here."

4

Sitting quietly, I observe my thought-beams split by a diamond prism, and shards of light cascade in all directions like laser knives. Ten thousand vestibules composed of crystal mirrors capture each beam, multiplying every shaft of light into a profusion of luminescent darts. Thus, every thought explodes each millisecond, momentarily staining the mind with various hues and shades—a marvelous, but constantly shifting kaleidoscope.

When one is chanting long hours day after day, visions constantly arise and fall away—new universes layer upon each other. Each hour offers enough psychic geology to be a lifetime of material for exploration into the collective unconscious. Wakeful reality has become blurred; I dream with open eyes. And when my eyes are closed, I consciously dance with shadowy spirits.

Each day for the last week and a half, I have drawn a tarot card from the major arcana to attune to the energy of the day. This morning, precognition was so strong, there was no past, present, or future. I knew as I chose from the pack which card it was. Before turning it over, I felt a sense of equilibrium between the subterranean domain and the physical world, as if I were standing in subliminal waters and their flow between the upper and lower realms connected on innumerable levels within my soul. I was certain it was the card called "Temperance," and was not even pleased at being correct; there was no room for doubt.

Last night, a moon-drenched meditation on the lawn just outside replenished my soul like a torrent surging through a deep canyon. Bundled in blankets, gazing at the stars, I felt profound wisdom permeating my marrow, not in words or concepts—rather a sublime sense of wholeness, as if a chrysalis were wrapped in these blankets and there was absolutely no longing for a butterfly to emerge; one is no more lovely than the other.

Our new home in Batesville, Virginia, rested on a low ridge nestled in the bosom of a mountain spirit, surrounded by a primal forest thick with bramble and thornbushes. It was the first home built on land newly subdivided into five-acre parcels with a couple of hundred acres set aside as community property.

We had to hack our way through thick vegetation to find our site. At one point, a large black snake lay coiled near my feet. A friend said it was a sign, and not really understanding, I acquiesced. Later, when we cleared the undergrowth, stone rubble of a century-old homesite was uncovered. We also found a small burial site nearby.

There was a large, brick country house at the front end of the four hundred acres. We had community meetings there, learned Sufi teachings one or two nights a week, and every Sunday afternoon we offered an open-house potluck dinner for visitors from near and far. On Sundays and holidays, we often practiced Sufi dancing in the back field or in the large, ramshackle barn behind the main building. Also we used the house for a weekly healing circle with the members of the Dervish Healing Order, whose leader was a founding member of the growing community. In the healing circle we meditated and sent wholesome prayers to people who were on the weekly list.

I was selected to be land manager for a while; but most major decisions were done by committee. It was a major project to develop this land with environmental and ecological consciousness. We had to have it thoroughly surveyed; a mile-long road was needed, as well as electricity and telephone lines. We also wanted to create a large pond.

As ours was the first house built, we lived in it for a year before the electricity was installed. Modern civilization abruptly entered our home the moment the electric switch was thrown. We acquired many appliances and conveniences, but soon came to regret the loss of a simpler style. Life had seemed more natural, somehow, with kerosene lamps, wood-burning stoves, carpet sweepers, ax-split fuel, and hand tools for daily maintenance. Most of all I missed the silence of our gas refrigerator when I realized how much the electric, automatic defrosting variety droned and gurgled in the background.

A separate building behind our house was erected as an office, study, and retreat sanctuary. From the day I had completed my retreat at Lama a few years earlier, I had thought of undertaking a forty-day retreat sometime in my fortieth year. There is magic in the number forty: Moses on the mountain, Jesus in the desert, Elijah in the cave, the Hebrews in the wilderness, the days of rain in the Flood of Noah.

Despite my good intentions, the demands of my business prevented me from taking more than a few days at a time during my entire fortieth year. I redoubled my resolve to complete this retreat before another year had passed. Many obstructions presented themselves, some of which seemed insurmountable. But a few months before my forty-first year was out, I forced the issue, blocked the time, and began a retreat that was to transform the course of my life, and Susan's.

This morning I had a familiar dream-vision, somewhat altered from the past: It was the presence of a huge being, a specter faintly glowing around a dark emptiness where a body might have been. Large shoulders supported a massive helmet—from inside, brilliant light arched out of tiny openings. This felt to me like a male counterpart of the goddess Kali; she destroys things by eating them. I felt a throb in my throat and began to gulp for air as my chest constricted. The being removed his mask for an instant, revealing a light that almost completely obliterated the faint face-skull barely distinguishable within the brightness. Then he covered his head once again.

In front of this fearsome creature was an egg-shaped mass. He smashed it open with one blow of a fist covered with chain mail. Two hemispheres fell apart, revealing a perfect, translucent orb. Somehow, I knew this was an essential part of my innermost being. He picked up this globe of radiance and carried it off.

A series of other visions quickly swarmed around me; I thought he was gone. But suddenly this power-spirit reappeared holding my soul-sphere. It had a new, strange light—and I was filled with a mysterious sensation of love.

Considerable time had been spent preparing for the forty days. This was not like earlier retreats, where I had made things up as I went along. Experienced meditators had told me that the best results would come from having a discipline and timetable. I asked advice from a number of people who had done retreats in the past. My schedule became full. I would arise at 3:30 A.M., or earlier, perform ablutions, chant, stretch with yoga, meditate, and repeat a number of *wazifas* (Sufi mantras).

This was the program before breakfast. Afterward, I would perform esoteric visualizations, read a page of something inspirational, write notes, practice a special meditation, rest, perform something physically strenuous, lunch, nap, spend the entire afternoon chanting carefully selected mantras or in silent practice, study Old or New Testament, Koran, Bhagavad Gītā, or Buddhist sutras, more yoga, sing a few sacred songs, eat a light supper, rest briefly, and then have an evening filled with Hindu and Buddhist mantras, *dhikr,* prayer, and a few extra, esoteric practices that I had sworn to keep secret.

After the first week, I was in a state of altered consciousness. Some of my mantras had daily sets of over a thousand repetitions. A strand of prayer beads was my constant companion so that I was sure to complete my quota. The fullness of my arbitrary schedule and the minimum daily requirements of a wide variety of practices melted all my resistance. I was completely devoted to the process; nothing was left in me to complain.

When I finished dhikr, *the moon had just set and dawn was beginning to show itself on the horizon. The instant I opened the door for a better view, a blast of icy mist charged toward the fire, scraping my face with sharp, moist claws, bringing me to instant wakefulness. The fire flared and hissed as the chilled air licked around the hairline cracks of the old wood stove. The ensuing light show seemed like thousands of fairies balancing luminous orbs on their fingertips and toes, dancing in wild gyrations on the walls and ceiling. For brief moments the flickering lights pushed aside shadow-veils, but the magical glow was soon absorbed by a thick, murky curtain that was the domain of the night-spirits still in command.*

The interplay of light and dark, morning and night, fire and dampness opposed each other like tantric counterpoint; there seemed to be a multitude of mantras within the Great Mantra of Creation.

These interactions were universal, and the beads of repetition formed an infinite strand of stars that crossed the heavens beyond the Milky Way. In those moments standing at the portal between inner and outer, I saw the measureless nature of the attraction of opposites, the unending process of merging, giving and taking, the fusing of polarities, and the continuous splitting apart that keeps the whole thing in motion; I saw how everything fits just right, exactly as it should; a perfect design.

The day began with ablutions, a new practice for me, and I discovered the potency of spiritual purification. Although scheduled for a 3:30 A.M. wake-up, I found the morning ablutions so captivating, I soon began arising at 2:30 so as not to rush the process. I first stoked the fire to break the winter-night chill and proceeded to sit on the floor with a small basin, washcloth, and soap. Slowly I bathed the sensory organs, eyes, nose, ears, mouth, hands, and feet. Each movement was accompanied by a ritual thought—for example: "May my eyes be cleared to see the truth. May my vision open the wisdom of all realities that I may see beyond the illusions of my own projections. May the light of inner clarity shine brightly."

Then the body itself would be washed; slowly, meticulously. Each *chakra* (metaphysical energy center) would receive special attention. Often associations would arise that helped me understand how things I had done in the past affected my physical, emotional, and psychic body. I tried to cleanse myself of these deeds, washing away the stains, purifying my consciousness as I imagined hidden pores opening, releasing the poisons of guilt, remorse, and anguish. The morning reflections during this process lasted an hour and a half. Then I chanted an hour of intense *dhikr*, sixteen hundred and one repetitions, to help transform and alleviate the repercussions of my past actions.

Our minds are amazing. Within the first two weeks, this exploration uncovered memories long buried and forgotten. Before I began the retreat, I thought I was fairly well acquainted with the person who uses my name. But in a short time an entirely new awareness infiltrated my being, and gaps appeared in my old identity. A part remained recognizable, but I had new eyes and ears, new feelings and expressions, and unquestionably a fresh way of understanding. It far exceeded my most profound drug experiences—this was a sustained altered consciousness with no side effects.

The new consciousness carried me to the heights of wonder, but I was also beginning to realize how my mind was filled with extraneous matter: old mementos, advertising jingles, movies, tapes, anger, frustration, fantasy, paranoia—an endless flow, usually repetitive, raged unimpeded throughout the day. There were moments of relative peace when the tap was suddenly shut off and everything became quiet. But they were rare. Sometimes my work with mantras was sufficient to block out this constant mental activity, but sooner or later, a thought would impose itself. Sometimes a seemingly inconsequential event from many years earlier would appear abruptly and dominate my thoughts no matter what practice I was doing. Each day became more painful because the busy mind would not remain quiet for long.

The blissful experiences I recorded in my diary were islands in a sea of enormous contrast: from doldrums of deadly boredom to gales sweeping froth across a mind racing out of control. This sea was inhabited with all sorts of weird creatures, including many mental thieves that steal time with impunity. They have common names, such as planning, rehearsing, wanting, not-wanting, reviewing, and reliving, as well as all the "coulds," "shoulds," and "if onlys." But these simple names are deceptive, for the actual entities of busy thought are vile creatures, parasites that feed on our vitality, leeches that drain us, leaving little with which to see, hear, or feel what is really going on around us.

This sea of mental activity stretches beyond the horizon, and its depth cannot be fathomed. It is so immense, it drowns the sun. If it were not for brief respites on islands that I discovered only on the inward voyages of my retreats, I would never have experienced the illumination whose brilliance permeates all creation. Yet, despite the irresistible luminescence of this source of light, it remains concealed in the swirl of mind activity. An Indian master named Thayumanavar wrote the following poem:

> You may control a mad elephant.
> You may shut the mouth of the bear and the tiger.
> Ride the lion and play with the cobra.
> By alchemy you may earn your livelihood;
> You may wander through the universe incognito;

> Make vassals of the gods; be ever youthful;
> You may walk on water and live in fire;
> But control of the mind is better and more difficult.[16]

We often consider mind activity a function of intelligence, yet sages in many traditions believe that most mind activity is really a sign of ignorance. This ignorance is not something that we eliminate through study, nor is it an emptiness that we can fill with knowledge. Rather it is the offspring of deluded thinking, the opposite of awareness. Wisdom teachings suggest that ignorance exists only in conjunction with ego, the sense that "I am something." When we are able to disengage from this misperception, ignorance immediately vanishes. One of India's wisest teachers in this century, Ramana Maharshi, said:

> There is no *avidya* [Sanskrit: ignorance] in reality. All *sastras* [scriptures] are meant to disprove the existence of *avidya*. It is ignorance or forgetfulness of the Self.[17] Can there be darkness before the sun? . . . If you know the Self there will be no darkness, no ignorance and no misery. . . . Ignorance never arose. It has no real being. That which is, is only *vidya* [knowledge].[18]

When mystics speak of knowledge, they are never referring to the kind of information we may glean from newspapers, textbooks, or libraries. They mean the knowing that grows out of the realization that things are not what they seem to be. Everything we think we are is part of the vast sea of forgetfulness; it is dark as pitch. One spark, one candle, and we begin to see the truth.

So the path of wisdom is not what we think. It does not require traveling, encounters with enlightened beings, or years of devotional practices. All of these are useful, but there is a requirement without which progress is impossible. Quite simply, we must find a way to sharpen our inner vision.

My practices on retreat revealed to me that one way to gain insight is through strong effort. But experience had taught me that this was not enough. Not long after each of these retreats, I was rapidly consumed by forgetfulness when I reentered the everyday world. Even spending an hour or two every day was not sufficient to maintain the level of awareness that developed during my periods of silence and solitude.

A majority of the thoughts that plagued me on retreat were related to events that had recently occurred or were expected to happen. As long as I reentered my world with the same patterns and habits of a lifetime, familiar thought forms appeared. The only way to change them was to introduce new activities and eliminate some of the things that continually imposed themselves in my mind. This was a process of purifying, casting off an old skin, opening more possibilities to encounter new islands in this limitless sea of forgetfulness.

I have been working with a practice in which I interrupt any thought or vision with a mental curtain called: "Hold it!" or "Stop!" or "Wait a minute." But when I do so, I find an inner voice asking: "Who is saying, 'Hold it'?" "Who is thinking, 'Stop'?" " 'Wait a minute' " for what? Then the mirror begins reflecting in an infinite regression: "Who is asking about who is saying. . . . "

Usually this process spins itself out like an exhausted top, and I wobble and flop into an inert mental lump. But only an hour ago something different happened when I was in the corridor of mirrors bouncing the "who is behind the who" back and forth. It was as if somewhere in that infinite string of images a new face appeared and the shock of this bizarre apparition broke through in one incredible moment: My mind cracked. In this tingling instant an electric wave of elation pierced my soul, revealing a rich golden treasure: The Buddha's smile illuminated every cell of my being, and I knew I would never be the same again.

Eighteen days after the retreat began I had a brief flash of *samādhi* that was the most sensual experience of my life. The afterglow remained for a number of days. I tried to reclaim the experience, repeating all of the things I had done before it appeared, praying that it would come back. The more I tried, the unhappier I became, until four days later I had used up all my resources and was exhausted by the futility of trying to grasp something that could arise only through grace. I was saddened to think it might never reappear; I wanted to keep it for the rest of my life.

My moment of mini-*samādhi* was a fluke. I would like to think it was a gift, but it was also a torture. It was as if an ideal friend, partner, teacher, or spouse materialized long enough for the taste of perfection—only to disappear. Every teaching I have read emphasizes that one cannot and should not hold on to such experiences. The teachers are correct, of course: We *cannot* hold on, and this is the torture. Once we have experienced pristine bliss, it is extremely difficult to release it completely, without any residual thoughts or longings.

My midday mantra was to chant HU! HU! HU! (one of the many divine names in Judaism and Islam) at the top of my lungs; today's prescription: ten thousand repetitions. During the chant, a vision arose of a Tibetan monk in beautiful robes wearing a high hat. He looked at me and put his finger to his lips, while my HU! HU! HU! was like lightning ripping apart my molecular system, thundering as it clashed back into a new form. The inner monk was trying to quiet this frenzy, but I was caught in the spirit of the moment—my beads told me I was only halfway done.

The monk sat peacefully for a while, but then his face began to contort, and his jaw and mouth extended directly into the center of my mind, into the place of absolute stillness that rests eternally serene even in the midst of a maelstrom of mental static. The lips of his stretched jaw opened, but no sound was emitted. Rather a lush, rich tree came out, brimming with plump, ripe fruit. I noticed each HU! was like a breeze passing through this tree. But I did not understand the message. My intellect suggested I should stop; but I felt I should finish what I had begun. And so I did—the vision faded long before I completed my daily round.

I was curious about the tree, and when I looked into my books I found the following: "The Tree of Life [Genesis 2:9] refers to the most profound spiritual experience. . . . The prophet reaches the highest levels of mystical experience, actually transcending the bonds that tie his mind and soul to the physical world. In accomplishing this he is actually approaching the Tree of Life. . . . "[19]

I felt something important had been revealed in that vision. The Tree of Life is a key symbol in the kabbalistic system, representing a foundation upon which the entire cosmology of mystical Judaism stands. I was forcefully struck by a recurring theme that seemed to appear in my deepest meditations. It had to do with something I could not grasp, but formed a continuing connection with Jewishness as if it were almost an encoded pattern in my genealogical structure. It seemed to transcend the cultural and familial connections. I was a fully assimilated twentieth-century generalist who had no religious upbringing, had rarely been inside a synagogue, and knew only that Jews fasted on Yom Kippur. Still, these visions continued to arise.

The previous year I had attended a Sufi conference in New York City, and one of the presenters was Rabbi Zalman Schachter-Shalomi. He began his talk with the Sufi invocation:

> Toward the One, the Perfection of Love, Harmony, and Beauty; the Only Being, united with all the Illuminated Souls who form the embodiment of the Master, the Spirit of Guidance.

I was impressed; here was a rabbi who could offer a universal perspective. In his talk that day, he said one thing that reverberated somewhere deep within. He said, "If there is anyone here who is interested in becoming a rabbi, please come see me."

There were over a thousand people attending this conference, but in that moment it felt as if the rabbi and I were sitting in his study, surrounded by bookshelves reaching to the ceiling, and he was penetrating to a core of being I had never before felt. For many months after this symposium, the words "become a rabbi" appeared at odd moments, dancing in my meditations, whispering to me in the middle of the night. Finally, I contacted Reb Zalman and arranged to meet with him one weekend at a seminar he was giving in Washington, D.C.

We sat on the grass, and I asked him what it took to become a rabbi. His answer: "You must feel authentic." My instant response was that I did not even feel like an authentic Jew, whatever that means. And his reply: "That's the worm that turns in the heart."

The next morning he asked me if I would like to wrap *tefillin*. I had no idea what *tefillin* were; I could not even pronounce the word. *Tefillin* are ritual items worn by traditional Jews during the weekday morning prayers. They consist of two small, cube-shaped leather boxes with black leather straps. Each box contains scripture written on tiny scrolls, and each is made entirely of natural material from kosher animals. One box is worn on the top part of the forehead—in the middle—and its straps hang over each shoulder; the other is worn on the upper arm—facing the heart—and its strap is wrapped around the forearm and secured on the hand.

I was forty years old and had never seen or heard of such things.

If I had, I probably would have reacted to them as a form of black magic, a kind of occult hocus pocus that has infected the world from time immemorial. But here was a respected and intelligent person suggesting that I try wearing these things. So I allowed Reb Zalman to wrap me in his personal *tefillin*. Then he directed me to the back of the room and asked that I sit quietly and meditate. Here's what I wrote in my journal after that incident:

A huge scroll is lying open, cushioned on a steaming bed of glowing coals, but the flames licking around its edges do not burn the pages. The pages themselves are shining, as if they are an iron brand in the fire. Letters on the pages are written in Hebrew script, and I "know" what they say, but my mind argues that I cannot read Hebrew. I "read" for a long time, the letters etching themselves on my soul.

In the background a candlestick arises, and I recognize it as a menorah. Alongside are giant loaves of bread; I count twelve of them. In the distance I hear a muffled trumpet, and I realize it is the call of the shofar. A flood of images then pours rapidly through this vision: priests dressed in lavish garments, crowds of people carrying lambs, the sacrifice of thousands of animals, billows of smoke and incense, on and on it flowed. Finally, a flaming sword arose from the ever-present bed of red-hot coals, and it was poised vertically before me, held by an unseen hand. Then it descended, splitting the middle of my skull, passing through my neck and straight through the body. I lost all sense of consciousness.

At some point, I heard Reb Zalman's voice speaking softly: "I think it is time to come back." My face was soaked in tears; I had no idea how long I had been sitting there. I was grateful in those first moments that someone had come for me, because it seemed that I would never have returned without a human touch.

This was my first extended episode with spontaneous images that had obvious Jewish context. I never resolved the mystery of Reb Zalman's *tefillin*, nor did I ever feel that he intended me to have such an experience. Wrapping *tefillin* is something that traditional Jews do every weekday, and he wanted me to share in the ritual. Nonetheless, I was shaken by this meditation. I had often had visions in my meditative work, but never with subject matter like this. I was astonished and bewildered: Where had it come from? I had never seen a Torah scroll, we never had a menorah in our home, I did not learn until much later the significance of the twelve loaves of bread that were part of the service of the First and Second Temples, I had never seen pictures of the high priest, and perhaps once in my teen years had I heard a *shofar* blown when a friend invited me to join him at Rosh Hashanah services.

There is a great deal of discussion in the mystical texts about the "Jewish soul." Most of it I find offensive because it is used as a point of division, separating humanity into categories. This is common in many traditions, each of which claims to hold the keys to heaven. But there is a more profound question having to do with archetype and myth, the collective unconscious and the transmission of inner knowledge. This was the focus of my fascination; how it was that after forty years I should begin to discover an aspect of my heritage that I had never suspected.

After my experience with Reb Zalman's *tefillin,* we began to discuss the process of becoming a rabbi. His educational approach was much less formal than following a curriculum in a seminary; it was designed to meet each student's needs. The course of study was not defined, but familiarity with a wide variety of texts, customs, and skills was the ultimate goal. I was intrigued by the prospect of following his program.

On this retreat, when my inner monk in his lavish Tibetan robes revealed the Tree of Life—which is at the centermost point of the Garden of Eden, the source of all mystical awareness—I knew that this was a continuation of the revelation of a spiritual stream that flowed deep within my essential being. Later in the retreat I was to perceive the full impact of this new reality as the Tree of Life offered me its fruit.

5

I heard a door close and slipped out of the house because I did not want to be disturbed while on retreat. Halfway up the path to my studio, I noticed it was dark outside. "Wait a minute," I thought, "it should be daytime!" At this instant I realized I was dreaming. But it was not like any dream I had known. I could sense my body on the edge of awareness, lying on its back in the middle of my retreat sanctuary; yet I was standing on the path outside, enjoying the brisk, clear night air. I was wearing a light shirt, yet felt no chill; when I walked along the path, there was no sound and the pebbles did not move.

I walked back to the house and passed through a closed door. Susan was seated in the living room reading a book. She did not seem to notice my presence. I sat next to her and read over her shoulder. The couch did not sag where I sat. In a mind-flicker, a part of me remembered that I was lying on my prayer rug fifty yards away.

I found myself beginning to float slightly above the couch, exhilarated. This kindled in me the lifelong desire to fly, and I wondered if I could pass through the ceiling and roof. I began to lift up, but I felt my mind tugging, and at that moment I felt my body begin to stir on the prayer rug. In an instant I was awakening, feeling the heat of the wood stove at my side, noticing the hiss of burning embers and the distant thud of an ax splitting wood. I got up from the rug and looked out the window, across the garden. Now fully awake, I saw the back door open, and Susan—holding a book—came out on the porch to stretch in the noonday sun.

During the third week, I began to have what I later learned were lucid dreams—out-of-body experiences. They were a delicate matter; I could impose a certain amount of will and maintain this altered state, but whenever I crossed an imaginary line of ego involvement, the dream would end. Over the years that have followed this first adventure into obscure realms, there have been many episodes, and I have become more skillful; but although my voyages in this condition surpass description, whenever personal ambition became an element, the experience abruptly disintegrated. I have learned to surrender to another hand that guides.

Susan was the guardian of my sanctuary. She related to me later that within a week after the retreat had begun, she was forcefully drawn into her own solitude because she so often felt my presence. A powerful bond takes place between a retreatant and her or his guardian. The quality of this bonding acquired new meaning for me when I reflected upon the dream experiences in which I discovered a plane of existence where thought and material substance are not clearly distinguishable from each other. How often was my presence on the couch next to Susan or she beside me in the retreat sanctuary, because of the focus of our thoughts?

Later she told me that as I was plunging into the unknown, she was drawn mysteriously, inexorably into her own exploration. Spontaneously, she began a retreat routine and soon was engaged in a rigorous practice. Throughout the remainder of our retreats she arranged for a neighbor-friend to be the guardian for both of us, and she then had the freedom to enter her own practice with full abandon. Our parallel retreats added a new dimension to the process.

Throughout the first half of the forty days, I focused on rites of purification because I felt contaminated by negative thought. My life had been dominated by a need for acceptance that translated into parental approval, achievement in school, success in business, devotion to friends, and a wide variety of mating games. On the surface, this was a common experience of many people in my generation—I was a solid citizen—but my inner being constantly squirmed at the bland mediocrity of acceptable behavior. In addition, I spent a great deal of time reviewing events and reliving them, as if enough repetition could undo what had happened, or rehearsing the future as if I could control the way things would unfold.

While on retreat, although the patterns of thought were familiar, I was able to observe them more clearly. The more I witnessed my mental functions, the less I was interested in maintaining the status quo. As Ibn al-Arabi, the thirteenth-century Sufi scholar, said:

> When the darkness of ignorance takes up residence in the heart, it makes it blind. Then the heart is not able to perceive those realities in respect of perceiving which is called a "knower".[20]

Many people rapidly discover on retreat that the witness is the part of us that "knows," while our thought process resides primarily in a dark zone of self-indulgence.

Face-images tumbled over each other, a thousand a minute. At first they looked like plain and simple folks, young and old, but then the visions melted into more grotesque forms: slobbering hunchbacks, hags with craggy teeth, demons breathing lizards, hollowed skulls, rotted flesh—it went on for a long time.

Then, pitch-black. A red glow formed, at first as a point in the distance, soon becoming brighter as an image approached. A neck-pulse beat against my collar when I recognized the face. It was ruddy and angular with shadowed eye slits, behind which nothing was visible; the cruel mouth had twisted scarlet lips that sneered around razor-sharp teeth.

This was Death; I was certain. Not the Angel of Death sent from above, but the Other Side, the demon to take me to rot in hell—to fulfill the curse that had been put on me.

I did not, could not, run. I had to have an answer, or die. I knew that I must have a sense of the Divine in my life; the spiritual gates must open. Otherwise, what was the purpose of saying I was alive if I was not really living? I looked my death vision in the murky emptiness where the eyes should have been and said, "Go ahead; I'm ready."

Death laughed in my face. It said that I was bluffing. A gun appeared, pointed directly above my nose. I could see bullets in the chambers. The dark, sanguine face behind the gun—no longer laughing—was intense.

There was no doubt in my mind. I would die if the trigger was pulled. As certain as a bullet in the brain, Death would take me in some way. I watched the gnarled, blackened, horn-nailed finger squeezing tighter on the trigger—it was my death warrant. For a moment, I hesitated. Deep within, a declaration arose: Yes! It was an affirmation of life—but not to continue this life. Yes, I wanted to live, but only on condition that I would be able to follow the light of the Divine. Otherwise, I wanted Death to pull the trigger.

We faced each other in this showdown. It was high noon, and I was prepared to die. I waited. Death stared at me, and I at it. Fear sucked at my vitals, everything was parched in this desert. Yet my resolve grew, and I never wavered. We gazed interminably, but nothing happened. Then, slowly, very slowly, the image faded. It disappeared. The trigger was never pulled.

Things were about to change on this retreat; I could sense something growing, but had no idea the direction it would take. I found myself praying—for the first time in my life—for help to gain freedom from my conditioning and the obsessive patterns that I had developed over a lifetime. Despite my ability in this solitude to spend time dwelling in realms that offered thorough satisfaction, my mind would often still fall into old patterns and self-destructive fixations. Also, I found sexual fantasy to be a dominant preoccupation, and it felt as though this was the time to gain objective distance, if that was possible. My prayers for release from these obsessions became impassioned. However, I was soon to learn that prayers are often answered in unanticipated ways that exact a price well beyond our expectations. Thus, we frequently hear an admonition, "Be careful what you ask for—you might get it."

Susan and I had an agreement that whenever one of us was on retreat, we would not pass notes except for serious reasons. Occasionally, an exceptional moment would occur when a love-rush needed to be expressed, and all rules would be put aside. We tried not to spoil ourselves, but sitting alone can prove alienating; thus it was comforting to know that a source of protection and love was nearby. Also, we found that occasional love notes were a benefit rather than a distraction on a retreat. So, when a note arrived at the time of my concentrated prayer for a light to break through the darkness of self-deception and spiritual ignorance, I smiled to myself, thinking it was a tender expression of support. The smile ended abruptly when I glanced at the note—it was terrifying. I had been found out.

During the last few months before I had begun the retreat, my wandering eye had caught the glance of another woman, and we had had a brief affair. A few days before I received the alarming note from Susan—by my calculation when my prayers began in earnest—this woman had confessed to her husband. His mind was now on murder, and it was no joke. This news had just reached Susan.

Her note was terse, frosty, and remote. She and I had been partners for six years. We had avoided marriage to maintain our so-called freedom, but early in our relationship experimentation had revealed that nothing was quite as destructive to our mutual trust and bond as extracurricular activities.

Things were bad enough when either of us found out about an infidelity, but worse when something remained undisclosed and the cheating was thought to be a well-kept secret. There are no real secrets in a long-term relationship. Whether secrets are spoken openly or not, a soul-ulcer forms on an essential level. When we are in the dark ignorance of our common, daily states of mind, we deceive ourselves into believing that circumspection and discretion can successfully hide the truth. However, in the sensitive altered state of heightened awareness, we recognize the subtle effects of all our actions. Nothing happens without having an effect upon the universe; our partners are influenced by our acts in ways that defy imagination.

The next few days were spent in enormous pain. The periods set for meditation turned sour. Chanting was dull, boring, and repetitive. I was haunted by images and harsh fantasies about Susan, the rest of the community, and, most of all, the irate husband appearing with a shotgun. I went through the routine of my schedule, but it was a facade. My mind burned in an inferno. I sent a repentant note to Susan, but nothing could cool the passions that ensnared us.

As it turned out, the husband had been encouraged by his therapist to confront me, despite the fact that I was on retreat. When he appeared, I was not certain if it was a lucid dream/nightmare, or really happening. Normally, I would have run the other way, but I still carried a powerful remnant of the work I had done during the first part of the retreat. Thus, I had a feeling of resignation, a sense of fate, and a strengthened belief that universal justice is absolute. When I saw him approach, I walked out to meet him, expecting to get my face smashed. It was my first conversation in almost four weeks.

He kept his hands in his pockets, but his enraged body trembled uncontrollably and he growled at me through chattering teeth. I knew that the slightest word misspoken would unleash his anger, and I could feel fear squirming in my gut. By the grace of providence, physical violence was avoided. Still, the verbal and emotional vehemence pouring out of him tore into my soul, a dark cloud enveloped me, and when he walked away, he might as well have left me a bleeding wreck; I was empty, abandoned, destroyed.

The rest of the day was spent in self-torment. All of the pent-up energy of weeks of sitting exploded in one vision after another of familiar faces in pain, sadness, and lonely despair. The retreat seemed to be over, everything was in a shambles. A continual thought whispered that I should give it up; but another voice kept murmuring something indistinct that drew me to it.

The following morning, as I performed my ablutions, I heard the whisper more explicitly. Was this not an answer to my prayers? Without a sledgehammer like this, I would have been unable to resolve my own dilemma, for I was trapped in my mind. Had I not faced this experience during the retreat, no matter what state of consciousness I attained through my meditative practice, sooner or later this past would have caught up with me, grabbed me by the neck, and, like a terrier, shaken me until I was nothing but a helpless rag.

Sweat pours; the cramps in my legs will not stop. Committed to be motionless for an hour, I peek at the clock. Only thirty minutes have passed. Oh, God, the pain is spreading to my hips.

OM MANE PADME HUM *is my mantra. A haze of pinkish gray fills the room; everything looks like an oozing sore of pus and blood. Perspiration clouds my eyes, tears begin to well. The pain is making me nauseated.*

The OM *groans on. I am now weeping without respite. Sobbing in misery, still I will not unlock my legs. Forty-five minutes have passed. Fifteen to go.*

Gone were the lucid dreams, visions of light, feeling of harmony and well-being. For the next few days I dropped into a bottomless chasm. I knew there was an answer, somewhere in the pain and suffering. An event like this might have happened any time. Why now, on this retreat? My thoughts constantly returned to the woman, her husband, their child—how lives pivot on events that may only have been momentary fun and games. This was not fun anymore; whole lives were profoundly affected. Moreover, I obsessed on the question of what was happening to Susan, and what would happen to us.

Meditations were filled with busy thoughts, fear, frustration, sorrow, and despair. If it were not that I knew something important was occurring, I would have quit. But all the traditions speak of pain and suffering as an important part of the process. I had enormous remorse, but my inner yearning—the feeling of separation from my spiritual core—held me steady and persistent in the ongoing meditation practice. My own suffering opened new understanding and compassion for the awful predicament of human existence. It helped in this process to learn the teaching that pain is a necessary part of transition.

Most of us want to avoid pain, but as Brother David Steindl-Rast says:

> If we live . . . the contemplative life of keeping the eyes continuously on the vision and then of translating that vision into everyday action—we will inevitably end up on the cross [i.e., profoundly experiencing the suffering of the world]. We may be reluctant to accept this, but in fact there is no bypass. . . . We have a choice of two attitudes, both of which are painful: we can either feel anxiety because we don't trust that life is a good gift, or we can exchange that anxiety for a positive kind of suffering, which is a growing pain. The second choice is the suffering of compassion, which is the joyful suffering of going with the grain, of realizing that it is narrowness that leads to life.[21]

At the end of the week, I gained new strength from maintaining the rhythm of a schedule. The more I meditated, the clearer my resolve became. I realized that I had reached my peak during the first half of this retreat, before everything fell apart. My limits were determined before I began. In mystical terms, we all live under the psychic burden of our actions. Even if this traumatic event had not become public, I would have carried it in my heart, and this heav-

iness, along with other deeds, now determined my spiritual potential. The only way to achieve anything more was through devoted
practice of purification, minimizing the constant addition of misdeeds and repairing, to the degree possible, the brokenness left
behind.

In the middle of the fifth week, I wrote a note to Susan. She
had been going through her own hell realms during this period.
My note was simple. I apologized again for the pain I had caused,
and I made a declaration that I had thought impossible: I vowed
fidelity to our relationship from that moment forward. We were so
in harmony that she passed a note to me at the same time. I was
shocked to discover that it contained essentially the same message
as mine to her. She had reached her own epiphany. As we read
each other's notes, we realized that our universe had shifted; in
the flash of a quantum leap we were now dancing to a melody we
had previously never heard.

I began making more journal entries during the last week of the
retreat. The writing revealed an inner truth that I had been unable
to derive in meditative contemplation. It became clear that I would
have to undergo a complete change of life-style if I wished to pursue the enlightenment process. A demanding daily practice was
needed to avoid falling back into old patterns; it had to have depth,
and it had to have passed the test of time. This led to the idea of
surrendering to a traditional religious path, despite my innate skep-
ticism. I reasoned that the precepts of a traditional path were designed to minimize the daily experiences that normally add to our
psychic burdens. In essence, traditional paths are natural routes of
purification.

Once it was obvious to me that the pursuit of such a path was
indispensable for my growth, I was still uncertain which path to
take. The Eastern traditions were familiar; I was particularly drawn
to Buddhism. The Western traditions were also familiar, and my
Sufi training up to now glowed warmly in my heart. There was
much to be said for Hindu teachings, and during the first three
weeks of the retreat I had experienced the remarkable glow of love
that I associated with the presence of Christ. I knew that any of
these paths would carry me to high plateaus, but a voice nagged,
"You are a Jew."

It was true that I had been born into a Jewish family; but we
were totally assimilated. My maternal grandmother was attracted

to Christian Science, and this certainly influenced my mother. I never went to Jewish day school, my folks were not members of a synagogue, I did not go through the ritual *bar mitzvah* that many Jewish thirteen-year-old boys experience, I had hardly ever been to religious services on High Holy Days. So I was a Jew by heritage alone. As an American Buddhist once answered when asked if he was Jewish: "Only on my parents' side."

I sat with this question for many days. Whenever I fantasized about putting on robes, shaving my head, or going off to India, Burma, or Thailand, my inner voice would rebel. After a while, I began to explore my feelings about Judaism. It frightened me, repelled me; I knew little about it, but it seemed constrictive, paternal, obtuse, exclusive, and completely archaic. Yet there was potential. The Sabbath is a day of retreat that occurs once a week. Passover and Sukkot could each be viewed as a week of spiritual retreat—one in the spring and one in the fall. Keeping kosher was an excellent purification practice. Moreover, there were many rules of daily living that would raise consciousness.

Throughout this entire process, the idea of becoming a rabbi was not a concern. My issue was with Judaism as a daily experience, whether or not it could be a spiritual practice that would enhance my personal growth. In the end, it was resolved through the ultimate question anyone can ask on a spiritual path: "Who am I?" or "Why am I in this particular incarnation?" For me this translated into "Why was I born a Jew?" If all paths lead to the source of Creation, then my own heritage might be a divine cue that I should follow. The more I considered this question, the more genuinely I found myself drawn to Judaism.

The other theme of my contemplation had to do with relationship. The spiritual path requires enormous commitment, as does a high-quality relationship. Some traditions compel the total loyalty of an aspirant. There is no room for the constant emotional distractions that are a normal part of human relationships. Thus celibacy is a primary tenet of many monastic communities, as well as for the clergy of numerous lineages. Moreover, in the traditions that include relationship as an integral part of the practice, almost all insist upon faithfulness to one partner.

A loud demon-voice in me hated this idea; it was infuriated. This was the one who wanted me to cross my fingers when I was writing the note to Susan; it wanted to couch the phrases in the note to leave some escape routes. It tried to bargain, plead, tease, cajole; it said repeatedly, "Aw, come on, you don't really want to do this!"

But the voice within that yearned to be in contact with the Divine, the part that found itself praying for resolve, the essential inner being knew that this was an important turning point in my life. The route of surrender to serious spiritual discipline seemed to be overgrown, dark, and scary; but there really was no choice. I had to follow this way, and I wanted to have a helpmate with me. Our only possibility for achievement was to have unconfused loyalty to each other, lest we wander off the path and be lost in the surrounding jungle.

I sent another note to Susan; this time a bombshell for *her*. The note asked three major questions: Would she be willing to get married? Would she consider converting to Judaism? Would she quit smoking? This proposal of marriage was our spiritual turning point—it was the fruit that the Tree of Life offered, and it dramatically changed our lives.

A major area of concern remained. If I resolved to follow the Jewish path because I was born into it, why not use the same logic for Susan to become more committed to her birthright of Catholicism? But she was not drawn in this direction. Her choice to follow my lead was more out of intuition than desire. She knew that we had to work together. It would have been easier, perhaps, had we both walked away from our heritage and selected an Eastern tradition. But we each followed our inner guide, and thus it turned out that she decided to convert.

Susan changed her name to Shoshana at the time of her conversion, a month before the wedding. She enjoyed telling the story with an impish smile that as difficult as it was to undertake a religious conversion, it had been even more difficult to give up smoking—which was accomplished by spending a few weeks on tranquilizers. But the deeper truth was that her conversion from a Catholic upbringing was a major burden.

There is always associated guilt in a religious conversion when one's roots are firmly set, and although Shoshana had some negative feelings about her Catholic training, she still was closely connected on a primal level. Moreover, she was clearly anxious about her family's reaction. Even during the wedding, which was obviously conducted in a Jewish atmosphere under a *chuppah* with a famous rabbi officiating, the issue was not confronted. It took years to discuss it openly. Indeed, it turned out that embracing traditional Judaism was enormously demanding for her—and for me as well. It was a much bigger decision than either of us imagined or could have conceived.

Pounding my chest as I chant HU! HU! HU! I feel the sheath of alienation around my heart begin to splinter. My schedule requires one hundred thousand and one repetitions of this sacred name during the last week of my forty days. As I chant, I suddenly realize that while we see only what we look at, the spiritual essence that I am calling HU! sees everything. When I soften my gaze behind the ongoing chant, I begin to see as HU! sees, and soon the entire room makes an impression. I know where everything is, even behind me.

HU! does not "see" in a way that attaches concepts, such as: that is a window or this is a table. Rather, a higher sense arises—a knowing that is aware of primal energies. In one direction is brightness, flickering shadows, smoothness, emptiness, and warmth. In another direction is darkness, roughness, sturdiness, and roundness. These are not "things" as we normally think of them, they are displays of a vital force; they weave, flow, and transmute constantly into new forms of expression, as a cosmic artist sweeps a brush across the canvas of creation.

We hear only what we listen to, but HU! hears everything. HU! hears essences: pitch, harmony, rhythm; it also hears hums, whines, groans, sighs, buzzes. The walls of my studio block many sounds, but HU! hears the cosmic symphony. Venus has her song, so too Saturn, Mars, and the other planetary bodies: the solar system makes glorious music. And HU! hears it all.

When the sun arises each morning these days, the forest around the studio explodes in a measureless array of harmonic notes. HU! consciousness leaves me far behind. This simple body, aching, confused, obsessed, and wounded is a granule at the bottom of a mountainous heap of impressions. HU! is the cry of whales haunting sea creatures for miles around; it is the howl of coyotes when the moon is full; it is the gnashing of teeth as life flows into new forms.

A hundred thousand and one HU!s is nothing, not a dust mote. Yet each HU! contains the universe; each is the cry of the infant or sigh of the dying; each reveals the secret of creation. Each breaks the outer shell of the heart a little more so that we can enter its core. Without a broken heart, it is said, we can go nowhere.

The puzzle of life lies before me in thousands of pieces. I have located the smooth-sided shapes that form the border; all the edges are matched together, and the frame is set. But the inside is empty, and many piles of odd-shaped pieces are gathered around the sides, organized by color. It does not feel to me that it takes brilliance to solve this puzzle; moreover, although we can learn clues and techniques to help us, nobody can teach its solution. In the end, however, it may be simple to complete the mystery alone, if we have the two necessary qualities: determination and endurance.

6

BATESVILLE, VIRGINIA: NOVEMBER 1982.
SEVEN-DAY RETREAT FOLLOWING AN
INTENSE YEAR OF WORK ON THIS
YEAR'S CONGRESSIONAL ELECTIONS.
MY RETREAT SANCTUARY IS STILL PILED HIGH WITH STACKS
OF COMPUTER PAPER AND DOZENS OF REPORTS.

The surrounding forest erupted this autumn like a volcanic display of gold and vermilion spilling down the mountainside, igniting the lower brush along the way until it felt like an inferno that would leave nothing but ash. It was a sumptuous feast of visual delight compared with the autumn browns, tans, and ochers of the lands around Jerusalem, desert scorched by the tropical heat of summer.

We returned from our Jerusalem honeymoon a year ago with plans to sell our home and our business, fully expecting to return to the Holy Land as immigrants. However, we soon became involved in community affairs, and the year was spent engaged in a flurry of business, expanding our garden, and helping our neighbors. It had been a vital and productive year. Shoshana and I had many late-night discussions, watching the stars through rising steam while we relaxed in the soothing waters of our hot tub. Objectively, life here was rich and we were well settled; an outsider might even have called it idyllic.

For many months we had second thoughts about returning to Israel. Business was better than ever—in just a few more years we would be certain to have a splendid money flow. We had put our house on the market, and only one buyer came along. One is all that is needed; but this one backed out at the last minute. If we believed in divine providence—and that was the belief system of the culture we were about to enter—all indications pointed to delaying our return until we were more financially secure, a minimum of four or five years away.

We had been in Jerusalem for only a brief time—a couple of months. Granted, it was love at first sight, but we wondered if it was infatuation. The decision to change our lives seemed so clear before we left Israel, but back in the comfort and familiarity of our home in Virginia, each day added more grist to the mill—and our disorientation grew stronger.

This morning I remembered a scene from our trip to Israel. For the third Sabbath meal, we had visited a hasidic yeshiva—an institution of higher learning—in one of the most religious neighborhoods. The rebbe sat at the middle of a long table; on either side were men, constantly stroking long gray beards, dressed in knee-length shiny black caftans, and large fur hats. The rebbe mindfully selected morsels of food from the large plate in front of him. Crowded around the table dozens of younger men, also in black, waited in hunched silence. The rebbe would take one bite from each piece of food and then pass it on—few honors are as exalted as eating from food tasted by the rebbe.

Every so often someone in the throng would raise a cup of wine, inspiring everyone with his toast: "L'chaim, l'chaim tovim!" ("To life, to a good life!") Every hasid in the room would drink and refill his cup from a bottle of wine that the rebbe himself had used. But when the rebbe began to speak, a hush swept through the crowd, and every word that passed his lips was absorbed like water dripping onto parched sand. He told the following story:

Once there was a king who had a son. This favored son did not appreciate the kingdom, nor did he understand the role of prince. He constantly played when it was time to study; he never took the affairs of state seriously. The king worried that the son would not be able to do his job when it came time for him to rule, so the king made the decision to exile the son temporarily from the palace so that he might learn from the school of life.

The prince was sent away to a distant land with only the clothes on his back. As he was not trained in any skills, he soon took to begging for his food, and he slept wherever he could find shelter. After a short time, when his empty belly gnawed, or his body trembled and chattered in the damp, cold night air, the prince truly understood what he had lost. He began to long for the palace and would have done anything to return.

But the king was concerned that the prince would soon again succumb to his wanton ways if he were redeemed too easily, so the king decided that he would not send for the prince until sufficient time had elapsed. The years passed, but unfortunately during this time the prince lost hope and began to distrust his own reality. He saw how many people lived in fantasy worlds, and the prince began to think that his own memories were hallucinations invented to bring some warmth into the otherwise bitter, chilly nights. After a while he gave up thinking about the princely life and thought only about food and shelter.

Finally, the king sent his envoy to find the prince and grant whatever his son wished. The king's ambassador did not have to look for long under the bridges of the distant land before he found the prince in filthy rags. He announced the king's message to the prince—that he could have anything his heart desired. The prince pondered the offer for only a short time and then asked for a warm coat and a plate of food. That was all.

You see, the prince had completely forgotten who he was and what he could be. The palace for him was a mere fabrication, and the idea that his father was king was, as far as he was concerned, a delusion. The prince thought the messenger himself was mad, for he knew the entire world around him was filled with insanity. Now the prince was like all the other beggars and vagabonds—and there was no escape.

Thus the rebbe ended the story. I had hoped for a happy ending, that everything would turn out for the best and the prince would be returned to the kingdom. But the rebbe was teaching that the predicament of our lives was exactly like the prince. We have been away from the distant kingdom for so long, we have forgotten who we are. If we want the story to turn out well for the prince, it is the same as yearning for the story to turn out well for ourselves. What then must we do to get back to the palace?

The group swayed quietly in anticipation of more wisdom teachings from the rebbe, but none were forthcoming. He silently nibbled on the cake that signaled the end of the meal, and passed on large pieces for his students to share. Finally, someone asked him if the prince was ever redeemed or if he was still wandering in rags. The rebbe looked at the earnest young man and, after a long, penetrating gaze, slowly

*smiled, and said: "The king still lives and continues to send his em-
issaries because he knows the prince will awaken. Each time we say
Shema Yisrael,[22] we are not only the messenger, we are the message
itself, and—listen carefully—we are the ones to whom the message is
addressed."*

The enormity of our decision to move to Israel awakened deep-
seated primal fears. We drew up lists and tried to analyze all the
implications, but whenever we thought we had a complete picture,
the variables seemed to multiply perversely. In addition to financial
considerations, family relations, career potentials, language skills,
support groups, and health care, we found ourselves turning to
issues such as self-identity, starting again in kindergarten, being
illiterate, and the constant threat of violence.

None of these issues had presented itself when we were in Jerusalem. People living in the religious world seemed sure that their
lives were unfolding according to divine plan, and they worked
diligently to improve the manner in which they approached each
task of the day. Men took their obligation to pray in congregations
three times a day very seriously, and many spent a large percentage
of their time involved in religious studies. We were never able to
understand how these families survived financially because many of
the men did not seem to work at regular jobs. Whenever I asked
about mundane matters like this, the usual response was a shrug
accompanied by the comment that "*HaShem* provides." *HaShem*
(the Name) is a euphemism for God.

Shoshana had to consider the dramatic impact this move would
have for her as a liberated person. In the religious world, roles are
more defined, and women assume major burdens including child
care, homemaking, and weekly preparations for the large meals of
the Sabbath and other holy days. Women often also have part-time
jobs, and many go to classes two or three times a week. Religious
families tend to be large, so the demands on the women are enormous.

Whenever I asked women direct questions about their lives, the
comments were invariably positive and assertive: they would not
trade for any other way. These were mostly women who had come
to the religious world by choice, often as university graduates, and
had been exposed to life as it is known in the developed world,
with all its conveniences—and its free thinking—yet they had cho-

sen this path. Nonetheless, this was cause for major concern for both Shoshana and me.

We finally made a breakthrough late in the summer. It occurred one night when we were reminiscing about life in Israel and we suddenly understood why we had been so captivated. While our experience in Virginia was successful and productive, there was something missing—a vital quality we had experienced in Jerusalem. Each day we walked through the ancient city, we saw and felt a remarkable sense of endurance, not only of the thousands of years that had passed, but a strength within the culture that seemed to permeate each moment. Living in Israel, we could not avoid experiencing our role in its unfolding history, and this feeling was enormously vitalizing, amplifying our sense of purpose. Clearly we could live full lives anywhere, but the pervasive sense of history in Israel was an unusual added ingredient, a spice that, once tasted, made all other dishes seem routine.

Moreover, having had a brief but marvelously sweet experience of talmudic learning, I craved the opportunity to pursue this uniquely Jewish path of spiritual development. It beckoned to me, calling me out of the consciousness of daily life, promising delicious rewards of new awareness. Between the potential for new growth, and the promise of a fulfilling life-style—albeit a complex and difficult culture—we found our resolve once again, and our plan to return to Israel became cemented in our hearts. We would return the following month, in December.

The rabbi told a story about when he was younger and had been engaged to make a speaking tour to Jewish communities around Europe. To make a particular point about the Sabbath, he would sometimes relate a story that had been passed on to him about a famous nineteenth-century rabbi known as the Chafetz Chayim, named after the title of a book he wrote about the laws of gossip. (It was a common practice for famous rabbis to be nicknamed after their famous works.) His real name was Rabbi Yisroel Meir Kagen, and it was said that he observed the highly detailed laws of proper speech so carefully, he attained a high state of awareness, and was known as a great tzaddik (saint) while he was alive.

One day someone brought his son to the Chafetz Chayim because the boy was constantly breaking the laws of the Sabbath. Like many teenaged boys, he found the rules silly, pedantic, and irrelevant—so

he went his own way. This changed the day he was taken to the tzaddik, *because after being in that room for only ten minutes the boy
ran out crying and never desecrated the Sabbath again.*

*The rabbi telling us the story said, "I used to say in my speaking
tour that if only I could discover what the Chafetz Chayim had said
to that boy, I would know one of the great secrets of our tradition."*

*The rabbi continued, "One day, when I was on a tour of Eastern
Europe, after I had been talking about the Chafetz Chayim and the
boy, an old man came up to me, his face drained of color. Shaking
with nervousness, he asked me where I had heard that story. I did not
remember. All I knew was that when I had heard it, it made a strong
impression on me. Then I asked the old man why he was interested.
The old man said, 'Because I was that boy! I did not know anyone
knew the story.'*

*"You can imagine," the rabbi said, "how shocked I was, and I
yearned to know the secret of what had happened in that room. So I
asked him, and this is what he said:*

" 'I walked into that room, and the tzaddik *was seated next to a
wall filled with books. He beckoned me to come over, took my hands
in his, and looked into my eyes. I saw his eyes begin to well up with
tears, but he said nothing to me but the words:* "Shabbos . . . Shabbos . . . Shabbos."[23] *("Sabbath . . . Sabbath . . . Sabbath.") That one
word, the way he said it, seemed to sum up the entire tradition of
Judaism. Some people say that it is not the Jews who keep the Sabbath
day, but the Sabbath day that keeps the Jews.*

" 'As the tzaddik *continued to repeat this one word, tears began
to roll down his face. Then one of his tears dropped on my hand—it
was like fire. It burned and burned as if someone had put molten
lead on me. It spread through my body, and I felt my heart begin to
burn, and the* tzaddik *kept saying:* "Shabbos . . . Shabbos. . . . "*

*" 'And I ran out of that room, my body in flames, his words etched
in my soul. I have lived with that fire for over sixty years, and every
week when* Shabbos *arrives, the place on my hands where those tears
dropped begins to burn, and I can feel them throughout the entire*
Shabbos *day.' "*

Once Shoshana and I clearly understood that we were committed
to this life change, it was fascinating to reflect upon the process of
decision making that brought us to this point. Logic was ulti-

mately discarded, and we discovered that our "will" to follow this path was not so much motivated by desire as it was mystically fulfilled by "letting go." Indeed, if we had strictly followed our desires, we would never have decided to leave our comfortable lives. The only real freedom of choice we had was to resist our desires—to allow some other force to draw us to it.

I had never been particularly religious; however, my retreats continued to open dimensions that illuminated my realization that things were not at all what they seemed. I became increasingly suspicious of my own mental process, and began to rely on more subtle cues. The more I explored the inner realms, the more certain I became that the universal intelligence communicates with us in all sorts of ways. A well-known story became one of my favorites:

A man was sitting on his roof as floodwaters rose around his house. A speedboat came up, and rescue was offered, but he declined, saying that he trusted in God. As the waters rose further, another boat appeared, but once again he turned down the rescue, saying that he really trusted in God. Finally the waters were quite high, and a helicopter came along to rescue him—but still he insisted on remaining, saying that God would help him.

The man drowned. When he came before the celestial throne, he was angry. He challenged the angel sitting there, saying, "I am a devout believer and have lived a faithful life. Now, when I needed your help, where were you?" Of course, the angel responded, "I don't understand your complaint. After all, we sent you two boats and a helicopter."

A famous Islamic saying can be paraphrased: "Trust in God, but tie the camel's knee." Trusting involves much more than simply waiting for divine providence. Moreover, it is a mistake to have preconceptions about the divine will. There was no booming voice coming from the heavens telling us to go to Israel—there were no obvious signs showing the way. In fact, almost everywhere we looked the message seemed to be "Do not leave." But despite everything we analyzed and every calculation we made, the universal intelligence was sending us other kinds of messages, and Jerusalem irresistibly drew us to it.

I sat awake most of the last night of this retreat. A crisp, sharp breeze heralded the approaching winter; the sky shimmered like a pool filled with precious stones. I found myself lured into its center, and as I dived through the sparkle, I experienced being drawn into a sense of union with the Divine, expressed in Jewish mysticism by the word *devekut.*

"Devekut," *is the mantra that arose.* "De-ve-kut," *I repeat as my body rocks in rhythm. It is a Hebrew word meaning "clinging" or "melting" into God. Jewish mystics believe this letting go of the boundaries of the self is a high state of illumination—giving up one's will in a union of pure love where there is no clear distinction between lover and beloved.*

An iridescent bell-shaped figure appears over my head. I continue to rock and repeat the mantra. The bell slowly descends until I am surrounded. My body is like a clapper; each time I rock and touch the inside of the bell, an eruption of flares casts sparks in all directions and I hear a sound that is not a sound—the sound of light splitting through a prism.

Soon the clapper itself begins to splinter into bolts of lightning, and the entire bell is filled with a spectacular tumult of shattering globes releasing white-hot gases. At the core of my being, something tells me this is the nucleus of an exploding galaxy. I am certain it is happening somewhere in the universe just as I am experiencing it at this precise moment.

Opening my eyes, I am stunned to find myself in the indifferent darkness of night. The contrast startles me like an icy plunge. Quickly I close my eyes, but now only the afterglow remains. Again, I look out of my window into the night and peer up into the star-filled sky for a sign. I see nothing with my naked eye, but my inner eye remains certain that up there, in that part of the heavens to the east, is an erupting nebula millions of light-years across.

7

Behind the Mount of Olives, the sky unfolds softly in tints of rose and lavender as an unseen artist applies thin streaks of melting light onto an ever-moving canvas. The golden Dome of the Rock stands at the heart of the city—some say the heart of the world—reflecting the changing hues like a great beacon calling out to the soul of humankind. Jewish mystics believe that every prayer uttered to God flies from around the world to this point on the planet—the Temple Mount—from where it is released to heaven. Now in the awakening dawn the reverse occurs: the celestial response to all our prayers flows through the sacred stone mound beneath this golden orb, and radiates out for all who are willing to hear.

Jews, Christians, and Muslims each believe God's response to the call of humanity is directed specifically to them because of their devotions. Over the centuries they have fought to control this particular piece of earth in the Middle East, as if somehow holding the keys is a divinely imposed obligation. Passions are strong and even violent on this issue; the subject does not lend itself to reason. There is no room for compromise.

I sit in meditation on the roof of an apartment building in the Old City of Jerusalem as the calm of early dawn gives the impression of peace and harmony. The Muslim call to prayer ended a while ago, and large flocks of chattering birds have performed their sunrise ritual, skimming just overhead in the direction of Silwan, to the southeast. Each morning I have noticed thousands of these little birds passing over al-Aqsa Mosque—at the south end of the Temple Mount—as they fly toward the rising light on the horizon.

In Arabic, the Temple Mount is called Haram al-Sharif (the Noble Sanctuary)—and it is the third holiest place in the world for Muslims, the others being the Ka'ba in Mecca and the Mosque of Muhammad in Medina. It is not the Temple Mount itself that is important, but the consecrated stone lying beneath the Dome of the Rock.

After crossing the silver dome of al-Aqsa Mosque, the birds fly near the City of David, just outside the current Old City walls. These are ruins of the original Jerusalem conquered by King David three thousand years ago. Some say that the prophet Gad revealed to David that this city would be the home for God's sanctuary on earth. David set his heart on building the house of God, the first Temple, but his son Solomon was destined to perform this work. Still, it was called the House of David because according to Rabbi Ishmael, "Since David was with his whole soul devoted to it, wishing to build it, it is named after him."[24]

The birds continue in their flight, and from my vantage point, they seem to land somewhere around Hezekiah's Tunnel, built twenty-seven hundred years ago to assure a steady supply of water for the city when it was under siege. At one end of the tunnel is the Pool of Shiloah, while at the other end is the Spring of Gihon. At the Pool of Shiloah are remnants of a church built over a thousand years ago to mark the spot where Jesus sent a blind man to be cured in those waters (John 9:7, 11). One Jewish tradition says that souls bathe in the waters of Shiloah before presenting themselves to the heavenly kingdom, but most Kabbalists agree that souls must be purified in a river of fire before entering paradise.[25]

Legend has it that Mary washed her infant's clothes in the waters of the Spring of Gihon. A biblical account tells us about another event that happened here a thousand years earlier than Mary—Solomon was crowned king. "[They] caused Shelomo [Solomon] to ride on King David's mule, and brought him to Gihon. And Zadoq the priest took a horn of oil out of the tent, and anointed Shelomo. And they blew the shofar; and all the people said, Long live king Shelomo" (1 Kings 1:38, 39).[26]

I envision these places from where I sit, knowing that in less than a half hour's walk I can dip my hands in the waters of Gihon. The collective unconscious of Western tradition centers here, and I could easily spend many lifetimes studying the history, stories, traditions, and wisdom teachings related to sites within a couple of kilometers. Everywhere I look, spiritual contemplation beckons. It is no accident that this city is the cradle of Western tradition—the kedushah *(holiness) is so dense, my feet are barely able to touch the ground.*

The mystical center of Jerusalem is an outcropping of stone covered by the Dome of the Rock—it is about fifty feet across. Many teach that this rock was called by the ancients the *even shetiyyah,* the foundation rock from which the cosmos was woven, the hub of the universe, the navel of the earth. Some believe this is the site of the Holy of Holies, the innermost sanctum of the house of God, where once each year the Jewish high priest—in the time of the Temple (two to three thousand years ago)—would commune directly with God on the holy day of Yom Kippur. Nobody else was ever permitted to enter. When the high priest was about to go into the inner sanctuary, his assistants tied a long rope around his waist, for if he had the slightest impure thought while in the Holy of Holies, he would die instantly and the rope would be the only way to get him out.

Tales abound about this sacred rock. Adam and Eve lived here; Abraham came here to sacrifice Isaac. In the future, the fountain of total awareness will bubble forth from this place. In Islamic tradition, Muhammad stepped off this rock when he took his famous night journey to heaven. Local guides usually point out to tourists an indentation in the side of the rock that is reputed to be Muhammad's footprint.

The Holy of Holies was the resting place of the Ark of the Covenant, which contained the tablets inscribed with the Ten Commandments, brought down from Sinai by Moses. The Ark also held the Torah, the scroll of the five ancient books written by Moses, dictated by God. On top of the Ark were seated two cherubs made of solid gold, facing each other with outstretched wings almost touching. Between these cherubs, God's presence was manifest, and all heavenly transmission was focused here. As one writer of Kabbalah notes: "The space between them [the cherubs] was also seen as an opening into the spiritual dimension. In concentrating his thoughts between the cherubs on the Ark, a prophet was able to enter the prophetic state."[27]

An interesting story is told in legend about how Solomon selected the physical location of the first Temple.

> He was long in doubt as to where to build it. A heavenly voice directed him to go to Mount Zion at night, to a field owned by two brothers jointly. One of the brothers was a bachelor and poor, the other was blessed both with wealth and a large family of children. It was harvesting time. Under cover of night, the poor brother kept adding to the other's heap of grain, for, although he was poor, he thought his brother needed more on account of his large family. The rich brother, in the same clandestine way, added to the poor brother's store, thinking that though he had a family to support, the other was without means. This field, Solomon concluded, which had called forth so remarkable a manifestation of brotherly love, was the best site for the Temple, and he bought it."[28]

There are thousands of stories about the *even shetiyyah*, the Temple Mount, the first and second Temples, and all that has taken place in that location during the two thousand years since the destruction of the second Temple. Despite the rich lore that is attached to this location, traditional Jews today are forbidden by religious law to set foot on the Temple Mount, because anyone in the proximity of the Temple sanctuary requires specific rites of purification defined in the Talmud—and these cannot be performed in our day.

Many Jews pray for the rebuilding of the Temple. Traditionalists mean this literally—take down what is there and put up a new structure. Mystics view the Temple not so much as a physical building, but as a level of God-consciousness. For them, the legend of Solomon gives us an important clue: that is, coexistence was a principle upon which the Temple was founded and is a necessary condition for its rebuilding. Almost everyone agrees that building the third Temple will require a miracle—but Jerusalem is the home of miracles.

One of the ten miracles of the first Temple was that although the physical space available within the boundaries of the Temple walls was not sufficient to accommodate the hundreds of thousands of pilgrims who came to Jerusalem each year, still everyone was able to get inside the walls by pressing closely together. This in itself was miraculous. But the miracle recorded by the sages was that when ritual required all present to prostrate themselves flat on the ground, which meant taking up at least four times as much space as standing, there was still room for the multitudes to lie side by side on the ground![29] No teaching could be more clearly symbolic: there is always sufficient space in any situation, if the level of devotion is sincere, even though the results may defy all logic.

Life in Jerusalem awakens a new inner cadence; it is not something that could be measured with bio-rhythms, rather it is in another realm, which I have labeled pneuma-rhythms, the mysterious flow of a spiritual source into the breath of life. And in the process, I am gaining fresh understanding of the nature of the Divine. My rational, pragmatic approach to life served me well in the material world, but it had not provided a clear sense of purpose. This is now changing, but not in any way that I can explain, for the entire experience is beyond the limits of reason.

I have fallen into an "in-between" world as I separate from the past but do not have a clear orientation to the future. Nothing fits as it should. I continuously wear a yarmulke, the head covering worn by a traditional Jew, but I still feel on the fringe. I do not dress in the pressed pants and light shirts of respectable Orthodoxy, the black suits of Hasidism, or the rainbow colors of the ex–flower children who have found their way back into traditional practice. In truth, I continue to have difficulties with organized religion, Jewish or any other.

My quest is spiritual and mystical. The religious life does not interest me as much as the potency of faith; I am not drawn to the ritual, but to the primal forces that are awakened. It is a search for the Soul: my soul, the soul of humankind, the soul of the planet and of the universe.

The Old City of Jerusalem is surrounded by walls of stone, hundreds of years old, massive enough to stop a modern tank. On the west side, Jaffa Gate opens into the Armenian and Christian quarters; to the south, Zion and Dung Gates provide passage into the Jewish Quarter; Lions' Gate opens to the east, and Damascus Gate to the north, giving access to the Muslim Quarter. These gates, plus a few others, are the only passageways through the majestic stone blocks of the Old City fortress.

Every day crowds of residents, tourists, and military platoons pass through the walls of Old Jerusalem in a steady flow. Sometimes, when the heat rises in the summer, life inside this stronghold begins to feel like a pressure cooker. The intensity builds, and the people inside must soften and become pliant, or the valves will blow. Whenever that happens, the scalding steam whistles out rapidly in a shriek that is often heard around the world.

Our first six months in the Old City were focused on integrating with the Israeli life-style. As we had experienced a year and a half earlier in Bayit VeGan, our social lives centered on the Sabbath meals. There were also gatherings for every *simchah* (joyous event), including engagements, weddings, births, *brits* (circumcisions), *bar mitzvahs,* and other special events, like naming a daughter, moving into a new home, or completing an important piece of study. *Simchahs* are frequent occurrences—rarely a month passes without at least one or two of these special celebrations.

We had celebrated Rosh Hashanah, Yom Kippur, Sukkot (one week long), Shemini Atzeret, and Simchat Torah on our first trip; in addition are the Holy Days of Hanukkah, Purim, Passover (one week long), and Shavuot. There are also some important observance days, including Tisha B'Av (mourning for the destruction of the First and Second Temples), the Fast of Esther (the day before Purim), and Tu B'Shevat (the festival of the New Year of Trees), in addition to many minor days of commemoration or fasting. Moreover, every new moon is a special day, the entire month of Elul (at the end of the summer) has significance in preparation for Rosh Hashanah, and there are forty-nine days of counting the Omer between Passover and Shavuot. Add to all this the national holidays, which include Independence Day and Jerusalem Day— one wonders how anything gets accomplished in between all the festivities.

It is difficult for people outside Israel to relate to the richness of the Hebrew calendar. In the U.S.A. we celebrate Easter, Thanksgiving, and Christmas, along with a half dozen or so national holidays. We may have a few *simchahs* in a year, but some years pass without any. We occasionally have guests for a meal, and try to go out for dinner and entertainment as often as possible, but most of our time is spent with the television, newspapers, or magazines.

Life in the Old City, on the other hand, was like having a close family of a couple of hundred cousins, aunts, and uncles all living within a mile. One day a week—Shabbat—was specifically set aside

for family affairs. No business discussions, travel, or outside entertainment was allowed on this day—the family sat together around
meals, in prayer groups, or in study sessions where the primary
topic was invariably one of religious contemplation.

This was also a close family in other ways. Whenever there was
a birth, and there were many, the new parents could usually rely
on having their meals prepared by neighbors. In times of illness, a
steady flow of visitors and helping hands would appear magically.
Child care was widely shared, and there were many layers of potential support for the multitude of minicrises that arise in everyday
life.

Our major effort at the time was to learn the language. It was
slow going, made worse by the fact that almost all of our close
friends were native English speakers. Although we worked inten-
sively in language school for four months, we did not make much
progress. Our difficulty with the language was a constant source of
frustration that was never resolved.

Daily life during this first year was intense. Fortunately, I had
developed a regular meditation schedule, and continued to take
three-to-seven-day retreats throughout this period. These days of
inner silence provided my spiritual grounding despite the highly
charged life-style of the Old City community. In many ways, my
time of solitude was necessary to assimilate the incredible flow of
information that overwhelmed us, and it was, as well, an important
source of nourishment for the transcendental being that lived
within—a being that was becoming ever more familiar to me
through my constant inward practice.

*The image stood by my left side, whispering into my ear, "What
do you want, David?" I answered, "I want to be stripped of my
conceit."*

*Two masked executioners appeared. They began to peel away my
skin. It was terrifying but painless. I watched in horror as they ripped
away layer after layer. Finally, I was merely bone from the neck down,
but my large head remained. There were also two jewel-encrusted
shields, one covering my chest, the other my back. They were some kind
of body armor, each an elongated diamond shape. I held on to them
fiercely. I did not fight the stripping of the flesh, but these body shields
I wanted or thought I needed.*

The hooded ghosts persisted in pulling away the shields. I let go reluctantly. I now looked really awful. I cried out for help to cover my nakedness, and was provided with a simple cloth of homespun cotton, like Gandhi used to wear. It was a humble cloth, secure, and it had a glow of its own.

"Are you satisfied?" the whispering voice asked. I said that I felt terrible, vulnerable, frightened—and I asked about the shields. "Pride on the front and insecurity on the back," it said. "The front one is the direct link to conceit, the other is the real cause of most bravado."

I felt helpless, but strangely calm. The voice said, "You can have it all back, if you want." I declined and sat shivering, seeing myself on a block of ice floating in an enormous sea. The ice was slowly melting, and I waited for the inevitable. But when my bony feet touched the water, it was warm. I floated away on the gentle sea; it was a new form of flesh, translucent, without boundaries. I now knew that I was completely safe.

"What is this?" I asked.

The voice responded: "The Nowhere of Selflessness."

Three weeks were spent cleaning the house in preparation for Passover. During this period traditional Jews do much more than a normal spring cleaning; they search for *hametz*. Literally, *hametz* is fermented dough, which includes anything made of five specific grains: wheat, barley, oats, spelt, or rye. Mystically, this represents a process of inner purification, removing anything that leads to pride—which is any quality of thought that isolates us from the awareness of our spiritual connections. According to the rabbis, pride "prevents us from performing the will of God."[30]

Thus, the entire house had to be meticulously cleaned. Every piece of clothing was examined to make certain not even a crumb of bread or morsel of cracker was caught in a pocket lining. All books were taken down and fanned to check for any food particles. Drawers were pulled out, rugs turned over, and the entire kitchen was carefully scrubbed.

The prohibitions concerning *hametz* include any pots, pans, dishes, or cutlery that have been used during the year—in principle, it is as if they absorbed the essential quality of the *hametz*. Thus all religious Jewish households have an entirely separate set of dishes and everything else needed to run a kitchen during the week of Passover. This first year we bought a couple of plates, a pot, and a few pieces of silverware—just enough to survive.

Although unleavened bread, *matzah,* is the symbol many people associate with Passover, the most engaged spiritual work of the holiday is done in the purification process prior to the actual *seder,* the meal in which the *matzah* is eaten. The constant physical cleaning, down to the minutest speck, invariably gives rise to irritation with trivial details and wasted time. To do the job well requires enormous patience and discipline, which are two primary ingredients of spiritual practice.

In addition, there is the study of a bulky catalogue of religious law related to Passover that must be reviewed and integrated during the weeks of preparation. It includes what may or may not be eaten, how food may be prepared, the specific details of the *seder* ritual, and the general principles that apply to the entire period of the weeklong observance. The weight of all these precepts packed into an event like this is usually sufficient to break the will of newcomers. The lengthy process requires distinct surrender, another vital ingredient for spiritual development.

The night of the seder *continued into the early morning hours. When we finally reached the words "Next year in Jerusalem!" marking the culmination of the long ritual, I leaned on my cushion and closed my eyes. Countless faces arose out of a silver mist, tumbling over each other, faces of many designs, but the eyes were all similar, expressing a mixture of anticipation and pleasure. I could not but contemplate how many tens of millions of* seders *had been conducted over thousands of years, in which people were searching for a release from the constriction of their own enslavement—the limits of the mind, the snares of language, the boundaries of thought, the constraints of concepts and notions about who we are and what life is all about.*

The story and ritual of Passover celebrates the possibility of escaping a prison that has infinitely high, impassable walls. How can we escape the limitations of our own minds through thinking? This is like asking the warden for the key. We must rely on something outside of ourselves to engineer the breakout. Thus, Passover celebrates the Jewish understanding that the ultimate path of enlightenment is revealed through the hand of God—not because we are deserving, but because the

*Divine Source imparts in some way, beyond all understanding, a
supreme level of freedom.*

*This Passover was the first time I recognized the extent to which I
was entangled in a web of my own making, a complex edifice of self-
identity and conditioned responses. I was shocked to realize the enormity of this jumble of perceptions, attitudes, and opinions. Until now
I had not fully appreciated the predicament; like a slave who is blind
and deaf, I had simply done what I thought was expected of me.
Suddenly my eyes and ears were opened, and the potential moved my
soul; I knew with a certainty never before experienced that there was
something else, something more, a truth that could shatter the prison
of my own mind.*

A couple of days after the *seder*, at two A.M. Easter morning, I
walked through the city's subtly lit corridors of carved stone walls
and listened to my steps ricocheting loudly in the hollow night.
Cats' eyes gleamed from moving shadows, as the animals stalked
an unseen quarry hidden behind loose rocks. The shadows fled
upon my approach, well out of striking range, following the ancient
wisdom of the jungle—the unknown may be dangerous.

At its quietest in these early morning hours, the Old City is the
most regal. Mundane street chatter awaits the signs of dawn, and
the city is given a respite from human traffic in the marketplace,
the gas fumes of tractors, and the tons of trash dropped by throngs
of tourists. Thus Jerusalem sighed quietly in the night as I crossed
from the Jewish Quarter into the Muslim Quarter on my way to
the Church of the Holy Sepulchre in the Christian Quarter.

The general consensus is that the Church of the Holy Sepulchre
marks the hill called Golgotha, and that the site of the Crucifixion
and the last five Stations of the Cross are located under its large
black domes. Marble stairs lead down under the church, where
there are caverns containing burial tombs, and many believe that
this is where Jesus was buried two thousand years ago.

All day Good Friday, a foreboding, sonorous bell in this church
had tolled every couple of minutes. It was compelling, the intervals
between the bells being just long enough to allow one to forget
the sound so that each bell jolted the awareness anew. As I walked,
the power of the bell vibrated an inner chord—something porten-
tous had happened long ago and was still happening.

Fortunately I had visited the church before, or I would not have been able to find it in the darkness. It is not on a main street, and the only way in is to push through unmarked gates that open on its courtyard. It was quiet and I was alone; but soon I was standing before the huge doors leading into the main dome.

The church was dark, dingy, Byzantine; the carved stone pillars were obscured behind water stains and mold. Lanterns with colored glass created an eerie feeling, like being in the bowels of a medieval castle, awaiting the black knight to appear from around the corner. A number of priests were gathered at an altar, dressed in black, carrying long, tapered candles and a huge incense burner spewing out clouds of pungent myrrh and frankincense. They did not look happy.

I walked around slowly in the dark. The church was filled with priests and portly middle-aged women dressed in black, with black scarves pulled tightly over their foreheads. Few of the altars were being used; it was quiet and solemn.

A dim light glowed in one of the stairwells, drawing me down to explore the lower caverns. After I had descended a few steps, the light began to brighten, glowing more radiant as I continued down. And then I heard melodious voices and knew that I had found what had pulled me out of bed in the middle of the night. This was not a dream, not a vision in my meditation—I was really here, this was really happening.

Rounding a corner, I saw a group of nuns, dressed all in white, dancing in a circle, singing a delightful hymn. There were about two dozen of them. Off to one side were four men dressed in white—I'm not sure what to call them: brothers? monks? priests? One song ended, and the next began; this time the men joined in.

I stood there transfixed, my heart thrilled to their music. It was like Sufi dances I had experienced. These people were ecstatic; the entire group glowed in the whiteness of their habits and the joy of their devotion. They continued like this for an hour, and I was so filled with emotion, I could hardly breathe.

Then they stopped for a while and performed an initiation or an induction of two men and one woman who had been standing on one side, dressed in ordinary clothes. The two leaders, a middle-aged bearded man, and a lovely middle-aged woman, stood before the group and administered vows in French. The young woman was initiated first, and then the two young men together, each lying prone on the floor with arms outstretched. When they stood up, they were given white robes, which the congregation helped them put on over their street clothes.

The dancing began again, with renewed strength and jubilation. Everyone was dancing together, and the hallelujahs rebounded throughout the caverns and subcaverns that were normally the domain of the dead, but were now fully bathed in light. On they went, singing, whirling, the most beautiful faces I have ever seen in a religious gathering—or anywhere, for that matter.

And then, suddenly, one of the young men glanced at his watch, and looked up with tears streaming down his face, whispering something—and then shouting for all to hear: *"CHRISTO RE-SURRECTE! CHRISTO RESURRECTE!"* ("Christ is risen!")

Something surged within me, and I shouted back: "YES!"

Then the rest of the group joined in, the men crying out, *"Christo resurrecte,"* while the women circled them, singing hymns of praise in a state of intense passion and ecstasy. One man ran up the steps toward me, saw my *yarmulke,* but also my smile, and we hugged, he whispering, *"Christo resurrecte,"* and I responding, "Amen, brother. Amen."

This was an affirmation of life. The purest, sweetest mystery of death and rebirth. I suddenly understood the parallels between the secret of resurrection and my newfound understanding of the profound meanings of Passover. They were virtually identical; the process of transformation from the limitations of constriction into the enlightened state of the Spirit. This is what is meant by messianic consciousness, the breaking of the bonds of Egypt and making the Exodus to the Holy Land. It was clear to me in those moments that the mystical message of Judaism, Christianity, and Sufism were all the same. The Paschal Mystery, the teaching of Christ as the sacrificial lamb, holds its epiphany in the realization of our illusion of being separate identities, and breaks through to Life, the mystical union with the Divine.

Clearly this is not the way religious traditionalists interpret these transformative events. Indeed there are obvious distinctions in outward expression and practices in different religions, but I was convinced more than ever that *Christo resurrecte, Allah Hu-Akbar* (Arabic: God is great), and *Shema Yisrael* (Hebrew: Hear O Israel) all come from the same source and speak to the same source, the Divine revealing itself to itself.

At the peak of this ecstasy and euphoria, dark shadows appeared on the stairs. We had been making too much commotion, sharing too much love, broadcasting too much light in the affirmation of the most significant message of Jesus Christ: Live! And the plump little women in black pushed the heavyset, sagging-jowled priests in black toward a confrontation with light. The message was clear—bright light reveals dust and cobwebs in the corners; uncontained joy interferes with solemn ritual. Thus, the congregation of light was asked to leave.

We all walked out together, quietly elated. The nuns glided down the road ahead, still in their habits; the men changed back into street clothes, and were indistinguishable in the early morning light. I watched the nuns walking away, and when it was too late realized that I had no idea where they worshipped or lived, or how I would ever find them again—but I hoped one day to dance with them once more, celebrating the unification of all humanity in messianic consciousness.

8

WASHINGTON, D.C.: DECEMBER 1984.
FOUR-DAY RETREAT IN A RENTED
SUBURBAN HOUSE JUST OUTSIDE
WASHINGTON.

This morning's meditation was agony. I have been trying a new style of pure silence—sitting quietly without any mantra, observing the breath, or working with visualization or focal point exercises. In earlier retreats I could chant for hours without any problem; in fact the chanting usually led to ecstasy. I could also do breathing exercises all day and attain a sublime state. But sitting perfectly still, focusing on emptiness, doing nothing, thinking nothing, is pure hell. Pain racks my upper back, radiating from the spine to the shoulders.

A few blessed moments have arisen spontaneously when I experience a perfect stillness; the pain vanishes instantly. During these interludes of supreme concentration, I feel as if I am floating in a vast cave with curved walls of marble that have the sheen of ebony. The blackness of the cave emanates a faint glow, a strange form of light. Unlike the gleam that is caused by heat, this is the illumination of coolness and imperturbability.

The negative side of my ongoing pain, however, is a foreboding sense of despair and depression. Most of my morning was overwhelmed by thoughts of destruction and death. My past deeds streamed before me; the imagined results of those events and the price that I would have to pay to redeem myself flooded my thoughts. Tears soaked my shirt; life was hopeless. The tears became a torrent, and for hours I wallowed in a salty pool of self-pity.

The rented house in our Washington, D.C., suburb seemed to be surrounded by barking dogs. When they were quiet, we could hear the sound of constant traffic a quarter mile away, interrupted regularly by the sirens that punctuate city life. Our quiet country home in Batesville, which had been deeded to new owners, was rapidly assuming new dimensions in our memories—becoming Paradise Lost.

After spending a year in Jerusalem, we returned once again to try to sell our home and make arrangements for the business. This time we were successful, but we had to complete the business year with the new owner before we could finally settle in the Holy Land.

During the year, it seemed once again as if the fates were against us. Our financial situation was bleak, and most of our friends and our respective families expressed enormous reluctance about the wisdom of the move. We also encountered new serious reservations in ourselves because of the political situation; not only was the economy tenuous, but Israel had gotten involved in a fruitless military adventure and was mired in Lebanon. We felt pummeled from all directions.

For a while it looked as if the business was going under and that the house would never sell; our return to Israel would have to be delayed, perhaps for years. When this became a real possibility, we discovered that the prospect of staying was more disturbing than the risk of leaving; this confirmed that we really wanted to explore living in Israel whatever the cost. Finally, at the end of June, our fortunes changed. An offer was made on our home, and the business turned dramatically. Although we had to vacate our home quickly, we were buoyed by the prospect of making a move to Jerusalem within six months.

We chose to move temporarily to a suburb of Washington, D.C., because it had a large proportion of Jews, quite a few synagogues, and was convenient to the city. Normally, we would never have been drawn to suburban life, with its rows and rows of houses and manicured lawns. But we had had such a welcoming in Jerusalem, we thought it would be interesting to get acquainted with the local Jewish community. This turned out to be a distinct misjudgment.

In many ways the people in our new neighborhood were more rigid than the Orthodox community in Jerusalem. I rarely saw an adult truly appreciating the Sabbath; dull suits and neckties were the uniform even when the summer temperature was a sweltering ninety degrees. There was very little interest in mysticism, Kabbalah, Hasidism, or any of the spiritual teachings that appealed to me. Indeed, it seemed to be the old story of form and ritual without substance, and of strictness without common sense—where was the joy?

Perhaps we missed something because we were newcomers. But the first—and only—time I went to the synagogue, the congregation felt distant and unfriendly; nobody said hello, or even smiled. It was worlds away from our experience in little Jerusalem *shtibls*. Except for some friends in the neighborhood whom we had met years earlier, only one family invited us for a Sabbath meal during our six months in this community.

The Jewish world wonders openly why its young people turn to so many other traditions. Jews spend a great deal of time agonizing about cults that entice away the lifeblood of the congregation, or about the high rate of intermarriage. The prospect of extinction is a constant reality for many Jews. It is a complex question; there are no easy answers. But I noted my own experience in this suburban Jewish community as a feeling of being in an arid wasteland. It would be the last place I would turn to nourish my soul—indeed, it was the polar opposite of our experience in Jerusalem.

Whenever I had a long weekend, I closed the door to my small room on the second floor of our house, and this became my retreat sanctuary and my own little synagogue, a haven for study and prayer, a space where I was able to create enough inner silence to ignore the noisy neighborhood. But the turmoil in our lives exacted its toll, and my meditations and periods of retreat were often invaded by mind chatter, anxiety, or the fear that we were making a terrible mistake.

Yesterday afternoon, my meditation became strong and steady; it was like a powerful jet, constantly building momentum, and it was almost airborne, just breaking out of my inner fog, when it smashed into a wall that suddenly loomed before me. I disintegrated and scattered in pieces around the room like a puzzle where nothing seems to fit.

I reflected upon the cerebral wall with which I had collided. It had begun as a few pebbles of wishful thinking, but had grown in a blink into a monstrous fantasy of aspiration and expectation. I never cease to be amazed at how quickly the mind careens out of control.

Ironically, my success was my downfall. The meditation had been going so well, I had tripped into the gluey quagmire of beginning to think about how well I was doing, and the inevitable crash occurred. Thoughts of success lead to images that seem sweet at first, but they soon become a noose of self-delusion, killing all taste, pleasure, and satisfaction.

This morning remained gray as my imagination replayed old tapes of inward criticism, a lifetime collection of self-loathing and dissatisfaction. I dug a deep pit, filled it with the muck of guilt, shame, and disgust, and then submerged myself in it. Sometimes I think we enjoy hating ourselves as much as we value loving ourselves. Perhaps it helps us feel more alive!

I was saved by Shoshana. As I stepped out to use the bathroom, a delightful yellow rose lay in front of the door. Tonight is the Sabbath, and I usually give Shoshana flowers on Friday—a habit we picked up in Jerusalem. This was her thank you. My heart flooded with a cheer that washed away all self-destructive thoughts. In an instant, this simple act of love cast a radiance that obliterated the gloom of despair.

Moses, our golden retriever, was with us. In these times of chaos and upheaval, Moses remained a comforting constant. Despite our regular fluctuation of moods, he was always in a state of canine joy. His world was filled with great expectations: the possibility of a chase, a new relationship, or a good fight. He was forever ready to wrestle or play tug-of-war—and when kids were around, he would accept punches, pokes, and general abuse with abundant good nature, never nipping or growling at a human being of any size. Although Moses had been occasionally troublesome, marauding around the land in Batesville, learning about porcupines but never about skunks, he still invoked a bountiful amount of humor and generated more than enough heartfelt love to pay his way.

We had left Moses with a neighbor in Batesville the previous year, assuming that he would have a better life ranging in the open territory of the Virginia hills than in the crowded streets of Jerusalem—but Shoshana sorely missed his company. Also, his newly adopted parents did not have our tolerance: he required attention, ate prodigious amounts of food, and was prone to battling other male dogs whenever the opportunity arose. As his hide got tougher, the fights became nastier. So, Shoshana and I relieved our friend by agreeing to take our dog back with us.

To acquire his immigration and travel documents for the trip to Israel, we were obliged to submit Moses to a thorough veterinary examination. This, fortunately, saved his life. The vet recognized some symptoms, had him X-rayed, and determined that his heart was about three times its normal size because of an infestation of heartworm. Moses would not have survived more than a few months in this condition.

The treatment was a form of canine chemotherapy, a large dose of arsenic that brought him close to death and killed the worm in the process. That was the easy part of the treatment. The hard part occurred during the following weeks, when the pulp of the dead worm was being eliminated from his system. He was never allowed to walk fast, much less at his normal trot, because it might push a clot of dead worm material into a place that would cause an embolism, which in turn could paralyze or kill him. So we had to walk at a slow stroll, constantly reining him in, until the danger was passed. This was just another chapter in the saga called Our Pal Moses. There would be more to come.

When I look in the full-length mirror, a squat fellow that assuredly is not me returns my gaze. A separate mirror alongside the first reflects still another creature—a long, thin critter with a bubble for a head. Definitely not me. In this hall of mirrors, I go from one distortion to another, looking for a "me" I can trust. Some mirrors reproduce a recognizable person, but each is a little different from the other. How do I know which one is right? How do I know if what I usually see and think of as myself is accurate?

A clown in this fun house has been following me, I think. I see him in the mirrors, but cannot feel him when I reach from side to side. He is always laughing, no matter how much the mirrors contort his face. Often he is grotesque, one eye on top of another, nose by an ear, but still laughing. A thought occurs to me: maybe he really looks like that grotesque image; some mirrors show his true reflection, while others give him the semblance of what we would call normalcy. He laughs.

My dream is becoming a nightmare. I want to get out; this hall of mirrors is no longer fun. The clown's laughter echoes like multiple

reflections bouncing from thousands of shards of glass. Familiar im-
ages, different faces of myself that I have seen over the years unfold
in every direction, as if I am standing in the inner sphere of a bee's
eye. Each part of the honeycombed wall surrounding me gives a
slightly different perspective—I am not any of them individually, but
I am all of them together.

There is no single authentic mirror for us to use; each reflection
distorts in some way. If not the mirror, then the viewer. If not the
viewer, then the fact that the object is constantly changing. We are
none of the images and all of them; this is why the clown is always
with us, always laughing. We think we can hold on to something, find
reality, know the facts—but the reappearance of the clown's hollow
laughter may be the only truth we will ever know.

A hasidic tale tells of a merchant and his servant traveling to a
distant market where the merchant goes each year for his annual
supplies. On the way, they stop to rest in a beautiful meadow where
they lunch and take their afternoon nap. The next day when they
arrive at the market and begin to select items, the merchant discovers that his money is gone.

They return along the road; the merchant is despondent. It was
all the money he had in the world, and now he is ruined. They
stop once again to rest in the same meadow. When they settle for
their afternoon nap, the merchant suddenly discovers his purse in
the tall grass and for a moment is overjoyed. But then he reaches
into the purse, withdraws half of the money, gives it to his servant,
and tells him that his services are no longer required.

The story goes on in long hasidic fashion to describe how the
wealthy merchant falls on hard times and quickly loses everything
he owns. On the other hand, the servant, who has always been
poor, invests the money he has been given and through a series of
wondrous events becomes enormously prosperous.

Years pass. The original merchant has become a beggar dressed
in rags. Traveling from town to town, he goes to the affluent part
of each community and hopes that the kindness of the people will
provide his bread. Sometimes this works; often he goes hungry.

One day good fortune seems to shine. The beggar calls on the
largest home in a new community. The man answering the door
of the mansion not only gives him ten rubles, a magnificent sum
in those days, he also invites the beggar to return in two days for

the Friday night Sabbath meal. The beggar is overjoyed. Everybody knows that a Sabbath meal in a wealthy home means an abundance of food, chicken soup, fish, meat, potatoes, and marvelous bread. Just thinking about it is enough to cause him to drool.

He returns to his makeshift bed under a bridge and falls asleep to dream about a fine table set for a kingly feast—and the fantasy banquet continues until the wee hours of the morning. When he awakens, the beggar discovers disaster has fallen. Someone has stolen the ten rubles he was given.

The day suddenly turns dreary. He must face the long hours ahead with an empty stomach. But all is not lost; tomorrow is the Sabbath. He sits most of the day watching the river flow under the bridge, and once again that night he dreams of a lavish spread.

The next day in preparation for the upcoming event, he goes to the public baths where the community allows beggars to bathe free. He lingers for a long time in the warm waters, but when he is done and returns to the dressing room, another disaster has occurred. His shoes are missing, and so are his clothes. Someone has stolen the rags he used for cover, and he is now naked, penniless, starving, and without a friend in the world.

The wealthy man who had invited the beggar to his house sat and waited for his guest. When an hour after nightfall had passed, he became concerned and sent his servant out in search of the beggar. The servant returned with the beggar (wrapped in newspaper), reporting that he had found the poor man dancing wildly in the park, singing with joy and laughing with glee. Everyone in the park thought he had gone mad, but he seemed perfectly sane.

The wealthy man had the beggar dressed in new clothes and welcomed him to his table. It was indeed a feast for a king, and when the beggar was well fed, he looked up at his host and recognized him to be the servant to whom he had long ago given half of his fortune. Of course the wealthy man had known all along that the beggar was his previous master, and that is why he was so eager to have him return to the Sabbath meal. He had been puzzled for years about why he had been given the money and sent away. Now there was an additional question: Why was the beggar dancing in the park after he had lost all of his worldly possessions?

As they sipped cognac at the end of the sumptuous meal, the beggar revealed his secret. He said, "I knew when I found that purse that it was such a propitious stroke of luck, I was probably at the height of my good fortune and that hard times were ahead. So, rather than carry you down with me, and believing I would have to discharge you at some time in the future when I was short of funds, I felt that it would be better to give you your wages for the next few years in one lump sum and send you on your way. As it turns out I was right—my luck was sinking while yours was rising."

And what was all this dancing in the park about? He said, "When I lost the last remnant of my clothing and everything had hit bottom, I knew that my luck had finally turned—things could only get better."

Sure enough, the beggar was correct once again. The wealthy man, when hearing the story, went to his treasure box and divided his entire fortune in half. Now both were rich in material things and in wisdom. It is said that they became famous across the land for helping people who had fallen to the depths, providing money and the training of skills so that unfortunate people could begin anew.

This story of changing fortunes meant a great deal to me. Our year had been the most difficult I could remember. I hoped that things were about to change. I found myself encouraged each time I reflected on the teaching of Rebbe Nachman of Breslov, who said:

> The greater the goal for which you yearn, the bigger the obstacles and barriers. . . . From this you can understand that if tremendous barriers spring up on every side . . . it is an indication of the importance of the goal you wish to achieve.[31]

Now that the time to depart was growing near, all of the links began to connect. The day the moving van carried away the many boxes we were shipping, the final linchpin was in place. There would be no turning back. A deluge of emotions swept us away, and we were buoyed on waves of exhilaration as we anticipated our imminent return to the Holy Land.

9

OLD CITY, JERUSALEM: JUNE 1986.
SEVEN-DAY RETREAT IN A RENTED HOUSE
BORDERING THE MUSLIM QUARTER.

I remember visiting Jerusalem in the early sixties, standing at the King David Hotel a few hundred meters to the west of the Old City, looking across the no-man's land, wondering why and how borders form between people. I also remember being troubled that I could not simply walk down the hillside and through Jaffa Gate to explore what lay behind the imposing walls built of huge stone blocks.

Since the liberation of the Old City in 1967, invisible borders continue to exist inside the city. The way they were formed is somewhat of a mystery. The first apartment we rented was at the entrance to the Jewish Quarter close to the Armenian Quarter. However, we were surrounded by Jewish families and there was hardly any interaction with our Armenian neighbors. Our next apartment, only one-half mile from the first, was on the opposite side of the Jewish Quarter, but it might as well have been on the other side of the world. This new apartment was located precisely on the unmarked but certain boundary between the Jewish and Muslim quarters, viewed by many as a dangerous frontier.

The windows on the south side of this new home overlooked a walkway that connected dozens of apartments occupied by Jews. The buildings were all relatively new, having been built in the previous twenty years. Everything was neat and compact, with electric, telephone, and television cable wires hidden underground. But the architecture for renewal did not include spacious living, and the density of the tiny Jewish Quarter was so concentrated that the physical proximity of our neighbors produced instant intimacy. Arguments, traumas, and daily events in family life flowed into the common courtyard and provided a living theater day and night.

On the other side of this small apartment—no more than twenty paces from one end to the other—large glass doors opened to a balcony, and when we passed over this threshold, we entered a different culture. The entire landscape changed; many of the buildings we faced had been built early in the century, and they showed the signs of wear, often covered with corrugated metal or patched with stone and cement. An agglomeration of electric and telephone wires cascaded in all directions—a clear sign that the modern world was an afterthought to the basic structure of a city built for kerosene lamps, donkey transportation, and grapevine communication, all of which in fact continued to function on one level or another despite the introduction of up-to-date conveniences.

Amid the many buildings was a wide expanse of uneven stone that looked like a huge, empty playground, but actually was a broad canopy of roofs interlocked to cover a lower tier of the city that contained a marketplace that stretched all the way to Damascus Gate at the far end of the Muslim Quarter. And below the marketplace, many layers of ancient cities are piled upon each other, some of which have been excavated by archeologists who have cleared large sections through twenty meters of rubble. At the bottom level, roads built by Romans and walls used for protection during biblical times still exist.

The archeological digs in the Old City are so rich, it is difficult to complete any building project without major architectural revision once the excavation begins. Living atop all of this, it was impossible for me to avoid the constant reminder that the buildings in which we stood would be the rubble of the future, and the Jerusalem that will stand a thousand years from now will be built ten to twenty feet above the current city.

From our balcony, we looked across a mere ten meters into the apartments of our Arab neighbors, once again sharing the intimacies of family interaction—experiencing the fragrant odors of unknown spices, the pleasures of unusual celebrations, the bickering of arguments in a completely unfamiliar language, and, of course, the humdrum of daily chores, which included the all-too-familiar management of laundry, house cleaning, and child care.

Shoshana soon struck up a friendship with a number of the Arab women. They found a way to communicate through facial expressions, gestures, and the shared experiences that transcend all the obvious distinctions of different cultures. Soon they began speaking—in a way. Shoshana used English and broken Hebrew; the other women used Arabic and bits of Hebrew phrases. The words were useless, but the communication reached profound levels of compassion and understanding.

Significantly, the men on the other side did not participate. They were rarely home, and when they were, they tended to sit alone or with each other. The Arab women and I were able to exchange smiles and waves, but we had a shyness that was not present when Shoshana was there. On one occasion, however, one of the women signaled to me and asked—with clear gestures—that I chase away some young Arab boys near her home who, with sticks, wires, and stones, were tormenting a wretched, bony dog. I hustled down and saved the creature as the small boys scattered in all directions. When I walked back to the Jewish side with the flea-bitten critter in my arms, the woman and I shared a smile that touched me to the depths, and in that perfect moment I knew we were of a single mind. From that experience, our neighborly relations with the Arab families seemed to reach a new plateau.

Shavuot is the day traditional Judaism celebrates receiving the Torah, the five books of Moses. This holy day comes fifty days after Passover; each of the forty-nine intervening days is enumerated in the evening prayers. This is called the Counting of the Omer,[32] and it has kabbalistic significance, being seven weeks of seven days each. This year I decided to retreat the last seven days of this counting period so that my retreat would culminate on the night of Shavuot, a time that traditionally is devoted entirely to learning Torah.

This retreat was the first time I attempted the practice of extended sitting—up to three hours at a time without any movement. Many masters remind us that long, arduous meditations do not necessarily produce results. A Buddhist meditation teacher, Achaan Chah, says: "Some people think that the longer you can sit the wiser you must be. I have seen chickens sit on their nests for days on end."[33]

Nonetheless, I was engrossed by the experience of prolonged meditation. I sat absolutely immobile—to the extent that I did not allow myself even the tiniest shifting of position—and after an hour or so, a profusion of images, visions, and epiphanies arose in abundance. I knew that much of this experience was self-indulgent, but I thoroughly enjoyed myself.

The night of Shavuot I spent in the company of Simeon bar Yohai, the mystic of mystics in Jewish tradition, who lived almost two thousand years ago. Legend describes him living in a cave with his son for a dozen years to avoid a death sentence that the Romans had put on his head. This was one of the longest "retreats" recorded in Western tradition.

Simeon whispered to me throughout the night about the seven levels of the higher realms and the seven of the lower; the archangels, the fallen angels, and the eternal battle that is fought between the Prince of Light and the Angel of Darkness. He spoke of the cherubs who stand in the Holy of Holies with their wings stretched over the tablets brought down by Moses, and of the angels whose names must never be mentioned for fear of invoking their awesome power. He discussed how the elements of water, fire, earth, and air are really the angels of mercy, strength, beauty, and dominion.[34]

This went on for most of the night, but in the early morning hours I read something in the Zohar attributed to him that spoke of the animal sacrifices during the times of the Temple, a subject that has always mystified me. Indeed a large portion of the Torah discusses sacrifices, and this may be the single most important reason why many people turned away from the Old Testament as an archaic document filled with primitive ritual. But Simeon bar Yohai teaches that these sacrifices are symbolic representations of archetypical forms: the ox, eagle, lion, and man,[35] which are the four faces of the prophetic vision recorded in Ezekiel (1:10). He goes on to teach that each act we perform nourishes the supernal worlds—the lower levels of creation arouse the upper, just as the upper arouse the lower.

Using this interpretation, we see that every act we perform reverberates throughout the cosmos; every thought has profound ramifications. And the idea of sacrifice can be transposed from its literal meaning to the perspective of our frame of reference. That is, when we realize that everything we do, feel, or think is a reflection of and reflects upon the universe, we find ourselves continuously "sacrificing" our identity as separate individuals. In essence, the entire concept of sacrifice is a pathway for spiritual development, and our task is to distinguish between those actions that are sacrificial on the highest plane—accomplished without self-interest—and those that are detri-

mental, such as misguided actions committed out of ignorance and self-delusion.

A few months after we moved into our new apartment, we noticed that activities in the Arab courtyard across the way had become charged with an infectious excitement. The women dashed from one place to another carrying wads of bright materials or large pots of vegetables and lentils. Three goats were brought in to wander freely in the enclosed area. Chairs were set out in a large circle. A big celebration was about to occur, and Shoshana and I looked forward to a vicarious enjoyment of the festivities. Knowing it was not yet time for Ramadan, the central holiday of the Muslim festivals, which lasts for a month, we thought at first that it must be a birth; many of the women were in various stages of pregnancy. But Shoshana was able to discover that one of the young girls was getting married.

The elaborate preparations continued for an entire week. Finally, one day the goats disappeared and the rich aroma of stewing meat filled the neighborhood. A huge pot on an open fire was constantly tended by women and men who kept adding various spices while they stirred the stew with long sticks resembling broom handles.

We knew that the bride and groom had arrived when we heard the greetings of ululating trills, the marvelous call of Middle Eastern women—half warble, half shriek—a sound that reaches primal triggers like the cry of a mysterious jungle bird luring its mate. The women danced in a circle around the bride to the sounds of drums and cymbals, while the men sat in a separate circle, smoking and drinking from small cups of thick, sweet coffee. Shoshana and I stood on the balcony and waved to the party, who waved back to invite us down—but we were much too inhibited to accept.

The celebration went on for days. The circle of chairs was constantly occupied by men eating stew, smoking hand-rolled cigarettes, and drinking the syrupy, black coffee that seemed to be omnipresent. Day and night the men sat quietly conversing, and the women glowed with pleasure, carrying large trays of food, tending the fires, or speaking quietly with each other in small groups.

After three days, the visitors stopped coming, the chairs were put away, and life settled once again into the normal daily routine. Even though we had not attended, Shoshana and I had the sense of being honored guests. Our neighbors in the courtyard would occasionally acknowledge us when we appeared on the balcony, and we could see them speaking to their distant relatives while pointing toward us. I imagined—and hoped—that they were saying positive things about their Jewish neighbors, and this strengthened our resolve to be goodwill ambassadors. It actually worked this way for some time after the wedding, until a disgraceful event occurred—about which I shall soon speak—that ruined everything.

Tu B'Shevat is the festival of the New Year of Trees, which occurs during the month of January or February. Many modern Jews celebrate this day by planting a tree in Israel or by contributing money to have one planted. Families involved in Kabbalah and mysticism prepare a special seder *meal on this day, mixing white and red wine in different combinations to represent the divine emanations through the four worlds of creation.*

The seder *also includes a wide variety of fruits that symbolically represent the relationships between a person's essence (the inner part of the fruit) and the persona (the shell or husk of the fruit). Some fruits are hard on the inside and soft outside, such as peaches or apricots, while others are soft within hard shells, such as coconuts. Many fruits are a combination—and many different metaphors are included as part of the Tu B'Shevat* seder *meal.*

Tu B'Shevat is a turning point on a mystical calendar that marks an important phase of the ending of winter and the beginning of spring. On our normal calendar, Tu B'Shevat occurs much earlier than the spring equinox, which is the time we might have expected a celebration such as this to happen—when the end of winter is clearly indicated by the warming days of spring. In mystical cosmology, however, the sap of life begins to flow well before we see the outward signs of renewed life. So when we see the buds and new leaves that normally mark the beginning of spring, something had actually occurred much earlier to initiate this process of rebirthing. In essence, all of nature begins at a point of initial creation that precedes conception. And thus Tu B'Shevat marks the day that a fresh movement of sap flows in the trees in a way that differentiates it from the quiescence of winter.

The mystery of beginnings has always been a major contemplation for me. What happens when a seed begins to grow—what is that initial quickening? We may notice combinations of things such as moisture, earth, warmth, nutrients, and sunlight. These all affect the outcome; but what is the original spark? Of course, this is the ultimate question of life. And the inner dimension of the festival of Tu B'Shevat is a celebration of life in its most quintessential form.

This year Tu B'Shevat occurred on a Sabbath. Just after sundown marked the end of the holiday, I received a call from the United States. It was my older brother, Ralph. The conversation began: "I have some bad news. . . . " My mother had died that day, suddenly, without warning.

We made the arrangements to return immediately to the West Coast, and during the long hours of traveling, I could not help but contemplate the connection between death, the absolute end, and the beginning of life as the primal sap starts to move in the trees. Meditating in the narrow seat of the crowded airplane, I felt a vision develop of my mother's energy spreading outward, across the horizon, encircling the earth—then expanding more, extending in all directions, as if for a moment the earth became a star radiating throughout the universe.

At the same time, I realized that the sap beginning to rise in the trees drew its source from the same vital energy that was being radiated: life and death, different sides of one coin, each feeding the other—and I knew for the first time that the mystery of the seed does not begin with the seed itself, does not really begin at all, but rather is a continuum where death is life in a different form, and life evolves through death's energy.

In a recent book, Dr. Larry Dossey says:

> Through the unbelievable richness of contact that every human has with the universe at large and with every other human being, our concept of death is wrong. In a universe of oneness, death is impossible. The richness of connectivity renders personal extinction impossible, because personal extinction is possible only in a universe of personal isolation. We do not live in such a universe. . . .
>
> The modern tradition of equating death with an ensuing nothingness can be abandoned. For there is no reason to believe that human death severs the quality of oneness in the universe. If we participate in the universal quality before our death, our survival after death is demanded.[36]

In many ways mystical Judaism is in accord with this view. The essential qualities of biblical characters, for example, are primal forces that permeate through all generations. Moreover, strong emphasis is placed on what happens in "the world to come," how things will be—our rewards and our punishments—after we depart from this physical manifestation and transmute into the spiritual realms.

But rabbinic Judaism has a different perspective. Death is evil and must be resisted at all cost. The fearful nature of death gains additional substance through the way Jewish law designates how we are supposed to relate to it. In fact, I had a shocking awakening when I faced rabbinic legalism at the time of my mother's death.

Just after I received the bad news from my brother, I called a rabbi to ask about laws and procedures regarding the death of a parent, and I made the mistake of telling him that it was my mom's request to be cremated, even though I knew this was unacceptable in Judaism. After a few moments of awkward silence at the other end of the telephone line, the rabbi said to me: "You are not permitted to attend that funeral."

I was appalled. The point for me was not that my mother had confronted Jewish law—I would have preferred that she had not decided on cremation—but it was her decision, and it should not have affected in any way my ability to pay respect to her and honor her memory. Never for a moment did I vacillate about returning to attend the funeral, but out of curiosity I called another rabbi for a second opinion. He proceeded to call quite a few other rabbinic authorities, and for many hours the issue was hotly debated among the Jerusalem religious hierarchy. Finally, a major rabbi gave his permission on the basis that my mother did not realize the consequences of her request, and ignorance in this case mitigated the religious law. Nonetheless, other restraints were suggested regarding the ritual I was to observe during the upcoming period.

If I had not been saddened and traumatized by the news I had just received about my mother, I might have found these rabbinic debates humorous. But there was nothing funny about it; rather I was sorrowed and dismayed by the self-imposed limitations of pure legalistic interpretations. This was symptomatic of a great deal that troubled me in the Orthodox Jewish world. There were so many deep, wonderful teachings, so much stirring ritual, such a rich lore, a mine of hasidic tales, a vast treasure of wisdom teachings—yet rabbinic legalism seemed to strip away the heartful aspects of the tradition, leaving a skeleton of rules, obligations, and requirements in a deadly cascade of law that added continuous detail and refinement to such an extent that it could never be fulfilled without some remnant of guilt. This episode with my mother's death added yet another wedge driving me away from full-hearted commitment to the Orthodox world.

After returning from my mother's funeral, I took a ten-day retreat and discovered—to my delight—new depths of understanding in the Jewish practices I had been doing: prayers that I had been struggling with for years began to resonate deeply within; teachings that had been superficial opened with intense, new vibrancy; ritual observance unlocked levels of awareness heretofore unappreciated; and all the exacting details of complying with Jewish law seemed to have ripples that not only affected me personally, but included the entire cosmos.

I realized that my frustration with Orthodoxy did not result from the substance of traditional practice, but from the way it was being taught. My fellow Jews in Jerusalem were not meditators; indeed they were not particularly spiritual—especially with regard to the teachings of world traditions. Thus, the way the Talmud was taught turned a river of robust and effervescent tradition into a dry desert of intellectualization.

In my meditations during that ten-day retreat, however, the juices began to flow once again. My prayer shawl became a close friend, my *tefillin* held the secrets of the universe, the sages of the Talmud became companions giving amiable advice instead of severe admonitions. In solitude and deep reflection, I fell in love once again with the breadth, depth, and mysterious profundity of the Jewish tradition.

It came, interestingly, through silence—a practice just the opposite of the animated discussions and arguments that are typical in a yeshiva environment where the Talmud is studied. The silence of extended meditations created a new quality of "listening," and in that state of mind all of the teachings assumed an altered form. They took on a life of their own, and I intuited that this was much closer to the authentic transmission of Jewish wisdom than my ongoing learning experience in yeshiva.

I stood alone in this belief and began interpreting the commentaries with more flourish than the conventional viewpoint. My teachers were tolerant—even interested—but they usually were afraid of stepping too far away from the teachings that had been passed on to them. We began to disagree and argue over many points, but these disputes were not so bothersome—Jews love to argue. My major difficulty, however, was that hardly anyone was interested in the power of silence or in bringing personal insight into the learning process. This was a vacuum that had to be filled, and it would influence my spiritual practice for many years.

The friction in the learning process also encouraged me to follow with clearer definition and greater intensity my own rabbinic track with Reb Zalman. He was someone who understood the problem and was clearly leading the vanguard to bring spiritual content to Judaism. I contacted him and thus gained a renewed emphasis and a fresh dimension to my studies.

Rav Kook, who was the chief rabbi of Palestine just before the creation of the State of Israel, continues to be one of my guiding lights in Judaism. He speaks clearly to the part within me that I know to be most real:

> *The inner essence of the soul, which reflects, which lives the true spiritual life, must have absolute inner freedom. It experiences its freedom, which is life, through its originality in thought, which is its inner spark that can be fanned to a flame through study and concentration. But the inner spark is the basis of imagination and thought. If the autonomous spark should not be given scope to express itself, then whatever may be acquired from the outside will be of no avail.*
>
> *This spark must be guarded in its purity, and the thought expressing the inner self, in its profound truth, its greatness and majesty, must be aroused. This holy spark must not be quenched through any studying or probing.*
>
> *The uniqueness of the inner soul, in its own authenticity—this is the highest expression of the seed of the divine light, the light planted for the righteous, from which will bud and blossom the fruit of the tree of life.[37]*

Rav Kook constantly spoke to the question of individual expression and of pluralism. As the result of his own outspokenness, he was often in conflict with other rabbis, particularly concerning his universal-

ism, his acceptance of fellow Jews regardless of their religious convic-
tions, and his desire to work out peaceful coexistence with his Arab
neighbors.

He remains controversial to this day, but for me is one of the true
inspirations of twentieth-century Judaism, a great mystic and sage
without whom I would feel almost completely estranged.

The intensity of life in Israel provided a continuous flow of con-
tradictions, wrenching us through the depths, carrying us to new
heights, and then down again and up again, extending our emotional range, squeezing us into new experiences we would never
have imagined possible. It was a Ferris wheel that went round and
round and did not seem to have a switch to shut it down; it continued until we were accustomed to the belief that these highs and
lows were the normal way of life. It was only when events and
experiences reached their limits that we were provoked to reeval-
uate the situation.

One such event occurred close to us when the tensions of hatred
and ignorance flared, sparked by a major incident in the Muslim
Quarter, where a Jewish school of advanced learning had purchased
a building and established itself to maintain a presence where Jewish families had once lived. In fact, many doorways in the Muslim
Quarter reveal angular slots in the stone on the right door frame
where *mezuzot,* the indication of a Jewish family, have been chis-
eled out and removed.

Despite the current "borders" that exist, the long history of the
Old City has many examples of integration and movement of the
artificial lines. Nonetheless, each time any integration is attempted
these days, it is a cause célèbre that often reaches proportions of
national—and at times international—attention. The yeshiva had
been in this location a number of years, and neighborly relations
were at a particularly low ebb when a local yeshiva student and a
couple of Arab boys got into an argument. It ended with the yeshiva boy being stabbed and killed.

That night, at four in the morning, when I had just begun meditating, I heard a loud crash nearby, and my room grew bright with
a flash of light. I heard someone running, a woman screamed in
terror, and when I jumped to the window, I saw one of the Arabic
apartments engulfed in flames. A gasoline bomb had been thrown
through its window in an act of revenge.

The fire was quickly extinguished, yet the screaming went on for a long time—not just the woman whose bedroom had been turned into an inferno and was now charred and smoldering, but all of her neighbors crying in shock, dismay, and disgust that such a senseless crime could have been committed. As daylight grew, the word rapidly spread through the Muslim Quarter, and hundreds of people came to witness the outrage for themselves.

Although the residents were not harmed, thank God, there was enough physical damage to require a renovation; but the true damage was incalculable. The faces of our neighbors and their friends who visited were changed forever. At one point Shoshana stood on the balcony with her hands outstretched and tears pouring down her face, but the women on the other side were too angry to acknowledge her. The young Arab men who passed through to see the ruins did not stay long, but when their eyes met mine, I knew that they would not hesitate to exact revenge at the first opportunity.

Shoshana and I understood how fragile our relationships had been across our little border, and we realized the enormous changes necessary in attitudes to overcome generations of animosity that instantly polarizes peoples when acts of ignorance inevitably occur. Our pessimism increased dramatically as a result of this experience, and our hope for peaceful coexistence in Israel diminished. We remained open to a wide set of possibilities for the distant future, but in the interim we wondered if we wanted to spend so much time in an environment of conflict and open hostility. This was another seed feeding the doubts about our move to Israel. It provoked many ongoing reflections, continuing a process that was to trouble us for several years.

I see the cage they built, and my eyes brim with tears. Their apartment had remained empty for a while after the walls were redone, the glass doors replaced, and the painting had been completed. I wondered how long they would stay away. Then the welders came and erected a steel cage across their entire balcony, holding a tight mesh that could repel any heavy object—and only after this was complete to assure their safety did they return.

Our neighbors on the Jewish side whose windows were exposed also began to install screens of thick metal. But the most obvious sign of difficult times is the large cage on the balcony across the way. The charred stone above their windows continues to provide witness for the event that will forever instill fear into their lives. The woman paces within that cage, her head and shoulders slump, her eyes are often dark from sleepless nights and melancholia—and my heart breaks every time I glance out of the window.

Whenever we drive in urban areas in the U.S.A., Shoshana comments on the number of homes that have bars over windows and doors, the number of enclaves that have armed guards at the entrances, and the degree to which we are erecting more barriers that provide a sense of security—even though the price we must pay is isolation and a continuing perception of alienation.

The cage across the way is a harbinger of sadness. We all live in cages, and our life's work is to break away. But when we surround ourselves with more burdens, more negative attitudes and judgments, we separate from the world just the same as if a thick mesh of metal surrounded our bodies. My sadness increased when I realized that an insane act of a few seconds could wipe out a bridge that had taken years to build.

I suspect that the cage will be there for a long time—as long as memory persists. And while it exists, it is a hallmark of pessimism. Whenever I visit Jerusalem in the future, I will return to HaBikurim Street, to see the market below and discover if the cage is still in place. I understand why it is there—I have built many psychic cages around myself—but I await the day when it will come down, when human consciousness becomes more expansive and inclusive, and we appreciate our differences as much as our commonalities. And as the Sufi poet Rumi says:

> *Once you have been delivered from this cage,*
> *your home will be the rosegarden.*
> *Once you have broken the shell,*
> *dying will be like the pearl.*[38]

JUDAISM

AND

BUDDHISM

10

MAQBARA HUT, LAMA FOUNDATION, NEW MEXICO:
AUGUST 1986. TWENTY-ONE DAYS, THE FIRST
SEVEN ON A GROUP RETREAT LED
BY JACK KORNFIELD, THE LAST
TWO WEEKS IN A SMALL CABIN
ABOUT TEN FEET IN DIAMETER
MAINTAINED BY THE
LAMA COMMUNITY.

A simple thing, the breath, yet so complex—muscles and tendons contract and release, vital organs constantly shift, blood chemistry adjusts equilibrium, bones of the chest cavity move, nerves fire, nostrils expand and contract, membranes undulate, billions of tiny movements are experienced in each inhalation or exhalation. As I repeat the mantra "Rising . . . Falling . . . Rising . . . Falling . . . " tens of thousands of times, the magnitude and intricacy of all these interlocking phenomena captivate my attention.

But today the "rising and falling" experience transcended conceptual thought and entered a remarkable level of awareness. No longer was anybody thinking, nor was it "my" chest and stomach rising. There was simply the experience of expansion and contraction in its purest form; nobody home—no sense of time.

It was delicious while it lasted. In this blissful state, nothing seemed complex or too big; even the sense of the divine presence was not overbearing. Everything fit perfectly into place.

Once again, as soon as I noticed how wonderful I was feeling, the experience began to dissolve. Bliss can be experienced, but not "enjoyed"—moreover, it can never be attained by merely wanting it. As the sensation faded, I took solace in remembering a teaching I had read recently by Shivapuri Baba, the guru who died in 1963 purportedly at the age of 137 years:

The bliss you experience in your moments of God-worship should not be cared for. If you know this bliss you meditate on the bliss and not on God. Therefore ignore this bliss and think only of God.[1]

At the end of this book of Shivapuri Baba's teachings is a fascinating dialogue between the author, John G. Bennett, and the guru:

Question: "Some, who have practiced seriously the method of deep meditation for several years, say that they come to a point where a plunge is made into the darkness. The consciousness becomes clear but empty of all forms. In this state, they not only feel bliss, and peace, but also the confidence that God was somewhere present. They want to know if this is the right direction."

Answer: "The final [goal] is God-Realization. This [bliss and peace] may be on the way, seeing such things. It may be hallucinations, or it may be some truth of their Guru's teaching; but this is not the final [goal]."

Question: "This experience of bliss and peace and confidence is not the final end?"

Answer: "No."

Question: "Is there anything else that should be said?"

Answer: "The sum and substance of my teaching is this: live the minimum life possible, subjecting body and mind to strict discipline. . . . Long for God, meditate on Him continuously. . . . It is by this that I saw the Truth, and I am happy. Yes."[2]

This is the advice of a teacher who not only sat in absolute solitude in an Indian jungle for a quarter of a century, he fully engaged the world for forty years, from age fifty through ninety, circumambulating the earth, walking over twenty-five thousand miles, meeting kings, queens, and leaders of many of the major nations—including Theodore Roosevelt, Queen Victoria, and Kaiser Wilhelm II.

Still, I must say it is difficult to get the message that bliss is not only insufficient, it may be a sidetrack that can pull us away from the ultimate realization of our spiritual practice. Life is so full of pain and suffering, a touch of bliss sounds marvelously inviting. The guru from India teaches us that this too is a deception, and I cannot help but wonder: How does this story of life really end?

My eight-sided cabin measures only ten feet at its widest, but many retreatants consider this one of their favorite sanctuaries.

Once again I am on Lama Mountain, in New Mexico, where I took my first serious retreat nine years ago in the High Hermitage, a few hundred yards up the mountain. This small hut, called the Maqbara (gravesite), is an homage to Sufi Sam Lewis, buried only a few dozen paces from here, who, as mentioned earlier, was a teacher and guru for thousands of flower children in Northern California during the heyday of the psychedelic sixties. He died in 1971.

As with the High Hermitage, the community of the Lama Foundation caretakes this sanctuary and the hermits that use it. Food and fuel are provided, as well as a wood stove, a small table, and a foam mattress that folds into a seat. On the narrow path in the woods between the Maqbara hut and the main part of the community, a tightly sealed trash can serves as a place for silent exchanges. When a retreatant has a request, she or he places a note in the can, and within a day, supplies await a pickup. Someone is always nearby, protecting the solitude, serving the "noble silence" of retreat.

Shoshana and I left Israel at the end of June and came directly to Lama to spend a couple of months for personal healing and to open our hearts. The previous year had been difficult for both of us in many ways. Shoshana had some health problems, which involved surgery, while I had struggled with an identity crisis. It was much more traumatic than I had imagined to leave behind a successful business and return to the first-grade level of Jewish education. My teachers were often in their twenties; they understood the mechanics and the doctrine, but were deficient in the natural wisdom that comes through the experience of living, and this proved to be a growing source of estrangement.

In addition, I had found that as I went deeper into biblical and talmudic studies—although they became increasingly profound—an insidious alienation occurred. As with all traditions, the studies invariably led to the syndrome of "us and them," stressing the differences between belief systems. This constant need to express distinctions was at first bothersome, but soon invoked my genuine indignation. I was much more interested in the wisdom teachings than in suggestions that one system was better than another.

Similarly, as a convert Shoshana reacted strongly to the exclusiveness of the Orthodox approach. She too was unsettled by the shock of living in a new culture, the intensity of the Old City, and the high pitch of emotions freely expressed by a wide variety of ethnic groups boiling in one pot. For Shoshana, the stew was much too richly spiced; her response was to withdraw through physical illness and occasional depression.

We knew it was time to take a long vacation in an eclectic community whose main focus was on individual growth, and Lama was our first choice. As soon as we entered the grounds and walked into the magnificent domed building that is the community's central meeting place, as well as its major landmark, we knew we were home. We became part of the summer staff, joining forty or so people who formed the official daily "circle," and we signed up for various tasks on the "wheel" that allowed for job rotation throughout the week.

We pitched our tent in a secluded grove and set up housekeeping. It had been many years since we had experienced the serenity of living in the midst of nature; indeed the solitude of our little campsite was a welcome relief from the fervor of Jerusalem. We soon felt an enormous release as our psychic armor fell off in large chunks. The natural serenity of the surroundings was enhanced by the community's commitment to a practice of karma yoga, openhearted service, and this spiritual practice permeated every activity of the day. The Lama community was not immune to problems faced by all communities—but it worked on these nuisances in a way that continuously melted individual resistance. This general acceptance of each other and the willingness to expose vulnerability was the other end of the spectrum for us, and a welcome relief.

The Lama community supports itself by providing a summer program of workshops, seminars, and retreats led by well-known teachers in various disciplines. There is a strong Sufi influence in the dancing and singing that is frequently part of the community activities, but there are intensive programs in all traditions, liberal and conservative, East and West. One week that summer they were offering a retreat in *Vipassanā* (Insight) Buddhism, which required constant meditation, sitting nine or ten times a day, and walking slowly in mindful silence between sits.

I had heard about this form of meditation a number of years earlier, but had been afraid to consider it as an option because of its reputed severity. This summer, however, I felt ready to take it on, and wanted to go even further than the ten days that were scheduled for the group practice. I arranged additional time for an independent hermitage so that I could continue my practice in the solitude of the Maqbara hut.

Once I got past the first few days of physical adjustment to the *Vipassanā* routine, it became a marvelous experience. There was no time to be distracted; all energy was focused on observing the mind and its process of associations, repetitions, and obsessions, as well as the wide spectrum of my mental states and the constant judging, criticizing, comparing, and evaluating of everything I encountered. It was amazing to sit quietly, doing nothing, going nowhere, simply observing the mind. There was never a dull moment.

When I look in a mirror, the image of my reflection seems to move simultaneously with me. But I know it does not move at precisely the same instant. There is a time difference—the time it takes for light to travel the distance from the mirror to my brain. In this infinitesimal hair's breadth where the speed of light is the only tool available to measure things, we can enter the links holding the chain of thought and can discover the presence of "will."

I am attempting to investigate the will itself, to catch its next move. It is not difficult to observe the expression of will, but I wish to experience the essence of the will—what sparks it, where does it live, how does it manifest? Of course, this is a kōan, a paradox. As long as I am engaged in trying to catch my will, my endeavor is energized by a will already in operation, aspiring to swallow itself like an uroboros—a snake consuming its own tail.

But I meditate nonetheless, the paradox of my effort notwithstanding, and the exercise brings me closer to the beginning of my thoughts, helping me grasp the initial stimulus or impulse that forms the trunk of a thought before it branches into a myriad of ideas. A glimpse of any thought-trunk immediately invites my awareness to the roots below the surface, the preconditions of thought, and I begin to understand the extent to which the residue of history profoundly conditions each moment and thereby has a stranglehold on the future.

Can this stranglehold be broken, or are we destined to continue forever the cycles of ignorance? Modern science assumes we are constantly making progress; but are we really much different from our parents? Or for that matter, when we read Greek classics or any ancient texts, are we not living the same dramas, suffering the same illusions, and applauding the same heroes and heroines?

A handful of spiritual teachers, however, assure us that we can elude the limits of our self-perpetuating system; we can escape history. This escape is simple to define, but difficult to learn. These teachers say the patterns of history exist only in darkness; the moment we let in the illumination of awareness, the pattern disappears. All we need do is clearly observe the aspects that precondition our thoughts, and these roots immediately wither, like spider threads touched by a spark, no longer able to ensnare us.

Thus I sit quietly, a cat at a mousehole, awaiting the whisker of will to make its appearance. I watch; I wait. A thought appears from a blind side. I realize I am thinking. With patience, I trace the thought back to its source. Usually I become lost in a maze of associations; but sometimes I am able to gain a flash of insight, and a new world awakens within.

Thus the cat continues to sit motionless before the tiny hole. If I am attentive and careful to scrutinize the concentration of this cat, every so often I notice a peculiar grin, a twinkle in its eye, a hair slowly rising on the back of its neck, and I know that it has touched a place of sacred knowledge—and one more thread of entanglement has fallen away.

Vipassanā was an impressive practice. In many ways I felt that all the years of meditation that I had done up until this experience were simply preparation. This was graduate school. I loved it.

When the seven days of group meditation ended, I moved into the Maqbara hut and continued in the *Vipassanā* style for another two weeks, meditating sixteen hours a day. Time and again I observed thoughts detonating in my mind, releasing a stream of associations that connected at lightning speed, branching in a multitude of directions until an internal universe was formed. It was like watching the Big Bang of creation occurring over and over again. Each universe was a reality in which the shape of my thoughts was the boundary of consciousness. Some of these universes existed for milliseconds, others lasted many minutes; occasionally I would be immersed in another world for the full hour of a meditation sit.

I soon learned that when engaged in my thought process, I missed almost everything that was happening around me. I did not notice the sounds of birds or wind, I did not see what was in my field of vision; my senses were overwhelmed by this internal universe as if a massive gate had been lowered. In one blink I could be present in the moment, observing everything; in another, I could be dwelling in the distant realms of imagination. As I observed this phenomenon of skipping between mental fantasies, the insight arose of how little time I spent being present. The realization—once again—that I missed most of what was really happening began to nurture a new bud of wisdom, and this soon blossomed into penetrating awareness.

My mental likeness floated like an apparition before me—nose to nose. It looked like me, but with a strange expression. The more carefully I watched, the closer it came into my mind. It began to infiltrate my face, like a plane intersecting a sphere. I could feel it shimmering with my breath, vibrating deeper into the center of my being—until it vanished and reappeared as a glistening, highly polished razor that was like a magical clock. One direction reflected what was approaching in the future, the other reflected what was being left behind in the past. This razor's edge was the exact moment of NOW.

I began a walking meditation. The edge of NOW was still with me. I did a slow, concentrated walk, and wherever my mind was focused the edge of the razor marked the moment. I was walking through the looking glass, coming out in the same room that I entered, but neither the room nor the person walking in it existed. There was simply a mixture of primal components: heat, wind, hardness, moisture, texture, color, form. As a composite of these components, nothing was as it seemed to be. It was like being in a room with a symphony orchestra, but hearing only individual notes from a selected instrument. Each note was not part of the whole, but complete in itself. It needed nothing else, neither the music that preceded it nor the other sounds with which to harmonize and resonate. In its purity, each note was its own universe. Thus captured by the elegant fullness of simple components, my sense of time virtually disappeared.

The simple act of shaking salt onto food became an exquisite display as dozens of grains gently tumbled through space. My perspective was as if I were viewing the revolving, box-shaped planet of each crystal world through the lens of a high-powered, slow-motion magnifier that stretched every moment into a millennium.

At one point in the afternoon, a brief shower of rain felt like an avalanche of light; each raindrop splintered the sunlight through its own prism, casting a spectrum of color that delicately settled onto an

*earth carpet of luxurious green—and the carpet mysteriously seemed
to sigh like a person whose aching thirst was finally quenched.*

*The curve of my meditation blanket slowly rippled with my breath,
and occasionally a mote of dust would spring up like a fish arching
out of water. When the dust mote landed, I could almost hear it
bounce from one fiber of cotton to another.*

*The elegant grandeur of this ever-present cosmic dance exploded in
my mind as if a small internal lamp had been connected to a million-
volt outlet. Every particle, every speck of creation revealed itself as the
object of the Unknowable's Awareness. This awareness IS the razor's
edge, and the experience of it flooded me with awe—and with joy.*

*That evening, as I felt my normal consciousness begin to reassert
itself, tears began to flow down my cheeks. I knew I could not inten-
tionally repeat such an experience, but the tears were more of gratitude than a sense of loss. I was at peace, true peace, for the first time
I could remember. It would not last—this was clear—but knowing
its presence was sufficient. My pillow was drenched that night.*

That summer at Lama was a splendid period. When I was not
on retreat, each day brought deeper connections with the people
on the mountain, sharing in the frequent work gatherings or the
times of inner processing that were a regular part of the weekly
schedule. Shoshana had more involvement with the staff than I—
because of my extended retreats—but both of us experienced intense relationships with many of the long-term community members.

When it came time for us to return to Israel for the High Holy
Days, we realized how profoundly we had been touched. Shoshana
had gone through a transformation, the kind of inner healing for
which Lama Mountain is famous. I too had discovered an essential
part within that until now had remained hidden, and I felt as if my
entire being had been recast—the old mold was no longer appro-
priate.

The community circle gathered on our final morning in the small
room above the kitchen, which still had the fragrance of freshly
baked biscuits, and after conducting the business of the day, the
group offered us travelers' blessings for our journey ahead. We
stood in the center of the circle, slowing turning to share soul-
glances with each of our new friends, and when the song began,
"May the blessings of God rest upon you . . . " the tears began to

stream. We had learned this song nine years earlier at Lama: It was the central music of our wedding, and its final words were inscribed inside Shoshana's wedding ring.

Shoshana began to sob; I'd never seen her release in public with such intensity. The song continued, *"May God's peace abide with you."* I saw that most of the people in the circle were also beginning to cry, and it felt as if we were melting into a different form: No longer a few dozen individuals, we were simply a presence, a unity of shared experience that transcended the limits of our separate personalities. This was the mystical midpoint between the I and the Thou; our group had entered a higher dimension—we were a new species.

"May God's presence illuminate your soul," we continued, and the collective heart of the gathering was touched beyond expression. For a moment, a pristine silence magnetized the core of our essence as we held our breath, and we all knew on the level of the soul that this communion was bonded by a mysterious gravity— the primal glue of the universe—unfettered, uncomplicated, unconditional love.

The power of love bathed the entire group in a glow of radiance, and I was not alone feeling the presence of a different reality. Many of the group confirmed later that they had felt beings from various planes of existence—angels and *devas,* fairies and dwarfs—gathered together with us as we sang in unison the final verse, which reverberated over and over, as if the universe were being aligned with the vibration of this sound: *"Now and forevermore . . . forevermore . . . forevermore. . . . "*

11

OLD CITY, JERUSALEM: OCTOBER 1986.
SEVEN-DAY RETREAT ON THE ROOF OF A
RENTED APARTMENT ON HABIKURIM STREET,
LIVING IN A *SUKKAH*: THREE WALLS
OF FLIMSY WOOD ATTACHED WITH
STRING TO A TEMPORARY FRAME; THE
ROOF IS MADE OF PALM BRANCHES.

Dawn approached the hushed city of Jerusalem like a parent entering a sleeping child's room—softly, gently, on tiptoes. It did not matter that the child had been naughty. Indeed, this child had been a problem for thousands of years. But she is special, endearing; she still draws the attention of the world.

I love walking the Old City's narrow, stone streets in the early morning hours. It is the time of transition, neither night nor day— a time when the spirits that live in shadows whirl and dance in one last frenzy before their murky playground recedes into oblivion. Pivotal points like this, the mysterious passage between moments, the blur where one thing is thought to end and another begin, are the gateways to other realms. In the hushed corridors of the slumbering Jewish Quarter, whispers of past eras can be heard—softly— like cats' paws on a dusty path.

For a while I went to the Old City *mikvah* every day to experience the ritual purification of immersion in "living waters"—water gathered naturally from springs, streams, or even the rain, in an amount sufficient to submerge the entire body at once. Many *mikvahs* are close to freezing, but through procedures approved by rabbinical ordinance there are ways to heat the water. The Old City *mikvah* has two pools: one quite cold and one deliciously warm. I preferred the warm.

Some things are dulled through repetition, but for me the *mik-vah* always had a profound effect. I also loved my daily routine in the Old City: getting up before dawn, practicing yoga with quiet concentration, walking the streets in contemplation of some mystical idea, submerging in the warm waters of the *mikvah*, and afterward going to the holy Western Wall to participate in the sunrise prayer service.

Jewish legend tells us that there were two stupendous beasts formed at the time of creation: the Leviathan and the Behemoth. They are magical creatures, but at the end of this era they must destroy each other in battle to make way for the world to come: messianic consciousness. It says further that the flesh of the Leviathan will be fed to those who are worthy of it, and after consuming this flesh the meritorious ones will live under tents made of the Leviathan's skin. The remaining skin, the part that is not needed for this ongoing feast, "will be spread by the Holy One, blessed be He, upon the walls of Jerusalem, and its splendor will shine from one end of the world to the other, as it is said: 'And nations shall walk at thy light, and kings at the brightness of thy rising' (Isaiah 60:3)."³

The Leviathan has intrigued commentators for two thousand years, and Kabbalists suggest this is a great mystery that holds within it the secret wisdom of creation. It is said that the Leviathan could easily destroy the earth. In fact, a talmudic text describes that the archangel Gabriel was given the task of dragging the Leviathan out of the sea. He succeeded in hooking the monster, but was unable to budge it. It turned out that only God could overcome this beast.

Another tale reveals a different, but similar aspect of the Leviathan's power. When Jonah was swallowed by a great fish, he was taken to the Leviathan, the master of all sea life; but when the monster saw that Jonah was one of the righteous people who in the days to come would devour him, he immediately fled.

Kabbalists believe that the Leviathan represents evil incarnate, which is more powerful than everything but the source of life itself. Messianic consciousness will come when evil is somehow conquered, when we transcend mundane existence and enter a purely spiritual life. All these tales conceal weighty secrets about the nature of evil. What does it mean, for example, that the light of Jerusalem, the holy city, will stream through the canopy of evil, resulting in messianic consciousness illuminating the world? It teaches us that our task is not to eliminate evil, but to search at its core for a spark that is a necessary element in the transition to higher consciousness.

This is a dangerous thought, and it is why the rabbis have been persistent in keeping kabbalistic teachings hidden and inaccessible. Like all mystical wisdom, if misused or misunderstood, it is the gateway to hell; but if our vessels are properly prepared to receive this light, it will illuminate a path to realms beyond our conception.

The Old City *mikvah* is on a side street that few tourists use; it is not easy to find. In the dressing room, an old man sat in a corner, bent over like a sunflower in autumn, his narrow, rounded shoulders formed a valley to cradle his chin where a chest had once been. His skin hung in little bags, like pouches of old memories, younger years in Poland when the *mikvah* was a mud hole in the summer, and an opening through ice in the winter. His *peyot,* the long sideburns that identify a pious Jew, hung below his chin; his beard would reach to his waist if he could stand up straight, but now it touched his knees. I wondered if he was past a hundred years in age—good chance.

On another bench a man and his son were getting dressed in hasidic garb. Both had shaven heads, but long, luxuriant *peyot* hung dripping down their cheeks. The floor was wet, and the man had to hop on one leg, doing the jig I had seen often, trying to get the second pant leg on without dragging its cuff through the muddy swirl on the floor. He slipped for only a moment, and a gray smear blotted his cuff. He shrugged briefly and then helped his son stand on the bench to get dressed.

I was dressed in yoga pants and a sweatshirt. A few of the regulars knew me; but many eyes stared across the room. I had tried to conform for a while by wearing the regulation slacks and white shirt of a yeshiva student, but people stared anyway. It did not matter what I wore, I did not fit in. So I decided to be comfortable, wear my normal clothes, and try not to be self-conscious. Nonetheless, I made it a point to come early, when there were fewer people.

Women are given privacy when they go to the *mikvah.* They are alone most of the time, except for the few moments when they are actually in the water; then a female observer is usually present to be certain that all body parts and hair are submerged at once. The *mikvah* is an absolute necessity for Jewish women at least once a month, as they are the vessels in which conception takes place— spiritual purity in this instance is essential.

Males also use the *mikvah* for spiritual purification, but more as a preparation for the fulfillment of daily practice and religious obligation, particularly prayer, study, handling or reading the Torah, or writing or saying the Holy Name of God. Male Orthodox practitioners regularly go to the *mikvah* just prior to the Sabbath or Holy Days, and many of those who are stringent in observance attend the *mikvah* every day before the morning prayers. Thus the male side of the *mikvah* is often crowded.

Aside from the implicit act of sanctifying this holy vessel we call our body, a good deal of the male ritual in *mikvahs* is similar to behavior we all learned in locker rooms. Like little boys who battle with their golden fluid swords streaming into a toilet bowl, men size up each other through the great equalizer of nudity. At the *mikvah*, we solemnly soap in the showers, rarely able to expunge the pervasive scent of maleness, and then immerse ourselves side by side in deep tubs of water; just as our Jewish brothers have done for generations; just as the Torah describes that the high priest had done in days of old. Some traditions beat drums, dance, hunt, and conquer for male bonding; Judaism uses the *mikvah*, prayers, and the constant process of learning Torah with a male partner.

The pool was all mine. I had waited a long time in the shower, peeking around the corner, hoping for a few moments of solitude. This was my reward: I was alone. As I hastened into the steaming tub, I pulled out the large rubber stopper in the wall that connected this water with an unseen source. The inflowing stream was cool. As the waters mixed, my tub was spiritually impregnated and validated as an authentic mikvah. *Somewhere within my being, I felt a charge when this coupling occurred. I was secure, encased in a womb, warm, wet, and peaceful. Spreading my arms, I floated a few moments, supported, caressed, gently rocked in the spiritual amniotic fluid, lulled by whispering steam leaking through exposed pipes near the ceiling.*

They say that every person has many souls, each of which resides on a different level; the highest aspects of the soul are connected with the angelic realms. Each time we sleep at night, one of our soul levels— called the neshamah—*flies away to the heavens, learning things of mystical delight. This soul force must return to us before we awaken, and the first blessing we make, as consciousness informs us that sleep* has ended, is a thanksgiving for the reinstatement of our soul—we could not live without it. The truth is, the soul would rather be somewhere else.

Today, when I immersed under the mikvah's waters, I felt my neshamah communing on ethenic planes. Bubbles streamed past my face as I slowly sank to the bottom in a fetal position. I felt myself melting into a unity, suspended in equilibrium—no gravity to remind me of my substantiality—and I lost all sense of body and form.

Echoes reverberated; a low, murmuring buzz that arose and fell from no particular direction was everywhere. The four Hebrew letters of the Holy Name etched themselves in my inner vision, and like a blast furnace pouring molten steel, flames streaked out from each letter. The fire intensified like mammoth sun flares traveling enormous distances, approaching me in slow motion as if through a gigantic telephoto lens, constantly coming nearer. I spread myself open, welcoming: "Come here, come to me; please."

There was a tug, an awareness, then another. My chest was straining. Something slowly realized that this body was under water—not breathing. The "I" consciousness began to return; there was a burning and ache deep in my lungs, far away. How long had I been here, and how long could I remain? I knew in that moment why the neshamah does not want to return. Quite simply, the womb of eternity is incomprehensibly serene, gentle, and loving.

I was curled near the bottom of the pool. The tugging became insistent. Slowly, I found the tiled bottom and pushed myself upward. As I broke through the surface into the world of mundane reality, I gently allowed my lungs to fill with the pervasive damp, warm air, and I knew something had been revitalized within me. In this daily experience of Jewish baptism was an affirmation and direct realization of a kabbalistic secret: We are reborn each day—indeed each moment—and we begin afresh with the possibility of new perfection in every breath we draw.

My favorite time at the Western Wall was three o'clock in the morning. I had always enjoyed this time of deep reflection in the stillness of predawn hours, but my recent *Vipassanā* meditation experience added a fresh perspective to my readings and prayers. In truth, up until this time, I had found the prayer service too long, too fast, and too repetitive. My goal had been to learn the pronunciation and to try to stay up with the prayer group. It was often a frustrating, numbing experience.

But now I began to prepare myself for the prayers by sitting quietly and emptying my mind. When I was ready, I would begin slowly, absorbing the meaning, dwelling in the rhythms, not concerned about how far I would get. Some days I spent hours on one phrase—and that was my prayer for the day; other days I felt the flow of the words pouring forth, and I would dance through dozens of pages, skimming the waves of emotion like a sleek canoe as I paddled from one poetic cove to another.

Not only did my prayers become more alive and more meaningful, the texts I studied assumed completely new voices. I had had glimmers of this earlier in the year, after my mother's death, but now the experience became robust, and I realized that these texts cannot be fully appreciated in everyday consciousness because their authors were themselves operating in an altered state.

Thus, strangely, my appreciation for Judaism was profoundly inspired by Buddhist practice. Indeed, if it had not been for the contemplative refinement of strenuous meditation, I would have missed a vast world of Jewish insight and wisdom that is hidden just below the surface—but few of the teachers or institutions I had yet experienced offered guidance along these lines. This was such an enormous void for me—and the fruits so readily available—I decided to pursue and gain some level of mastery with the meditative technique, all the while deepening my relationship with Judaism. Thus, I spent months going to the Western Wall long before the crowds appeared, and sat alongside the huge blocks of granite for many hours—in stillness—absorbing the aura and history of the Jewish people.

There were always a few devotees at the Western Wall who spent entire nights as self-appointed guardians of the sacred space, but normally wide sections of the ancient stone blocks were unattended, and I could sit and meditate without being disturbed. When dawn approached, large numbers of men began to fill the square, and my meditations had to cease. Many *minyanim* (prayer groups with a minimum of ten men) formed, each with its own style and pace. The cumulative effect was chaos. This was diametrically opposite to the atmosphere of my silent meditations. Visitors to the Wall who are not acquainted with Jewish prayer are often shocked or amused that every prayer group, and every individual within each group, seems to be going off in a separate direction.

Religious law requires the morning prayer to take place within a certain period after sunrise. It also emphasizes praying in a *minyan*—Judaism is a communal tradition—and so pressure is brought to bear on all individuals to join in group prayer. My experience had been that few groups had a rhythm or orientation to prayer that was compatible with mine, but I found a way to meet these group obligations at key moments during the prayer sequence while still cloaking myself in a kind of invisibility—a psychic separation—so that I could continue the quality of my meditative prayer. I longed, however, for a like-minded group who could meditate and pray together because the power of a group working harmoniously in spiritual efforts far exceeds the sum of its parts.

My spiritual solitude was never a deterrent for dozens of *shnorrers,* people who ask for money, who always appear at the Western Wall on weekday mornings during the hours of prayer. Although I could manage to gain some distance from the other people praying, it was hopeless to try to avoid the *shnorrers.* Nothing stops them.

Americans have a difficult time with collectors of charity because most of us view begging with disdain. *Shnorring,* however, is a highly honorable profession. Many of these people are collecting money for others as well as themselves, and their self-image is that they are vehicles through which other people can do good deeds— because it is a great *mitzvah* (good deed) to give money to the poor. Thus a *shnorrer* "expects" people to give, and is not particularly grateful when they do—which is misinterpreted by many uninitiated contributors as arrogance.

It should be noted that this attitude is not unique to Jewish beggars. A well-known Zen story tells of a man named Umezu who brings five hundred gold pieces (called *ryo*) to his teacher, Seisetsu, for the expansion of his school building.

> "Seisetsu said: 'All right, I will take it.'
> "Umezu gave Seisetsu the sack of gold, but he was dissatisfied with the attitude of the teacher. One might live a whole year on three *ryo,* and he had not even been thanked for five hundred.
> " 'In that sack are five hundred *ryo,*' hinted Umezu.
> " 'You told me that before,' replied Seisetsu.

" 'Even if I am a wealthy merchant, five hundred *ryo* is a lot of money,' said Umezu.

" 'Do you want me to thank you for it?' asked Seisetsu.

" 'You ought to,' replied Umezu.

" 'Why should I,' inquired Seisetsu. 'The giver should be thankful.' "[4]

I made it a rule when in Israel to try to give something to every person on the street who begged openly. It did not matter what the individual looked like or how aggressively he or she approached passersby. The less I felt inclined to give, the more I made an effort to increase the amount. Almost every time I tried to pray at the Wall, a *shnorrer* would approach me from the side, peek into my prayer book to be certain I was at a point where acknowledging him was permitted, and then lean close to my face, mumbling something. I always tried to have pocket change handy, so when this occurred I would transfer coins to him without removing my eyes from my book as if this were simply another component of the morning prayers.

Many people resent this kind of intrusion and will avoid going to the Western Wall for this reason alone. I had little difficulty with this, however; my distraction came from the crowded conditions— the loud voices of many prayer leaders, the shoving and elbowing of people jockeying for space, and the general mood of socialization, all of which contributed to the disruption of my concentration. The *shnorrers* were simply color added to the grand swirl of events that fill the canvas of the epic work known as Daily Life at the Western Wall.

The mind tenaciously grabs for something each moment, like a frog unrolling its sticky tongue to capture an insect, and instantaneously a mosquito is buzzing in my thoughts. Sometimes I track it through an aimless series of associations; other times it is joined by a swarm of images flooding into repetitive patterns—and I forget where, and what, and who I am.

Indeed, there is more forgetting than remembering. Only in moments like this do I realize that I live almost entirely in a state of forgetfulness. When I am able to cut off the drone of these thought-mosquitoes, I have a twinkling of remembrance. It never fails to shock me, this remembering; it dwells in a radiance that instantly soothes my aching psyche. It brings me back into the garden filled with delight that has often been my home—a place of serenity and perfect peace.

Around the garden's perimeter a fruit tree grows. The scent of it offers irresistible promise: divine wisdom. But the instant the fruit is tasted—in the repetition of the mythic cycle—the veil of forgetfulness descends and we are condemned to an endless motif of remembering and forgetting.

This is our mind. Constantly seduced by the aspiration for divine wisdom, only to discover it is not something to be attained but is inherent in our own stillness. Yet the paradox remains that in the stillness "we" no longer exist, and the fear of absorption into this nothingness fuels the endless chain of forgetfulness. Our ambition is self-defeating; letting go is our only hope.

The seven-day holiday of Sukkot was nearing its end. The morning prayers during this seasonal celebration are the most festive of the year. Each person carries four distinctive plants: an unopened palm branch, called a *lulav;* three branches of myrtle, called *hadasim;* two branches of a willow, called *aravos;* and the fruit of a species of citron, called an *etrog.* Each person has his own set of the four plants, and at a specific time during the prayers he waves them in six directions. According to one of the major Jewish mystics, Isaac Luria, the directions must proceed in the following order: south, north, east, upward, downward, and, finally, west.

This ritual is not only a thanksgiving for the harvest, it is a rain dance. A circle is formed around the Torah, and the men chant songs of praise as they circumambulate the holy scroll. At the end of the week, the willow branches are beat against the ground, and the prayers for rain begin in earnest.

When I first learned about and participated in this ritual, I was rudely awakened to the fact that Judaism has a fair share of primitive ceremony, and I was embarrassed to be involved in what appeared to be superstition and magic. But the more I became involved in these activities, the more I appreciated the power of our primal nature—its mystery transcends the farthest reaches of the intellect. Modern man continues to admire the amazing abilities of Aborigines who commune with nature, but most of us have surrendered this link in the name of being civilized. Religious traditions, however, have often retained rites that actually open passageways to a wondrous primeval energy within us.

Thus, over the years, the Sukkot ritual has become one of my favorites, particularly the requirement to dwell for a week in the *sukkah*, with its roof open to the skies, completely dependent upon the vicissitudes of nature. Sukkot has become for me the Jewish paradigm of an annual spiritual retreat—I love its raw, primitive flavor and the profound mysticism that is associated with it. The days of Sukkot each autumn provide a marvelous combination of spiritual insight that never fails to inspire new and penetrating self-realizations.

My etrog *this year is long and thin, with a plump tip called a* pitom. *Many hasidic stories tell of people spending their last cent on an* etrog—*devout believers are enchanted by the power of this* mitz-vah. *It is as if the individual's world is balanced on the* pitom *and if he fails to fulfill this particular commandment, everything will come crashing down.*

I am not sure what long and thin means for the year ahead, but when I hold the etrog *in my hand, it emanates a sublime vitality. Each day, when I pick it up, it softens me, and I feel the core of my being melting into it—perhaps this is what is meant by the idea that an* etrog *is a person's heart. Also the spine of my* lulav *is straight as an arrow, and the tip is in perfect condition. Another symbol, I hope, for a good year ahead.*

I spent hours this year among the vendors of Mea Shearim (the oldest and most orthodox neighborhood in Jerusalem), standing shoulder to shoulder with other potential buyers dressed in long, black caftans. Many of these shoppers used small magnifying glasses to examine the tips of their lulavim *to be certain they were not split, even a tenth of a millimeter, and to scrutinize the skins of the* etrogim *for any microscopic spots that could invalidate the fruit because of rabbinic requirements. In back alleys long lines of men stood, holding their choice* lulav *or* etrog, *awaiting final approval from one of a handful of experts in such matters. Almost all of the vendors allowed a person to carry away expensive items for approval without a deposit or even taking a person's name. Everyone knows that stolen items never can be used for a* mitzvah.

A few years ago, one of the first times I did this shopping, Shoshana came along to help. Our initial purchase was a long, narrow plastic container that was used to protect a lulav *and keep it moist. Then we spent many hours checking hundreds of* lulav *candidates, mainly looking at the tip to find a perfect specimen. Finally, I found my* lulav *and with great relief slipped it into its container and closed the zipper along the length to seal it in.*

Then we continued the search for another lulav *because I had promised a friend that I would buy her one as well. After another hour and a half, I found a good choice, but just to make certain, I compared it with my first selection. The two together looked wonderful, indeed the second choice looked more perfect than the first. When Shoshana replaced the first* lulav *in its container and began to zip up the side, in one heart-stopping moment I saw the tip was not completely in the plastic and the zipper was closing on it at lightning speed. Instantly the tip was caught in the zipper and ripped beyond repair. I doubled over in existential agony as I remembered the early childhood memory of pinching my young male organ in my pants' zipper! Oy vey, my* lulav *was ruined.*

Shoshana was mortified, I was numb. It was one of those splendid moments when everything materializes in slow motion, and each frame freezes for an instant, providing testimony for a lifetime of memories.

I ended up spending five more minutes and bought the first moderately acceptable lulav *I could find. I gave my friend the really good* lulav—*I felt it was hers—while I adjusted to my second choice and wondered what message this comedy of errors would have held for the mystics.*

I have noted that the Jewish calendar is filled with days of ritual celebration. When I first encountered this ongoing procession of Holy Days, I was impressed by the experience of reflecting on the past, reliving ancestral events thousands of years old. Having repeated these rituals for many years, however, I have found that while the cycle invites contemplation upon the past, each experience—although repetitive—seems to sharpen my awareness of the present moment.

Long ago, I read about the famous Dr. David Livingstone, who was found in the African jungles by Mr. Henry Morton Stanley, the news reporter. One day Livingstone was attacked by a lion, and was virtually in its claws before the lion was killed by a gun bearer. When asked later how he felt, Livingstone replied that when he realized there was nothing he could do, his terror transformed into an oceanic calm, a peacefulness he had never before experienced.

When I first heard this story, I thought Livingstone's euphoria was the result of an ultimate release in the clutch of death, the final realization of: "So this is how it is going to end!" In later years I discovered an important nuance in this supreme level of resignation: simply that the utter release of our survival impulse leads to breaking the bonds of all sense of past and future. When we are not clinging to life, we enter the continuous experience of the present moment. And so it turns out, paradoxically, that our grasping for life is self-defeating; it is only when we let go completely that we can be fully alive.

Similarly, whereas the ritual of tradition at first draws us into the past, its repetition, year after year, begins to generate a feeling of an endless cycle. Eventually, this leads to the realization that although we have a degree of choice, we are also encapsulated in our bodies, limited by our minds, products of creation bound by the laws of this universe. While we might conclude that the reality of being constrained by the nature of existence would result in a sense of fatalism, the actual experience is quite the opposite. Just like Dr. Livingstone, once we clearly recognize that we are securely in the jaws of fate, we release into that sublime state of transcendence that is commonly known as being fully present in the everlasting NOW.

12

INSIGHT MEDITATION SOCIETY, BARRE, MASSACHUSETTS: JUNE 1987. TEN DAYS ON A GROUP RETREAT LEAD BY JOSEPH GOLDSTEIN AND SHARON SALZBERG.

The Insight Meditation Society (IMS), located in the Berkshire Mountains near Barre, Massachusetts, is housed in a large mansion that was once a Christian seminary. There are accommodations for over one hundred people to experience the intense form of Buddhist retreat in the *Theravāda* tradition that utilizes the meditation technique of *Vipassanā,* which loosely translated means "insight." It had been almost a year since I took my first *Vipassanā* retreat, and I was eager to explore this method in more depth. The facility at IMS is generally considered one of the best places in North America to experience this kind of Buddhist practice.

Outwardly, the IMS estate is similar to many that can be found in New England, with its impressive driveway, enormous lawns, and columned entranceway. When I arrived, the main building revealed signs of disrepair, and many places beckoned the eye, calling for cosmetic or more serious maintenance. But despite the outward appearance, the inside was filled with a warmhearted familiarity. The moment I passed over the worn, chipped threshold and felt the pervasive silence within, my heart opened.

I placed my bags in the foyer and before going to the office to register was drawn down one wing of the building into a large room with highly polished floors. I slipped out of my sandals and with bare feet felt the texture of the wood. Over the next ten days, during the periods of walking meditation, I became intimate with the grain and knots of every board in this floor.

Huge windows lined opposing walls of this room, in which there was not a single piece of furniture. At one end, the windows were made of stained glass, depicting a Christian scene. Just past these windows was the entrance to a much larger room, the meditation hall, where a statue of the Buddha overlooked row upon row of cushions. In these two rooms I would spend fourteen to sixteen hours each day, alternating sitting and walking meditation, constantly observing my thought process.

I gazed into the library next to the registration office, and my heart soared. It was filled with a wonderful selection of books from all traditions, and had an especially fine selection of Buddhist works. I knew that I would allow myself very little time reading during this retreat, but I was already convinced—within the first fifteen minutes—that I would be returning often to this place.

My love at first sight never changed, even though there were often difficult hours, filled with excruciating pain, particularly during the first few days. Many people would not like this highly disciplined routine, the absolute silence, the lack of all social connection, the austere sleeping arrangements, and the grinding effort of constant engagement in meditation. For me, this was a five-star retreat facility; pure luxury. It was warm, dry, secure, protected; there were hot showers, plenty of blankets, comfortable foam bedding—and the food was outstanding. But the important thing was that the teaching and guidance was clear, simple, and as powerful as anything I had experienced in years of spiritual practice.

Twelve paces from one door to the next, I am repeatedly measuring the hallway—with a slow contemplative stride—waiting for my interview with Joseph Goldstein. Lifting, moving, placing each foot, noticing my mind was being pulled by something—perhaps anticipation of the upcoming meeting—while another part of me tugged to bring the attention back to the movements of my feet. What is pulling? Who is tugging?

A spider is moving along the wall. It invites me, drawing my attention into the beginning of a contemplation. In a hop-skip-jump of dozens of associations with intricate junctions, I find myself walking carefully in a dense jungle, pushing aside thick, lush palm fronds as I peer ahead for signs of life. The temperature is sweltering, and my neck is covered with slick, oily sweat.

Jungle drums beat in a slow rhythm in the distance. Two booms and a long silence; another two booms and a silence; still again, another. I realize I am walking to match the rhythm, and then I discover the pounding drums are my own inner voice as I mentally note the movement of my feet, each syllable exploding like an echo in a large cavern: "lift-ing (boom, boom)," "mov-ing (boom, boom)," "plac-ing (boom, boom)."

The door opens, and the person before me exits. I slowly walk into the room, but my concentration has been broken as thoughts now flood my consciousness. I rapidly review all of the things I want to say during the next few minutes. I am not observing my breath, nor am I aware of my body, and I begin to lower into the chair facing Joseph. All the while I am moving very slowly, pretending now that I am being meticulous in my meditation practice. He watches me and calmly says: "lowering-lowering, turning, sitting . . . " I realize he is trying to bring me back into the moment. My pretending was foolish; anybody could see that my mind was racing around a dozen speedway tracks at once.

We talked a short while, and when it was time to leave, I began to lift myself from the chair—but Joseph held up his hand and said: "rising-rising, bending, stretching . . . " We both smiled, sharing a moment of recognition that most people live in a state of constant forgetfulness and move unconsciously in rote patterns; most of us are conditioned to act, think, and feel in predictable ways, rarely noticing what is going on in our minds and what we are doing with our bodies. Now I was standing, and, smiling, I was turning-turning, twisting, and then I was lifting-moving-placing each foot, one after the other to exit the room; lifting-moving-placing, lifting-moving-placing.

The third day I broke an unwritten rule and placed a long-distance telephone call to inquire how our dog, Moses, was doing. He had been diagnosed as having cancer, a canine lymphoma. Many months earlier he had stopped eating and had become lethargic; I could feel the swellings in his flanks and behind his ears. Our Israeli veterinarian did not offer any hope, but he did not want to put Moses to sleep.

A pet could not replace the child we wanted and never had, but

Moses was nonetheless a surrogate for a tremendous amount of our affection. In return, he was a paradigm of love, filled with joy at a moment's notice; his comical, drooping eyes would accent a porpoiselike smile, his butt would wiggle and quiver uncontrollably, and he would perform an inimitable dance of circles and twirls punctuated by moist, delirious yelps of rapturous delight.

When the vet gave us the news of a terminal illness, we did our best to make his last days comfortable. I decided to encourage his food intake and began to prepare the archetypical Jewish cure for every problem known to humankind: chicken noodle soup. I boiled the entire chicken—kosher, of course—and then picked through the glob carefully with my fingers, separating out every bone so that he would not choke. When this glutinous, rich mixture was combined with his dry food, Moses could not resist, even though he was a very sick animal. He began eating again and actually got friskier.

But then he slowly deteriorated. A few weeks before we were due to leave Israel for our annual summer trip to the U.S.A., it was clear that Moses was not doing well. We took him back to the vet in the hope that this was the right time to send him to dog heaven. But the golden retriever breed is exceptionally gregarious, and the moment we entered the vet's office, the smell and presence of other creatures excited our dying dog so much, he began to jump and frolic as he had from the time he was a puppy. When the vet saw this happy dog, he wondered openly why we were there, and our sense of guilt at conspiring to rid ourselves of a companion who had been with us for ten years sent us slinking out of the office, with our tails between our legs.

We brought Moses with us on the plane back to the U.S.A. The length of the trip required an overnight stay in Brussels so he could have his medicine on time, and we could be sure he had the necessary water and food. It was a complex, difficult saga bringing him along, far more exhausting than his trip as an immigrant into Israel a couple of years earlier; but we made it somehow to Shoshana's parents' home in New Jersey. By this time, Moses did not appear well at all.

When I called to inquire about my sick friend, the answer, although half expected, came as a numbing shock. He had simply lain down the day after I left and refused to move. They got him to the vet, who took one look and could not understand why her

Israeli colleague had ignored the evidence—the poor dog was a walking corpse. His body was completely riddled with cancer, and despite the outward look of fullness, his once thick head was now hollowed at the temples and there was very little flesh left on his ribs. Shoshana reluctantly agreed with the vet's observation, and cradled in her arms, Moses had been given a lethal injection. He had died less than a week after returning to his birthland.

Many meditations after this news were filled with reflections of events that had occurred during this dog's life. Almost all of the time Shoshana and I had been together, he was our companion. Thus, thoughts of death and destiny became a theme that interrupted my inner silence for a couple of days.

Most of us live on a track of "becoming"; we are constantly leaning into that future period when we will have enough money or enough free time; when the vacation will arrive, the kids have moved out, the promotion will be awarded, or the credit cards are paid off and everything will be okay; when we will find the right relationship, the ideal job, or the quality time of retirement, and all the pegs will fit into their proper holes.

This constant feeling of "becoming" is a treadmill we construct in our minds that not only exhausts us, it deceives us into believing that this is the way things work. We are like hamsters running in wire cages that pivot in circles—our food rests on the other side of the wire, just out of reach—we run and run, thinking that in a few more steps we will have it.

Our hamster cage is called "self-perception"; as long as we are running, we can feel ourselves. If perchance we misstep and begin to fall off the track, we lose the sense of ourselves, and as there is no direction in the void, we cannot identify who we are. This emptiness is terrifying, and we claw to get back aboard the treadmill that at least helps us believe in the illusion that "This is me."

As long as we cling to our need for an identity, we remain trapped; we can never delve into the true sustenance that will free us. Krishnamurti discussed this question:

> *Tomorrow is the invention of thought as time, and if there is no tomorrow psychologically, what happens in life today? Then there is a tremendous revolution, isn't there? Then your whole action undergoes a radical change, doesn't it? Then you are completely whole*

now, not projecting from the past, through the present, into the future. That means to life, dying every day. Do it, and you will find out what it means to live completely today.

Isn't that what love is? You don't say, "I will love tomorrow," do you? You love or you don't love. Love has no time, only sorrow has time. . . . So one has to find out for oneself what time is, and find out if there is a "no tomorrow." That is to live, then there is a life which is eternal, because eternity has no time.[5]

This basic teaching of "being" versus "becoming" opens the paradox of timelessness. Most of us are snared in the web of time, either reflecting upon the past or preparing for the nebulous future—waiting for something: hamster food.

Krishnamurti's point is that when we are able to ignore the sense of the future, when we release ourselves from the idea of tomorrow, we become whole just as we are, and this leads to a radical change in perspective. It inspires a new level of self-assurance that I am what I am, complete in this moment, waiting for nothing—and everything is exactly as it must be.

On the sixth day of this retreat, slow-walking in deep meditation along the driveway, pacing about twenty steps in each direction, back and forth, I suddenly saw IT! The IT that I saw was the realization that this practice really worked, every moment of mindfulness was complete in itself—there was nowhere else to go. This idea—as simple as it sounds—dramatically affected my practice from that moment on. There were no flashing lights, supernal beings, or ultimate realizations; simply a clarity, a step through a mental time warp, a powerful insight that dwelt in my soul like a warm fire on a foggy night.

The spark for this realization came during an interview with Sharon Salzberg. She suggested an elementary practice that turned out to be of enormous benefit. The idea was to approach the upcoming breath, or the upcoming step, as if it were the first breath/ step I had ever taken, and the last I would ever take. This idea sounded simple and obvious, but the power of working with it in a meditative practice had a phenomenal effect. Each breath/step was like a snowflake, unique, unrepeatable, enormously interesting, stunning in its rapid transition through existence, blossoming out of the heart of oblivion through the membrane of awareness, and then . . . nothing, except for the mind's insistence on clinging to the image, turning it into a thought, a world, a universe, which itself grew out of nothing and ultimately faded into the void.

From the moment I left Sharon's office I was doing the One-Step Dance, as I called it, and soon its consciousness penetrated every act. This was the only time I would reach for this fork, feel this movement of arm and hand, touch this texture, taste this flavor, see this shadow, hear this sound.

The One-Step Dance became all-consuming; everything else was put aside. Thoughts of past and future, plans, ideas, fantasies, everything was gone. Soon I realized that there were so many messages coming in through the senses, I could discern merely a fraction, like a toothpick out of a giant redwood. Nonetheless, a growing sense of harmony with the universal flow began to evolve, and this is what brought me to the realization of the mysterious IT.

The ten-day retreat has just ended. Once again I feel revitalized on my spiritual path—the Vipassanā *technique opens increasingly higher layers of awareness in my Jewish practice. Indeed, the practice of silence and the intense meditation I did during this retreat inspired more clarity into a mystical world that transcends religious distinctions. On this last day, after the closing talk, I went to the library, which I had put off-limits as a self-imposed restraint, and fanned through dozens of books from many different traditions: Christian, Islamic, Hindu, Taoist, Shinto, Zoroastrian, as well as Buddhist and Jewish. I saw that although the forms differ distinctly, the transcendental descriptions of mystics within each sounded curiously familiar. When I read the words without first reading the title or book jacket, it was impossible to identify the tradition. Mysticism is as universal a language as music.*

I left the library and walked around the grounds of IMS. Most of the flowers had already peaked, and the summer burst of greens was luxuriant. The large, organic gardens to one side of the building were past the sprouting stage; leafy plants reached up with outstretched arms, soaking in sun and gathering rain. They seemed to be laughing.

I lay down spread-eagled in the grass this last day, welcoming the life-force heat generated at the center of the solar system, and the inner lotus unfolded. I remembered almost twenty years earlier lying on a Mediterranean beach, my body dissolving in an LSD rapture, melting in the sea of sand, completely calm in a world exclusively composed of light and warmth. In this grass it was the same phenomenon, but something today offered a clarity that the drug never revealed. Everything I ever wanted was right here, within, always accessible; it was more than bliss, happiness, tranquillity—it was peace; simple, pure, serene, peace.

13

Shoshana returned with me this year to the Insight Meditation Society to take her first forty-day retreat. Last summer I was so enthusiastic about the *Vipassanā* meditation, we went to California for a ten-day retreat before going home to Israel. It was Shoshana's first experience with *Vipassanā*. She loved it. Those ten days inspired her to plan an extended retreat, and we carved out forty days to live in seclusion at IMS in the woods of Massachusetts—living in the same building but alone.

This was a new adventure for us. Except for my forty-day retreat seven years earlier, we had never been out of communication for such an extended period. Yet we discovered that despite the silence, we communed more profoundly than we ever had during the first thirteen years we were together.

When we arrived at the center, hundreds of flowers were budding around the perimeter of the main building. A frosty chill in the early morning air intimated that winter's trace was still present, but the warm spring winds and the midday sun would soon erase all signs of the previous season. The building was empty except for staff and a few "long-term yogis," others who were engaged in independent retreats of varying lengths of time.

The first evening, before beginning our retreat discipline, a friend invited us to the staff dining room for dinner. It was good to meet with these folks, but the inevitable discussion arose about the political situation in Israel. Almost every time I have been involved in a discussion about the relations between Jews and Arabs, I have found that emotions run high, and the subject invariably deteriorates into a quagmire of uneducated opinions. Despite the fact that we had a home in Israel, we often felt uninformed ourselves because the politics are intricate, the personalities are complex, and—as in American politics—the statements of public figures in the government cannot be trusted; we knew only that many meaningless deaths occurred on both sides—and there did not seem to be a clear solution. So each time this discussion arose, I experienced the feeling of despair and sadness when I heard the blind accusations, insinuations, and blatant anti-Semitism.

We were acutely conflicted about the situation in Israel, and the most frightening part was that we were becoming accustomed to a life where it was normal to be paranoid, where every package on the street might be a bomb, where a large percentage of the population openly carry weapons. Gunshots in the distance were daily events, hatred and bigotry were expressed openly, and a life of division and separation between peoples seemed to be an unresolvable fact. I wanted it all to go away, and I hoped that by ignoring it, by numbing my reactions, I would miraculously turn the ugly mess into a field of flowers. But it seemed to be getting worse, not better, and we struggled to gain clarity.

In truth, violence is much more rampant in the U.S.A. than in Israel. There are far more murders, knifings, rapes, muggings, and thefts in any American city with a population of a million or more than in the entire State of Israel. But things are taken more personally in Israel, and a single act of violence that is ethnically motivated is normally nationwide news. Thus when Americans become self-righteous about Israel, most Israelis are infuriated by the hypocritical attitudes. Nonetheless, as Shoshana and I straddled the two nations, we were left with aching hearts and spent long hours trying to ascertain where and how we fitted.

Both of us were looking forward to this retreat, not only for the spiritual practice, but for the quiet time away from the intensity of Jerusalem. We each longed to walk peacefully in the woods without looking over our shoulders, to sit silently for hours without concern about the news of ongoing civil disturbances.

The day after we arrived, I began my retreat discipline, and within hours I was into a routine of absolute silence. After a few days my concentration intensified, and as frequently happens to me on extended retreat, I remembered once again what I always forget when I am engaged in the world: I remembered what it feels like to enter the sweetness of complete release into silence—no appointments to keep, no deadlines, no time demons, nobody to engage, nothing but the simplest routine in a safe, warm, dry sanctuary.

My practice for the next six weeks would be to start the day at two-thirty each morning with yoga, and begin the first hour of sitting meditation at three A.M. From then on, I would continue walking and sitting meditation all day, except for eating and brief periods of rest. Bedtime was set for nine P.M.

As the days passed, I approached each hour of sitting or walking with ever-increasing interest and curiosity because I could never predict from one to the next what was going to happen. One hour I might enter into states of sublime bliss, exquisite and profound; the next I might drop into a process of circular thinking, anger, boredom, fantasy, desire, or aversion.

After weeks of these vacillations between extraordinary pleasure and intense distress, I began to understand that the mind states arose and evaporated on their own, and I realized through direct experience the magnitude of the teaching that one was not preferable to another. Mind states come and go; we try to hold on to them or push them away. But we cannot succeed in either case. Our choice, then, lies in continuing in this self-torment of trying to grasp or repel mind states, or we can choose not to have preferences and be with whatever arises. When I started this practice of "no preference," a special quality of mind began to grow—a unique understanding and affirmation of the way things are—and I discovered something extraordinary: the heart of stillness sits perfectly balanced in the middle of chaos. This is the true dwelling place of the soul.

On his deathbed Aldous Huxley was asked to reveal the wisdom he had gained through his rich life experience, and he responded that he wished he had been kinder to people. I am touched by this thought. How do we learn to be kinder to people? I believe it has to do with the sense of unity, sameness, the realization that we are all caught in this predicament called life. When we feel separate, alone, isolated, how can we feel kind to others? But when we empathize, when there is a common touch-point that evokes our memory of personal experi-

ence, such as when the child scrapes its knee or a friend suffers a
personal loss, then our hearts melt, we feel a flutter in our midsections,
and lovingkindness flows easily.

As long as people are unaware of the mechanics of the thought
process, we are caught in the grip of a tenacious dragon called Mind.
It often breathes fire, searing us in the heat of our own illusions,
setting our blood boiling, but most importantly, causing us to believe
that we live in a cave and that our job is to prevent anything from
entering. The mind-dragon keeps us separated from the world.

The only way we can attain the wisdom teaching of kindness is to
slay the dragon. How is this done? By realizing that this dragon
thrives in the darkness of the cave but cannot survive in the light. As
we observe our mental process, we bring a light to bear on the mind-
dragon, and sooner or later it will melt away. And then, without
additional effort, the lovingkindness within each of us will find clear
expression because our essential nature dwells in the realm of com-
passion.

As my meditations became clearer and the state of "no preference" more dominant, I began to feel an outpouring of tenderness
and warmth that had never before found this depth of expression.
Every person in the room, every bird and insect, the plants, the
grass, everything that pulsated with life shared my own heartbeat.
The intensity of these feelings multiplied a hundredfold when I
glanced at my beloved Shoshana out of the corner of my eye. As
I drank the elixir of these feelings, I began to see the creation anew,
as if my entire visual field had muted and softened into a magnificent Renoir, and all my senses were bathed in the warm waters of
divine harmony.

When I later read the ninth-century Sufi poet Bayezid Bistami,
I was shocked by the familiarity of the image he developed. A
thousand years ago, he wrote as if recording the words of God
speaking:

> My servant [anyone devoted to serving God] ceases not to
> draw nigh unto Me by works of devotion, until I love him; and
> when I love him I am the eye by which he sees and the ear by
> which he hears. And when he approaches a span I approach a
> cubit, and when he comes walking I come running.[6]

The "works of devotion" about which Bistami writes are acts of complete surrender, a constant mode of giving. The implication is that the more we give freely to the divine source of life, the more we are empowered to give. It is not one for one, rather each portion of giving is returned many-fold. This realization soon opens the gates of awareness, and we realize that it is not us giving, but we are vessels through which the energy of creation is conveyed. This flow of energy is nothing less than Pure Love.

We cannot attain Pure Love through aspiration because the ego is attached to desire, while genuine unconditional love is void of self-consciousness. We can only learn how to give. The art of giving will transport us to higher realms; generosity is a true path of self-realization. Thus, I discovered, the essential act of loving is exclusive of all demands and expectations; it is simply the ability to open our hands, to give, to release, to break out of the bounded ego by acts of utmost generosity.

I remember a lecture I attended last year—the rabbi stood behind a podium stacked high with large, well-used books. The room was filled with students of Talmud, taking a break from their studies to listen for an hour to this wise man who had spent a lifetime of constant reflection on the holy books. He talked about many different aspects of Torah, and his arguments were too complex for me to recall. But I recollect one important point about which he gave us an example and posed a question. Here it is:

One man walking down the road saw a dirty beggar in a ditch who swore and spat at the man as he approached. The man was disgusted by the beggar but realized that he had not given charity that month, and he was obliged to give away ten more dollars to meet his quota for tithing. For a moment he considered giving the money to a more likable cause, but then he handed the money to the beggar, who grabbed the cash with a sneer and turned away without a word of thanks.

Another man walking down a different path saw a beggar in rags. Even though the man's monthly quota for tithing had been fulfilled, his heart was touched by this poverty and he automatically reached for a dollar to give the beggar. He gave the money, and the beggar smiled in gratitude.

The rabbi asked: "Which act of charity is higher—giving out of obligation or giving from the heart?"

All of us in the class were inclined to respond that giving from the heart had something more in it, but we knew the rabbi was going to tell us just the opposite, because in spiritual teaching nothing is logical. We were not disappointed.

"Giving from the heart is a wonderful thing," the rabbi said, "It is a very high act and should never be demeaned. But there is something much more important that happens when somebody gives charity out of obligation.

"Consider who is doing the giving. When somebody gives from the heart, there is a clear sense of oneself doing something; in other words, heartfelt charity always involves ego gratification.

"However, when we give out of obligation, when we give at a moment that every part of us is yelling NO! because of one reason or another—perhaps the beneficiary is disgusting, or it is too much money, or any of thousands of reasons we use to avoid giving charity— then we are confronting our own egos, and giving nonetheless. Why? Because we are supposed to. And what this means is that it is not us doing the giving, rather we are vehicles through which God gives.

"Understand, however, that obligation is often confused with guilt, resignation, or a sense that one is making a payment to be recorded in the heavenly ledgers. Each of these is a wrong interpretation because each is pervaded with self-consciousness. As long as the sense of oneself is present, charity is on a much lower level. Obligation is founded on the principle of spiritual clarity—it is an understanding that this is the way things work; we do what we are supposed to do without regrets or expectations. Even when a beggar spits and maliciously turns his head in disgust, a person with spiritual clarity walks away without a second thought. Moreover, the person giving charity easily could have passed the man by and still fulfilled his religious duty by contributing his monthly tithe to a different recipient, but an opportunity presented itself and he just did it.

"You cannot appreciate the true experience of this high spiritual level from the story, you must yourselves give at every opportunity, give until it hurts, give until it is clear to you that there is no stickiness on your fingers and nothing clings in your mind. Give until it flows freely, and then you will discover one of the greatest gifts God has offered us—the ability to let go of our grasping nature; to attain the true realization that God is constantly sustaining and replenishing us, that no matter how much we give, it comes from the infinite well of God's love. This is the gift of overflowing abundance, which is *always available to us but which can be experienced only through giving."*

The kabbalistic imagery often used to describe the process of giving and receiving is the relationship between vessel and light. A vessel can hold only so much light. Each aspect of creation is the vessel for the light of the Creator. The vessel is the receiving side, and light is the giving side. The vessel of humankind is unique in that it can consciously give its light away. This is what it means that man is created in the likeness of God—this likeness is the ability to give. But no matter how much we give, as the light of creation is infinite, the vessel is immediately replenished. Thus, we never view this as a sequential process—that giving may lead to receiving—because the process is simultaneous; receiving occurs instantly and automatically whenever we give. As Chögyam Trungpa said:

> Compassion has nothing to do with achievement at all. It is spacious and very generous. When a person develops real compassion, he is uncertain whether he is being generous to others or to himself because compassion is environmental generosity, without direction, without "for me" and without "for them." It is filled with joy, spontaneously existing joy, constant joy in the sense of trust, in the sense that joy contains tremendous wealth, richness. . . .
>
> Compassion automatically invites you to relate with people, because you no longer regard people as a drain on your energy. They recharge your energy, because in the process of relating with them you acknowledge your wealth, your richness. So, if you have difficult tasks to perform, such as dealing with people or life situations, you do not feel you are running out of resources. . . . There is no feeling of poverty at all in this approach to life.[7]

A kabbalistic concept describes all creation as having a "will-to-receive."[8] The mystery of why things become what they are, their shape, their color, their smell, or any other attributes, including consciousness, are all related to this "will-to-receive."

This idea is based on the belief that the Creator of life is infinite and thus is all-giving. The infinite, by definition, has no possibility of receiving anything. It is always full. Creation, on the other hand, is continuously in need of sustenance, and thus in each and every moment it must receive, or it will disappear.

This paper I write on has the will to be paper, so to speak; this pen has the will to be a pen. I have the will to be me. Obviously this is a different kind of will than that which we commonly describe as the basis of motivation, or willpower, or free will. It is not "my" will, there is no attachment to ego; indeed the will to be me is identical with the Creator's will that I should exist. The Sufis express this through poetry:

> One went to the door of the Beloved and knocked.
> A voice asked, "Who is there?"
> He answered, "It is I."
> The voice said, "There is no room for Me and Thee."
> The door was shut.
> After a year of solitude and deprivation he returned
>   and knocked.
> A voice from within asked, "Who is there?"
> The man said, "It is Thee."
> The door was opened for him.
>
> Rumi[9]

Attuning to this flow of creation, we can develop a new relationship to life as vehicles through which light is constantly transmitted. The Kabbalists believe that the highest form of spiritual perfection is the person's ability to transmute the will-to-receive into a will-to-bestow. They recognize that humankind can never divest itself completely of its natural acquisitive instinct or desire. This instinct on the physical/material level is closely related to the survival instinct. However, on the essential soul level, the survival instinct is not relevant because the soul dwells in a timeless, deathless realm. Thus, as our awareness increases, and the true nature of our inner being freely asserts itself, our selfish, acquisitive, ego-centered behavior is transformed into lovingkindness, compassion, and generosity.[10]

I used to wonder, "Why did the Buddha return from *nirvāna*?" I envisioned *nirvāna* as the ultimate stage of realization, total absorption in the Oneness, the revelation of absolute truth where nothing is hidden. I thought that surely the wisdom of *nirvāna* exposed the limitations of the world, including the obvious fact that throughout history only a handful of spiritual aspirants have even come close to attaining this exalted state. How could a wise, enlightened being engage in the seemingly futile effort to raise the masses to a pinnacle upon which, it seems, only a few can stand. It would be like shouting in a pitch-black cave filled with a maze of blind tunnels, "Here I am!"

I discovered this question as a teenager, sitting on a Lake Michigan beach with a friend who joined me in solving the problems of the world. We had the wisdom of youth, the self-assurance that we could resolve problems that had plagued philosophers for thousands of years. Yet for some reason this riddle completely baffled us. For the next thirty years I found myself occasionally returning to ponder this mystery. I imagined what it might be like to inherit all the wealth heaven had to offer, and wondered what would possibly bring me back to the poverty of mundane existence.

In a meditation during this retreat, I was struck by an insight that offered a new perspective. As often happens with enigmatic questions, there was a problem with the question itself. It assumes that *nirvāna* exists as some other realm exclusive of this world. However, the Buddha revealed an enormous secret: ultimate enlightenment requires compassion and charity, which means working in relationship with others. Quite simply, engaging the world is an intrinsic part of the enlightenment process—*nirvāna* and service to humankind go hand in hand.

We have learned that the Buddha taught the world about the true nature of things. However, we do not usually appreciate that his act of teaching was part of his own continuing illumination. In fact, there was no choice; the Buddha did not choose to return, he was here all along. *Nirvāna* is not an end point; it is simply a consciousness that opens the floodgates through which a torrent of unrestrained compassion and love will stream.

Love and compassion are themes that permeate all the world's spiritual traditions; indeed in the West, the vital impetus of creation is love. Without it, nothing would exist. Some have even said, "God is love." This is not a description of a divine attribute, but a definition whereby one cannot be separated from the other.

A well-known Kabbalist from the sixteenth century, Moses Cordovero, developed the idea that the highest human expression was the "imitation of God." In Kabbalah, one of the ten major components with which God created the universe is called "wisdom."

Cordovero describes how human beings should imitate wisdom in the following way:

> [A person] should constantly pray for mercy and blessing for the world just as the Supernal Father has mercy on all His creatures. And [this person] should constantly pray for the alleviation of suffering as if those who suffer were actually his children and as if he had created them. . . . He should think of those that are cut off, seek those that are young, heal that which is broken, feed that which standeth still, restore those that are lost. . . . These are the qualities of Wisdom, of the father merciful to his children. Furthermore, [this person's] mercy should extend to all creatures, neither destroying nor despising any of them. For the Supernal Wisdom is extended to all created things—minerals, plants, animals and humans.[11]

The idea of imitating the love that personifies the essence of the Creator extends well beyond any conception of love regarding relationships that we experience. Rather it is an ideal with respect to all creation, experiencing the realization that the existence of everything is continuously empowered by the creative force and thereby contains the "love" of God.

All of these marvelous feelings have renewed truth in the altered consciousness that naturally arises in silence and solitude; I am awed by the possibilities of human interaction. If only we could imagine that we are really imitating God, so to speak.

I notice Shoshana's presence, even when I do not see her. I hear a person enter the large empty meditation room, and I know when it is her. I feel a presence in the community kitchen, and I know she is there. I try not to think about her too much because I am certain that our thoughts intermix and I want to be respectful of her inner quiet. Strong thoughts could be as disturbing as a meaningful glance or even a touch. So when I feel her presence, I flow into it with love and then quickly pull myself back into my meditation practice, aware of the breath or the movements of my body.

Nonetheless, with all this careful discipline, every so often I dissolve into a mind state of warm cuddlies, hugging her, radiating my love, sharing a sweet caress that extends beyond time and space. Recently, this transcendental embrace carried me into a new province of love.

It was beyond personal need, fear, desire, pride; beyond any sense of other. It was a psychic meltdown, two cups of life-spirit flowed together and could never again be separated. This had nothing to do with our individuality as vital, independent, creative human beings—it was strictly on the higher planes, the sympathetic vibration of a musical note of one instrument in perfect tune with another. Impossible to articulate in words, it is a knowing, a mysterious connection, a whole new quality to my experience of love—a delicious, superb, delightful warmth in my soul.

14

As a long-term yogi I soon felt that IMS was my home. People coming for scheduled retreats hauled in assorted worlds with their arrival baggage; but they departed the retreat center with a freshness glistening in their eyes and a secret in their hearts. They had touched something within, and it gave them remarkable strength. At first I found myself annoyed when new people arrived—as if they were disrupting my solitude—but my spirit soared when I observed the profound transformation experienced by so many retreatants.

Each of the three retreats scheduled during our six-week stay was unique in the type of instruction offered and in the character of the group that attended. The first was somewhat more "orthodox," given by a monk with a clean-shaven head, an Englishman who had taken Buddhist vows and was now clothed in the orange robes of his order; at mealtimes he carried a large, wooden begging bowl. His flowing robes, and the Buddhist pacifism they exemplify, hung ironically on a muscular body hardened by street wisdom. Indeed, his craggy pocked and scarred face gave the impression of a past life with a motorcycle gang, and I often envisioned him dressed in black leather, standing tall with a chain wrapped around one fist.

This monk was a brilliant presenter, ironic, self-deprecating, and with provocative ideas. As he was not well known, the group he drew was fairly small, composed of more adventuresome retreatants who were willing to try a new experience. They were not to be disappointed.

When this first retreat ended, there were a number of days when the whole facility was empty except for a half dozen long-term yogis and the staff. These inactive times were when I felt most comfortable in my daily rhythms. Routine chores of the retreat center required more attention when there were fewer hands, but this was compensated by the emptiness and hushed ambience of the large meditation rooms.

Even though the few other long-term yogis rarely talked, we gained an increasing sense of intimacy as we became familiar with each other's body language and temperament. The others had been there longer than us, some for many months, in one instance over a year. The command they had of their practice greatly influenced mine, and I noticed—whenever I sat or walked in meditation alongside one of these people—my heart often glowed with a serene inner smile that added new warmth to my spirit. In those eternal moments, a root quality connected in some marvelous way, I knew we were bonding for life in an unspoken, spiritual wedlock.

This bonding is the adhesive force of the Sangha, one of the triple gems upon which Buddhism is based—the two others being the Buddha himself and the Dharma (the path, or the way). The Sangha is a living entity that is formed by like-minded individuals who are genuinely involved in a spiritual practice; the word *sangha* originally described a group that composed a monastic order. A Buddhist practitioner can take "refuge"—gain spiritual protection—in any of the three gems: the Buddha, the Dharma, or the Sangha.

Nowadays in the West anyone undertaking Buddhist practice is considered part of a Sangha bound together by a common thread of spiritual aspiration. In the vernacular, we sometimes refer to our fellow retreatants as "Dharma buddies." In a way, this is like alluding to our spouses as good friends or pals. Although a spouse may be a friend, this image falls far short of the magnitude of the relationship. And while "Dharma buddies" is a good description of the social level of the Sangha, when people work shoulder to shoulder in the passionate effort to uncover universal truth, something is awakened within each person that reveals—like a mirror—the commonality of all existence, and this is the essential wellspring of the Sangha. My own understanding of the Sangha is its universal nature, extending far beyond Buddhist boundaries, including the part in all of us yearning to be at one with the true nature of our existence.

The second retreat was led by another European, a German, who had been a monk at one time, but now dressed in ordinary clothes; he gave the impression that he enjoyed and was very much at peace with the anonymity of an undistinguished appearance. His approach to meditation practice was much more relaxed, liberal, and multidimensional. There was a larger group of participants in his retreat; the atmosphere was more festive and social. This was difficult for me because I was thoroughly into my solitude by the third week and did not want to be distracted by the conviviality of the group. I spent a great deal of time meditating in my own room.

The last retreat was given by two of the founders of IMS, Joseph Goldstein and Sharon Salzberg. Once again the style of teaching was distinctive, having a clarity and simplicity mixed with an acute sensitivity to the problems of beginning meditators in a Western environment. The retreatants drawn to this ten-day session were mostly people who had attended other retreats given by Joseph and Sharon—it was more of a family gathering. People in this group had spent many previous hours in silent communion with each other, and mutual affections flowed like warm springs under the exterior terrain of personality. I was quickly attracted to this group and found myself in remarkable harmony with the meditation practice as it unfolded during the retreat.

A group of retreatants gathered in a small room to share with a teacher and each other. Usually these sessions are one on one between student and teacher, but occasionally they are structured as a group experience because it is helpful to be exposed to the problems and experiences of others. Sitting in this group, I was reminded of my earlier days and the problems most retreatants face. I have learned to bear pain without a grudge, and submit to tedious repetition or boredom without complaint. Through experience I have a small list of rules for the road: Accept whatever comes, the highs are always followed by lows, do not try to hold on to anything or chase anything away, be steady, do not change practice in the middle of a meditation, and, above all, persist—never let doubt get a foothold.

Many questions were asked in this group, as in others, about pain and patience. Retreats are hard work. Things move slowly; glimmers

*of progress are quickly erased by a single difficult meditation period.
Even monks who work with strenuous daily disciplines for dozens of
years admit that they often experience pain, confusion, racing
thoughts, and the fear of getting nowhere—just like beginners.*

*Yet despite the difficulties, many people who begin this practice
continue for a long time, perhaps for a lifetime. The initial lure may
be the goal of enlightenment. But soon we gain the wisdom that the
act of sitting in itself is the essence of enlightenment—for enlightenment is a process, not an end point. The penetrating truth we discover
is that the merit of a practice is simply doing it. The score of the game
becomes unimportant; the way it is played is crucial.*

*Some of the faces in this room I have seen on other retreats. They
ask different questions now; their bodies and minds seem to move with
greater awareness. The work done on retreat transforms the conditioned, rote, indifferent activity of everyday life into more mindfulness, consciousness, and alertness. This is why people come back again
and again. Our inner voice calls us, a voice that itself is connected
to eternal, infinite awareness—it is that still, small voice calling us
to the luminescent center of our beings.*

The long days of constant meditation reminded me of my days as
a sailor. There were periods of slack winds, the sails hung limp, and
I drifted aimlessly in a state of mind like a thirsting castaway on a
sun-scorched raft. These were intervals of great aridity, boredom,
and a sense of futility. At other times the breeze was steady,
constant, and I was attuned to the slightest shifts of wind and sea,
constantly making minor adjustments to keep on course. These were
the periods of greatest insight as I became more alert to inconceiva-
bly subtle nuances.

Occasionally a storm would brew, and I had to hustle to reef
the sails and tend the vessel to avoid being swamped by the sea
monsters of anger, fear, frustration, anxiety, self-pity, or dozens of
other dangers in the ocean of consciousness. At these times, my
emotions were overwhelmed, and the sense of hopelessness could
be contained only by trusting that this would pass—as it always
did.

My lifeline throughout these shifting mental states was the fif-
teen-minute conversations I had every other day with one of
the teachers—usually Sharon. I would talk about whatever was

most prominent in my thoughts, and she would offer encouragement, support, or tidbits of wisdom teachings that might be applicable. At one point, during a stretch of doldrums in which I had sunk into an abyss of insipid repetition, Sharon offered advice that became a major focal point of my meditation. It had to do with "interest" in the primary meditation object upon which I was concentrated. The idea was to get so close to the object of meditation, there would be a sensation of mentally "rubbing" against it.

It took a while to accomplish the experience of a tactile feeling as if I were touching something with my mind. My primary focus all along had been to observe the rising and falling of my breath—until now that seemed to be a process of deadly monotony. But as I experimented with this idea of rubbing my breath with my mind, I realized the breathing process had enormous complexity. I began to view the breath through a mental microscope, and as I turned up the magnification, the results were astonishing. In a short time, I became so interested in my own breathing, I was drawn completely into the moment—overcoming my wandering mind. This was the precise guidance I needed to break the tedious obsessions that had been plaguing me.

Most people think of meditation as a game of quiet attentiveness that, through a touch of divine grace, ultimately rewards a patient student. Many meditation techniques follow this basic idea. But here was a different approach, an aggressive technique of forceful meditation that required strong, disciplined, concentrated efforts—there was no sitting back.

As I became more engaged in this method, I found that although strenuous, it paid dividends far beyond the elimination of boredom. My concentration became enhanced—just as exercise strengthens muscles—and I discovered that everything from that time on became more interesting. This new "interest" in life decisively influenced my relationship to time.

I used to spend a great deal of time worrying about wasting time! I thought that every moment should be filled with meaningful activity because preparation for the future was an imperative. In that state of mind, whatever I accomplished was not enough because my inner critic constantly nagged that I could have done it better. I had the feeling that somehow other people knew how to live life while I was being carried helplessly on a tidal wave of obligations. As a result, life went by in a blur; I did my assigned chores, and time ticked on.

Now, in my quiet meditation, as I was doing nothing—the ultimate time waster, I would have thought—everything became enormously interesting. My inner world was a marvel of fascinating reflections. I was mesmerized by the awareness of my own body—this exquisite, complex, awesome organism contracting, expanding, pumping, intaking, outflowing, observing, and cogitating. The rising and falling of the breath led to worlds within worlds as I visualized tiny molecules flowing through my nostrils, past my throat, into my lungs to be absorbed into small pockets of tissue, drawn into the bloodstream, pushed through the heart, and sent to all the extremities as well as my brain—my awareness followed the intricate pathways as if I were a miniature observer, the incredible shrinking man of a science fiction movie.

At times, I would be caught by an external phenomenon. A subtle waft in the air would brush gently against my cheek, and I would know a person was passing silently on the other side of the large room. A brief twinkling of light would reflect off a dust mote, and I would be aligned in a moment of full integration, sensing the connection between the sun nearing the horizon, the dancing of heated molecules pushing that speck of dust, and the relationship of my awareness with a photon energy packet released by burning helium millions of miles from this spot. I saw tiny creatures living behind windowsills in the dozens of plants that lined the rooms, or along shelves and cupboards—and each insect had a personality, each a profound life story; each had a lesson to share. Indeed, sitting quietly was not monotonous at all; so much was happening, it was overwhelming, the surrounding life was vibrant, the panorama in each moment was exhilarating.

I had experienced heightened awareness in many of my previous retreats. Colors were sharpened, food tasted better, nature's abundance was breathtaking, and all sensory input gained a new quality. But this process of attentiveness and increased interest raised sensory awareness to new heights. I was appreciating not only the physical delights of my sensory world, but—in addition—emotions, thoughts, intuitions, and insight blended together. Nothing was as it seemed, boundaries were blurred, and every experience I had was a metaphor revealing profundities of universal wisdom. All this arose from the effort to concentrate more strongly, and as the days rolled on, filled with silence and meditative effort, I dropped deep into the stillness of pure awareness.

I sat on the foam mattress in my room thinking, "I'm average, mediocre, nothing special—enlightenment will definitely not be mine in this lifetime, nor will I achieve anything unusual. I'm just simple folk doing my simple little act to maintain a tidy life." In the past this thought had always been depressing. Today it was a fundamental truth, and the relief of not having to be anybody unique began to warm my heart until I became exhilarated.

Sitting there, I automatically began to concentrate on my breath. In a moment, my conscious self-identity disappeared, and this bag of bones called David effortlessly slid into the longest-lasting state of emptiness it had ever experienced. There was no "I" observing, simply an awareness. Pure breath, no body. Each rising thought was noted in its most nascent form, a spark generated like a stone against flint. Each spark dropped into the tinder of the mind, and a matrix of associations formed images into contextual thought—which flared and then quickly evaporated. The entire mental process repeated this scenario dozens of times each minute, mechanically. And the observer watching this sat absolutely immobile for two hours; there was no pain whatsoever.

Then I noticed a mind state of fear. A thought had arisen that perhaps I had fallen into a catatonic condition that would never end. This fear arose, disappeared, arose again, disappeared again, and I noted a body experience—the beginning of a flutter in the midsection—that was filled with memory. Fear crept in, and I felt its tentacles spreading through my body and mind. Soon the fear of catatonia became a full-blown fantasy, and I imagined what would happen when they found me in a few days or weeks, sitting here, frozen. They would call an ambulance, and men dressed in white would carry me away to a mental institution.

Of course, the instant the fear had given form to my self-identity, as soon as there was an "I" in the picture, the state of pure awareness that had been present ended abruptly. Immediately my self-consciousness returned, the normal pains of extended sitting appeared—became intense—and in a matter of minutes were strong enough to compel me to shift my position, thus ending the meditation.

Interesting, that fear. The great masters somehow overcame it. In an introduction to the life and teachings of Ramana Maharshi, we read:

> In 1896 a sixteen-year-old schoolboy . . . driven by an inner com-
> pulsion . . . abandoned himself to a newly-discovered awareness that
> his real nature was formless, immanent consciousness. His absorp-
> tion in this awareness was so intense that he was completely obliv-
> ious of his body and the world; insects chewed away portions of his
> legs, his body wasted away because he was rarely conscious enough
> to eat and his hair and fingernails grew to unmanageable lengths.
> After two or three years in this state he began a slow return to
> physical normality, a process that was not finally completed for sev-
> eral years.[12]

*That "inner compulsion" holds the secret. It suggests a willingness
to surrender life itself in the pursuit of true understanding. However,
as we have enormous propensity for self-delusion in this pursuit, our
fear is often a sane and healthy reaction to our potential for self-
destruction. Thus we are left with the central dilemma in the search
for truth: When do we leap from the precipice, and when do we turn
cautiously away from its edge? Beyond that dilemma is a more existential question: Do we really have a choice, or is that also an illusion?*

The process of spiritual growth is not a smooth curve upward,
but a series of spirals that rise and fall. One moment we may be in
an illuminated state, the next we return to a mundane frame of
reference. In the past, I thought that once a plateau was reached,
the new level of consciousness would be mine forever. Now I have
discovered that while I may realize a high plateau of awareness, it
is not a permanent residence. Soon I will slip back to my regular
experience of life filled with emotions and monkey mind. In any
single meditation period, I may bounce many times between expanded awareness and the prison of contracted thinking.

People who are not familiar with this process are often confused
when they see a spiritual aspirant revealing "unenlightened" behavior such as anger, fear, frustration, egotism, greed, hatred, or
other expressions of small-mindedness. We have an expectation
that inner work assures constant growth, which reveals itself
through saintly conduct. But the sages teach that it does not op-
erate this way. They teach that the process is ongoing, climbing,

slipping, constantly wrestling our way up the path, hopefully—over a lifetime of effort—to rise more than we fall, to attain some new level of awareness.

This is frustrating for an aspirant who wants nothing less than to be at the mountain's peak. But the alternative is to not ride the merry-go-round at all, and then we are left outside the gate in a gray world that receives its meager light from the faint luminescence whose source is somewhere near the central pole around which the merry-go-round turns.

This morning I noticed that Shoshana is not as serene as I thought. In the breakfast line somebody took the last two bananas just before Shoshana got to the fruit bowl. One person with two bananas; big trouble. Whatever equanimity Shoshana might have had evaporated in a flash of anger. I saw her stomp into the kitchen. A few minutes later she came out with her own banana. I chuckled: Life centers on major issues like this.

On retreat, these trivial experiences give rise to insight into how the mind works, where thoughts come from, and what we do with them. Every experience holds seeds of enlightenment. Hundreds of stories in Zen, for example, show satori *arising out of simple events like being offered a cup of tea, pointing one finger in the air, or getting slapped at the perfect moment. When we actually experience how our thought process functions, immense curtains of self-delusion fall away and the ensuing light is what we call wisdom.*

It has been fascinating to experience how my basic needs bubble into my thoughts. One moment I am communing with the angels and feeling complete in every way; the next moment I am having fantasies of running off to the woods with Shoshana. Or to a motel.

Next week is our seventh wedding anniversary; we've actually been together thirteen years. This retreat has been going on for about four weeks—a long time without a hug. Most of the time I avoid thinking about sex, but every so often I get kindled and become almost nutty with desire. Then, with a couple of deep breaths I am once again in my practice, each moment arising in choiceless awareness, and I feel in perfect harmony with the universe.

Near the end of the six weeks, the days began to flow into one another in a rhythm that obliterated awareness of time as we know it—seconds, minutes, hours, days, months, years. This form of time was invented for the marketplace—to conduct business—and for the world of the intellect, to identify events and sequence. Universally agreed time is also imperative for navigation, to help us determine where we are when there are no clear landmarks. The world simply could not function without keeping time.

But I had entered a world completely indifferent to clocks and calendars. There was nowhere to go, no appointment to be kept, nothing to accomplish, no decision to be made. I awoke automatically after a few hours' sleep. Immediately upon awakening, I noticed the flow of my breath and dwelt in this realm of rising and falling without a sense of beginning or end. At some point, I noticed that awareness was attending the emptiness that precedes willful thinking—and the mental preparation to move a body part was revealed like a huge book used by mechanics showing how all the parts of a complex machine work. In the premovement state of mind, my awareness awaited the mental ignition necessary to send a message through nerves to muscles and tendons. This awareness observed, to the degree possible, the entire progression from the desire to move a body part to the actual movement, a process that is executed at lightning speed. In this new contemplative universe where artificial time was not relevant, each change in the status quo was a source of measureless fascination—getting up and out of bed was an act saturated with insights.

The retreat routine absorbed all necessity for decision making. I sat, walked, prayed, sat, walked, ate, napped, walked, and sat throughout the day; bells announced beginnings, endings, and food service. Except for the division of these segments, all other relationship to hours and weekdays evaporated. The only thing that kept me attuned to the calendar was my commitment to light the Sabbath candles on Friday night and to be aware of the Sabbath for the following twenty-four hours. But my experience of timelessness from Sunday through Friday was really no different, and the final two weeks were like one perpetual Sabbath.

During this period, my spiritual passion strengthened as the wisdom hidden in prayers and psalms unfolded in ways I had rarely experienced. The clarity of this altered consciousness was like a beacon in the murky labyrinth of my logical thought process. In this mind state I could easily recognize the difference between the eternal truth of profound teachings and the nonsense that fills the books of all traditions. My Jewish practice was strengthened in many areas, while some aspects were simply dissolved. The mystical elements expressed through Buddhism, Hinduism, Christianity, and Islam all resonated within and blended into a unity, while the exoteric forms became little more than features of a broad landscape.

Most of all, in the natural flow of the retreat rhythm an entirely new feeling of harmony carried me like a feather wafting across polished oak floors and manicured lawns—everything seemed to be in remarkable equilibrium. Although many of my meditation periods were filled with busy thoughts, I had a new sense of objectivity and was fascinated to discover that occasional digressions into monkey mind did not in any way change my overall sense of contentment.

In this state of heightened awareness, I entered into a rapture, experienced everything merging together in consummate perfection, and promised myself that I would follow the contemplative path the rest of my life. It seemed inconceivable that anyone could choose to remain asleep once the ecstasy of this path was made available.

My previous retreats had opened hidden gates; they had helped me make major decisions and had drawn me into serious spiritual introspection. Indeed, my life path had been detoured from the fast track of business success onto the bumpy road of religious inquiry. Now I realized that all of this was a prerequisite to an even stronger commitment—to enter a life of intense inner work.

In a different era, this would have been the turning point to carry me into a monastery. I had not the slightest doubt or resistance to committing to a life of contemplation. But Shoshana was part of my life, and we had to search out some way that would meet our needs as individuals and as a couple. The big question I had near the end of the retreat concerned Shoshana's state of mind—was she having anything like the feelings I was experiencing, or was she sick of the whole process?

The retreat has come to an end in a mind-blazing finish. Friday I passed a note to Shoshana to set up our time for candle lighting, and to make a "lunch date" for Saturday because people on the current retreat were going to break silence at that time. We met at a bench a short way into the woods behind the retreat center and sat quietly for a long time eating our lunch. This was going to be our first conversation in six weeks, and we savored lingering in the cradle of silence for a while longer. It was wonderful being together, feeling each other's warmth, comfortable in our stillness.

Slowly we began to share our experiences, and after a while she suggested that we needed to find a more peaceful place to live because the intensity of Jerusalem was not conducive to contemplative life. Then she revealed that she too had found a new level of serenity during this retreat and was considering taking an entire year to explore a continuous meditative process in some secluded environment.

We contained ourselves throughout this conversation, knowing from past experience that we were like pressure cookers under a full load of psychic steam. She was beaming, and I too felt aglow; it was more intense than sex. After an hour of this we had to pull apart, and each of us returned to the meditation hall to integrate our reentry into the world.

My first sit after this meeting was a jumble, as could be expected. But during the second meditation, I came to the full realization that Shoshana and I had been on parallel tracks throughout the entire retreat, and that now there was a real possibility of following a contemplative life-style. We would be a unique experiment—married, loving hermits. Occasionally in the world; but much of the time devoted to our individual inner processes. As I thought of this, I began to weep in pure joy. The tears filled my beard and then began to drip onto my hands. I did not know where we were going, I could not envision the future. But all that mattered was that we would follow our hearts.

We slipped off again later in the afternoon and continued our conversation, this time in a much more animated way. I was excited at the prospects and began to think in terms of a much longer commitment than one year. In some ways it was frightening; we had no idea where we were headed or what it meant for our relationship.

I went from being excited—thrilled—into bliss; and I knew the pressure cooker's seal had blown. I almost fainted with the rush of euphoria that swept through me. My inner censor kept whispering, "Be careful!" but it was too late. My fantasy mechanism was liberated after all the weeks of tight constraint, and the world became paradise. The retreat experience had revealed a clear and irrefutable affirmation: We all have eternity within us if only we allow ourselves the opportunity to perceive it. Once seen, it alters our lives forever.

15

SINAI DESERT, EGYPT: JANUARY 1989.
A BRIEF RETREAT AND JAPANESE TEA CEREMONY
AT THE FOOT OF MOUNT SINAI.

Jerusalem is feeling more and more like a maiden whose spirit is being broken by a cruel stepmother. Her clothes are torn and ragged, she is unbathed, and her mood seems so sad. She continues to suffer from psychic violence that too often turns physical; the intifada *(the Arab uprising and demand for independence) is an abrasive nail scraping against a wound that constantly weeps pus because it is not given time to heal.*

Outwardly the city displays its magic, but in form only, a facade of antiquity that requires serious renovation to keep from disintegration. A dark mood filters the ancient glory; people are afraid to enter many parts of the city; the arch-covered walkways of the Old City are often deserted—uncollected trash litters the area, adding to the feeling of decay.

It is not so much actual violence that tears the city apart; compared with most urban areas in the world, it is fairly calm. But fear, fatigue, and sadness contribute to a depression for everyone, Jew and Arab alike. We all agree, "Enough, already!" but nobody knows how to begin to resolve the situation.

Now we were caught on the horns of a dilemma. Our contemplative practice was enormously rewarding, but it lacked the vitality and the nurturing of the Jewish practice. Judaism was our extended family environment, but it was dry and technical without the contemplative insight.

Each practice was enhanced by the other. As I had listened to many of the Dharma talks during our forty-day retreat—the discussions given by the teachers to inspire the practice—I found myself broadening the scope of these teachings by silently adding colorful, rich Jewish fabric to the Buddhist weave. And when I was engaged in my Jewish learning, prayer, and ritual, the added perspective of meditative and contemplative insight was not only invaluable, it was crucial for the level of understanding I needed to vitalize my experience.

Yet the two disciplines seemed unique and in opposition to one another. Judaism is communal, social, verbal, relationship-oriented, dependent upon authority, somewhat rational, and theistic; Buddhism is individualistic, intuitive, silent, dependent upon direct experience, and nontheistic. But from my perspective, the oppositions gave balance to each other, sharpening perspective and awareness in marvelous counterpoint.

However, it would be difficult to do silent retreats in the intensity of Jerusalem, and it would be equally difficult to maintain a consistent Jewish practice in a cabin in the woods. The resolution of this issue soon became apparent—we had to find a way to explore each tradition as fully as possible, and this led to a harsh reality neither of us was willing to face at the time. It was simply this: The expression of Judaism in Jerusalem's Orthodox community would not tolerate any exploration of other traditions. On the other hand, the broad spectrum of Judaism in the U.S.A. openly invited these kinds of investigations, much to the concern and fear of the Orthodox world.

I found myself drawn once again more closely to Reb Zalman's ideas for Jewish renewal, even though they were in open conflict with Orthodoxy. Here were people who were not afraid to explore meditative techniques—indeed, they were drawn to them as much as I was. They were not afraid to experiment, and although I was often shocked by the experience, I appreciated the effort and struggle to bring meaning into a spiritual practice.

I often thought of my discussion with Reb Zalman many years earlier about what it takes to be a rabbi, and I now knew that I could never feel "authentic" cloaked in rigid, legalistic Judaism. I carefully observed the "laws" for purposes of spiritual growth, I found the self-discipline exceptionally beneficial, but I was never caught by the ideas of sin or disobedience. Nonetheless, I felt that

I could be authentic as a guide for people interested in the contemplative side of Judaism as I was discovering it. So I contacted Reb Zalman and reaffirmed my commitment to work with him on the rabbinic track. It meant that sooner or later we would have to develop a base in the U.S.A.

Jerusalem's groans of suffering and her visible distress tore at our hearts; how could we ever leave in her time of need? Moreover, despite her wretchedness, she still offered a flavor so sweet that a small drop could nourish the soul for weeks. She would always be our spiritual mother; we never really wanted to be weaned. And so I hoped—and prayed—that we would find a way to develop our contemplative Jewish practice, explore the vitality of American Judaism, and maintain an ongoing commitment and connection with Israel throughout this process.

I have been learning about the ten plagues that occurred before the pharaoh sent the Hebrews out of Egypt; the richness of the metaphors in these tales relates to every individual's struggle to escape the bondage of our perceptions and gain liberation in the realm of awareness.

Egypt is always viewed by the Kabbalists as the archetype of constriction, the place we dwell when we sequester ourselves in our own minds. The pharaoh is the force of desire that operates within us, the grasping element that can function only as long as we have something to grasp and therefore, by its nature, causes us to feel separate. The power of this elemental clutching is so great, it continues to "harden its heart" in isolation despite the overwhelming evidence that we cannot stand on our own against the creative impulse of the universe. When we are caught by our inner pharaoh, even the immanence of death is not sufficient to shake the illusion that we are distinct identities.

The teachings of the plagues become increasingly enigmatic as Moses keeps raising the ante to get the pharaoh (our desire to be a unique individual) to understand the universal nature of life. In the first plague, the Nile's water—some say all the world's water—turns to blood, which represents a new level of awareness having a life-force that changes our perspective of reality forever. The tenth plague, the killing of the firstborn, is a complex metaphor that involves the need to understand, acknowledge, and surrender the precursor of each and every thought and action—to relinquish the initial spark upon which everything that follows is dependent. Once we realize the cause behind the spark, we are liberated by an entirely new perspective and world-view.

Each plague is fascinating; I have been focusing primarily on the ninth, the plague of darkness. The verse says:

> *And the Lord said to Moses: Stretch out thy hand towards heaven, that there may be darkness over the land of Mitzrayim [usually translated as Egypt], darkness which may be felt. And Moses stretched out his hand towards heaven; and there was a thick darkness in all the land of Mitzrayim three days. They [the people of Mitzrayim] saw not one another, and none rose from his place for three days: but all the children of Israel had light in their dwellings.[13]*

The ancient sages—and medieval commentators—focused on four textual questions: What is darkness that can be felt? What is thick darkness? What does it mean that nobody moved for three days? How were the children of Israel able to have light simultaneously at the time that Egypt was enveloped in darkness?

The oral tradition of Jewish legend—the Midrash—adds its own dimension to the mystery:

> *The darkness was not of the ordinary, earthly kind; it came from hell, and it could be felt. It was as thick as a dinar [a large coin], and all the time it prevailed, a celestial light brightened the dwellings of the children of Israel, whereby they could see what the Egyptians were doing under the cover of darkness. . . . The darkness was of such a nature that it could not be dispelled by artificial means.[14]*

What is this darkness that comes from hell—a darkness that is thick and palpable? What is this darkness that can be defeated only by celestial light, which is such that some people can utilize it while others in its presence miss it altogether?

One of the great hasidic masters, Levi Yitzhak of Berditchev (eighteenth century), suggests a fascinating notion to resolve these questions. He says that the plague of darkness was not caused by darkness at all, but rather by a primordial light, a light so penetrating that it blinded everyone who did not have the means to apprehend it. This light in Kabbalah is called the Or Ain Sof—the infinite light. It is the light in which original man—represented by Adam—lived before the descent into the form of humanity as we know it today; in other words, it is the infinite awareness of our primeval nature. In this state of awareness, "Adam could survey the world from end to end."[15] *That is, the celestial light has nothing to do with vision; rather, it is the light of perfect knowledge.*

Light as we know it in everyday life is the light of hell; it is in fact a form of darkness out of which "the visible and the invisible were created."[16] *The idea of visible and invisible represents the aspects of creation that are bounded, separated—by our illusion—from Oneness. Indeed, this sense of separation is born when we devour the fruit of the Tree of Knowledge of Good and Evil, because the seed within this fruit is the essential function of the intellect—this seed has the qualities of distinguishing, comparing, and judging upon which our mental faculty depends.*

According to the Midrash, the light we now use comes from a "cold" place in the lower realms, where "a gloomy fire is always burning. And all [of] that place has fire on all sides, and on all sides cold and ice, thus it burns and freezes."[17] *Simply stated, as long as we dwell in the light of self-delusion—which is our normal state of mind—we reside in hell.*

Perhaps the most revealing teaching of all is the Midrash that says eighty percent of the Hebrews living in Egypt before the Exodus were killed during the plague of darkness. Why? Because they really did not want to leave. Although they were ostensibly slaves, they were afraid of the unknown. They fancied the material comforts that they were given by the power of constriction to lull them asleep; the price of freedom was—for them—too great a sacrifice. As a result, along with their masters, they too were blinded by the light and were thus destroyed.

This is a poignant legend as we reflect upon our own enslavement. The light may surround us, but we miss it. Our comfort is our prison; our sense of separation is really the result of a sweet, almost irresistible fruit that we are unable to set aside; we live in a darkness that is actually palpable, but we are stuck and most probably will stay here, given the choice.

This idea is so frightening, most people are unable to gaze into its face; only a relative handful have truly searched for a resolution. What is the part within us that is ready to build the vessel that can embrace the infinite, celestial light? This is the question posed to us in wisdom teachings that have extended over the millennia: Knowing

*now comfortable it is to remain asleep, how do we cultivate the cour-
age to pay the price and finally meet the challenge of expanding
awareness?*

I rededicated myself to study, meditation, and prayer richly
spiced with ongoing meditation and frequent short retreats in a
separate room of our Jerusalem home. We registered for a long
retreat the following spring with U Pandita, a Burmese master in
the *Vipassanā* lineage. The retreat was to last two months, and we
planned to take an additional forty days on our own to maximize
the experience. In all, we had committed to a hundred consecutive
days in silence—a magic number for us.

Thousands of people in the Far East—especially Burma and
Thailand—take annual three-month retreats. We in the West—
growth- and production-oriented—cannot imagine sitting quietly
for such a long period; it seems an appalling waste of time. And
this is not all: Most of us are terrified at the prospect of being
isolated from the general community for such an extended period.

There are some Westerners, however, who resonate completely
with the path of silence and solitude. A few have a natural affinity;
others have learned the power of contemplation or meditation
through experience. Priests, nuns, and monks usually appreciate
the retreat practice, and when people from different traditions
share their own experiences of intense inner work, all external
boundaries of religion and personality seem to fall away. Spiritual
aspirants recognize in each other a similar yearning, a soul-essence,
an appreciation of paradox, and a sense of eternal struggle; most
important, we see the luminous glow of wisdom in the eyes of the
others who have experienced the pain that every sincere meditator
comprehends.

*I delight in the Muslim call to prayer that echoes across the city
five times a day, and the church bells that seem to peal spontaneously;
I love to watch nuns approach the Western Wall with tiny notes that
they jam into the crevices—a Jewish custom—sending written prayers
to the Divine. And I never cease to be thrilled by black preachers who
occasionally stand at the Wall and cry out to Jesus, or—just as poignant—the solitary Buddhist monk who walks across the city beating
on a peace drum.*

I remember one day breaking down in tears as a troupe of black

evangelical men, led by a stout woman wearing a paisley dress, strut-
ted through the narrow market streets and out Jaffa Gate singing a
magnificent syncopated gospel song. I thought that this kind of de-
votion was universally appealing, but I was sad to see that most people
stood to the side with blank expressions, unable to savor this splendid
emotion because they were stuck in the dogma—and loneliness—of
their Jewish or Muslim upbringing.

This sadness, more than anything, is the focal point of my struggle
with life in Jerusalem. The intensity of the city cloaks every issue,
adding weight and density so that lightness and joy are often missed.
The thickness adds a kind of armor, inviting segregation, and strong
opinions are expressed in simplistic terms of black and white. Whether
the issue is religious, political, economic, sociological, psychological,
physical, or ideological, there is little or no room for compromise. This
hardheadedness is in direct contradiction with my sense of potential
for harmony and order; and the gulf between my expanding aware-
ness of the unity of life as opposed to the pervasive perspective in the
Middle Eastern environment of duality and separateness is becoming
an unbridgeable rift.

A few minutes east of Jerusalem is the desert. The hills are dotted
by the ragged awnings used as tents by Bedouins. In late January
with its winter rains, a wispy, light green ground cover delicately
rests on patches of rock-hard earth; the green hue will quickly burn
away under iridescent skies in the spring. As the road drops to sea
level and below, the hills become brown and yellow, pocked and
scarred, covered with assorted rocks like a giant game of checkers
being played by the desert winds and floods—each game lasting a
millennium.

We were headed for Mount Sinai on an excursion into the desert
to prepare ourselves in some way for our imminent return to the
U.S.A. and the one-hundred-day retreat. To the northeast—just
ahead—was Jericho, where the walls came down at a shout. Today,
Jericho is two cities—one in which Palestinians live; the other a
ghost town with rows of decrepit mud-and-stone shells of houses
that were last inhabited a few decades ago, before Israeli tanks blew
out walls and roofs during the Six-Day War. In the short time since
then, under the blaze of a white-hot desert sun, the original city
had come to resemble the two-thousand-year-old remains of Pom-
peii sitting in the ashes of volcanic dust.

We bypassed Jericho and turned south, driving between mountains and a large expanse of water so salty and full of minerals, nothing could live in it: the Dead Sea. The green hills of Jordan could be seen on the other side of this oily, uninviting sea that was dotted near the shore by white flecks of small, floating salt-bergs.

Qumran, less than a mile to the west, was hidden in towering curtains of eroded rock walls hundreds of feet high; the deep folds of stone contained hidden caves and secret passages. Not many years earlier, in one of these caverns, parchments sealed in jars were discovered, untouched for thousands of years; and in them were scrolls, providing new grist for academic mills concerning the authenticity of biblical texts. The Dead Sea Scrolls are now housed in their own atmospherically controlled building in the middle of Jerusalem.

As we drove past miles of arid land, where the sun incinerates almost everything exposed above the ground, we came upon the canyon oasis of En-Gedi. A spring of water from high in the mountains had transformed a narrow strip of desolation into a ribbon of lush foliage, stretching a mile, almost to the sea. Near the top of this canyon David, soon to be king, hid from the armies of King Saul. According to legend, as the troops were about to investigate the cave in which David was hiding, Saul noticed a spider's web across the entrance and called off the search. How many times has the spider's web of coincidence altered our lives?

We drove past the hot sulphur baths where health-oriented tourists lather themselves in steaming mud and then wash themselves in the Dead Sea waters of sulphur and minerals. This really should not be called water because it could kill anyone drinking it; an accidental mouthful is nauseating. Moreover, the liquid of this sea is so dense, the tourists float on it sitting upright.

Soon we passed Masada, a high plateau in the desert built as a fortress by Herod. Two thousand years ago a small band of Jews defended this small summit against the Roman army and held them off for years. The Jews were ultimately defeated by Roman engineering and technology. The Romans used slaves to build a ramp of millions of tons of earth to the crest of the plateau; then they hauled their war machines up to the wall of the fortress Herod had built. The night a breach was certain, the defenders made a suicide pact, and all but a few died before the Romans entered. Today special forces of the Israeli army use Masada for ceremonies to keep alive the memory of Jewish martyrdom.

Just after Masada, the Negev desert begins. The city of Sodom was in this desert. Its memory shrieks a warning, a message from the wasteland. Beware of self-indulgence! It reminds us that we are free each moment to escape from the illusion we see when we look into mirrors. But when we have been successful in our emancipation, we must not turn around to gaze behind us into the funhouse filled with these alluring mirrors, for they will draw us back inside its walls onto winding passageways that lead nowhere—and we will be lost once again, no more vital than a pillar of salt!

After a hundred miles of bleak desert, the city of Eilat arose in shimmering waves like a mirage. Many Jerusalemites believe Eilat is a modern Sodom, with its topless beaches, shrimp and pork restaurants, tourists in short-shorts, and decadent hotels with morning poolside aerobics classes. In addition to its regular population, Eilat is a watering hole for modern nomads, a new subculture that has inherited the good, the bad, and the ugly from parents and grandparents who themselves were beatniks, hippies, freaks, and punks.

We were not as morally offended as many of our friends, and we enjoyed Eilat's vibrant life on a number of occasions, but as this journey was intended to be a pilgrimage to the desert, we bypassed the main city and drove south along the beach to a more secluded area. Here we rested overnight and prepared ourselves for the border crossing into the Sinai, and onward to the mountain, where we would meditate and commune with the spirit of Moses at the place where some say he talked with God face-to-face.

> And the glory of the Lord rested upon Mount Sinai, and the cloud covered it for six days: on the seventh day He called to Moses out of the midst of the cloud. And the sight of the glory of the Lord was like a devouring fire on the top of the mountain in the eyes of the children of Israel. And Moses went into the midst of the cloud, and went up into the mountain: and Moses was in the mountain forty days and forty nights.[18]

I have always been curious as to why the scripture says that Moses was "in the mountain" rather than "on the mountain," so I searched the Talmud and Midrash for clues. The biblical version of this legend is that the people with Moses heard the voice of God coming from the mountain, fell back in awe, and were so overwhelmed by the experience, they immediately accepted the divine rulership of the one and only Creator. This seems reasonable—if we could imagine being in the presence of the Almighty, there would not be a moment's hesitation. The biblical text says:

> *And all the people perceived [saw] the thunderings [voices], and the lightnings, and the sound of the shofar, and the mountain smoking: and when the people saw it, they were shaken, and stood afar off. And they said to Moses, "Speak you with us and we will hear; but let not God speak with us, lest we die."[19]*

This is all well and good, a natural unfolding of the drama at Sinai. But we find a curious addition to this legend recorded in the Talmud:

> *The Holy One, blessed be He, lifted the mountain over the [heads of] them [the people], like a basket [upside down], and said to them, "If you accept the Torah it is well; if not, here shall be your grave."[20]*

How could this be? It suggests that the people were not overwhelmed by the presence of the Divine, but that they had to be intimidated into accepting the word of God. As one of the sages pointed out, if they accepted the Torah only under threat, they would be free to practice nonobservance once the threat had passed.[21] In the Talmud, the sages resolved this issue by saying that the Jewish nation reaffirmed its acceptance at other times, when the people were not threatened with annihilation. But there is a more profound, mystical understanding.

The Midrash teaches: "[During] the awful vision on Mount Sinai . . . [the people] heard the visible and saw the audible—the privilege was granted them that even the slave women among them saw more than the greatest prophet of later times. . . . "[22] This teaching is derived from a literal reading of the Hebrew in the text: "All the people saw the voices. . . . " (Exodus 20:15). How does someone see a voice—and in this instance, how is it that everyone saw voices?

This idea of "seeing a voice" is of the same paradoxical nature as being "in a mountain," and from it we learn that there is a state of altered consciousness that transcends the limits of logic and enters a realm we normally experience only in dreams. In this nonrational state, a more profound level of truth is revealed—a truth not bounded by the limits of the mind—and this level of awareness equals or exceeds the experience of prophecy.

Following this viewpoint, there is a completely different interpretation for the image of God holding a mountain over the heads of the people. Whereas our first inclination would be to imagine being squashed under the weight of the rocks and earth, the legend makes a clear point of indicating that the mountain resembled an overturned basket—that is, it could enclose the people without crushing them. Thus, it was not the kind of threat we thought initially; rather it was a teaching: if the people accepted and followed the path that was being offered, they would be enclosed WITHIN the mountain; if they rejected the guidance, they would continue to wander in everyday reality, which, according to this teaching, is not much different from dwelling in the grave.

Therefore, the mountain of Sinai represents a spiritual realm in which we may choose to reside. Enclosed in this sphere, we gain an entirely new perspective on life and our reason for being. Scripture suggests that the experience of being "in the mountain" is the arousal of the penetrating light of awareness, the light that emanated from Moses to the degree that "the skin of his face glowed" and he had to wear a veil because of his awesome appearance (Exodus 34:29–35).

Crossing the border between Israel and Egypt was tricky. Not many Israelis had crossed since the time—a year or two earlier—an Egyptian soldier had gone berserk and shot a group of Israeli tourists camping on a Sinai beach. It took us one and a half hours to get through the layers of bureaucracy even though we were the only private car crossing that day. We entered the desert with strict instructions from the Egyptian officials not to wander off the main road—for military reasons.

We were a caravan of one lonely vehicle accompanied by billions of ghosts who inhabit this desert. Although encased in our steel cocoon, powered by iron camels flying on the wind at one hundred kilometers an hour, I could feel a presence with us at all times—this desert never forgets. Its stillness seems to be constantly reflecting on past events. Each event is a momentous occasion in a land where rocks remain unturned for centuries, no one to kick or push them, nothing to budge them but tempests or earthquakes. Sinai evokes a different kind of seclusion from any I had felt before; it is like a sugar-coated sweet that covers sheer dread at its core.

After a number of hours, we arrived at the monastery of Santa Katarina, which sits wedged in a valley cleft. These days, its fortress walls are a barricade against a heartrending silence that prowls the mountains. This is a pure silence whose origin is in Nothingness, a numbing vacuum that absorbs all mind-chatter and leaves a person splayed open, no boundaries to define the self, nowhere to hide. For thousands of years this experience has drawn pilgrims, many of whom continue to reside inside the monastery in a heap of sun-bleached skulls.

The mountain alongside this monastery, according to some, is the actual Mount Sinai where Moses walked. It was easy to imagine a congregation gathered in the expanse below where the valley opened to enormous desert flats in which people would seem like ants, an area so vast, it could readily accommodate the earth's entire human population. Watching the desert shimmer, I could hear the bleating of trumpets, and a transcendent voice boomed across the mass gathering of spirits, melting untold numbers of minds over the centuries into one Great Soul.

We climb a short distance along a rocky trail. Boulders around us are sculpted by wind and water as if a rock-eating giant had sauntered from one immense rock to another, tasting the flavor of each. Shoshana situates herself in a small, flat clearing and sets up her straw mat with the implements of Japanese Tea Ceremony. I discover a rock throne etched into a huge boulder, and as I settle into it to meditate, the rocks around me begin to look like gnomes who have stood there for centuries surveying the valley below.

The desert invites a clarity I cannot attain in other environments. New voices are heard within, resonating and blending with secret worlds I rarely acknowledge. Scenes arise in my mind; they are more than imagination. What are they: dreams, visions of the past, precognition? My inner field of vision is brimming with images that burst the barriers of logic, time, and space. People in headdress dance in ritual initiation; horses bearing heavy armor carry men with maces and spears, all dying of thirst in the desert heat; tanks roll across the plains firing laser-guided missiles at moving targets miles away, hitting them on the first try; a group of men and camels lie low in a rising sandstorm, and slowly disappear into oblivion.

Suddenly I realize Shoshana is standing beside me. I did not hear her approach and do not know how long she had been there. She is offering me a small pond of delicate green froth floating in a bowl of shining black lacquer. The blackness of the bowl is a cave leading into the heart of the mountain; the greenness is the garden in the world to come—after this parched land is redeemed through toil and strife. My heart bursts with love and appreciation as I accept this offering of tea.

We sip tea in silence until dusk. The power of the Sinai Desert and the prominence of this mountain lend a quality to our meditation in only a few hours that is similar to the experience of altered consciousness that arises after many weeks of silence and solitude.

As the sun sets, shadows creep through the piles of boulders, and I feel the presence of prophets and sages who have climbed this great mound of stone and rubble for over two thousand years. These prophets never sleep. They cast a vague light among the shadows—not like the sun that reveals things, but a light from the center of creation that permeates everything in existence. This light of prophecy is the source of all human endeavor, it is the light of the burning bush—the light of transformation.

Shoshana and I traveled to this sacred mountain because we wanted to enter into its spirit. But we did not need to make the physical journey; we discover in this afternoon of tea and contemplation that the mountain is always within us and we within it. Its light is a potential in every shadow. Its spirit protects us not as an outer shell of hardened earth, but as an ember at the core of our being that can never be extinguished. Thus, throughout our lives we are entering the sacred mountain to the degree that the light within us illuminates our awareness and the truth of our existence.

16

Our long-awaited one-hundred-day retreat did not begin as planned. When we arrived in the U.S.A., Shoshana and I flew separately to our respective families in Florida and California to assure them that we were relatively sane; obviously they were concerned about the upcoming period of seclusion. When Shoshana arrived in Palm City, Florida, she was told that her stepfather, Bill, was being treated in the hospital for leukemia. Her mother, Meg, had kept it a secret for the last few weeks, not wanting to worry us. His prospects did not look good.

We instantly switched the schedule that had been worked out months earlier and began to recast our lives. I flew to Florida and spent the next couple of weeks immersed in the issues of mortality, fear, and pain. We soon became experts on blood counts, chemistry, physiology, esoteric medicine, chemotherapy, diagnostics, and vital signs.

As a nurse, Shoshana knew her way around the hospital, but medicine had changed dramatically during the ten years since she had had hands-on experience. We had to remind ourselves constantly that beyond all the numbers, formulas, statistics, and professional guesses of the doctors, there was a lonely, frightened person suffering the incalculable dread of impending death. I was dismayed to realize how little the physicians really knew and how much they camouflaged themselves behind data and probabilities.

One of the few physicians who has spoken out on this question is Dr. Larry Dossey. He says:

> Modern medicine has learned to look at the hard sciences as models, hoping to embody the precision and exactness demonstrated most notably by classical physics. Believing we have actually found that precision, we in medicine refuse to listen to the message that has come from physics for over half a century: *the exactness never really existed.* Today's medicine is like a loser in a shell game: once we saw it, now we don't.[23]

Unfortunately, they guessed wrong about Bill's disease and began a chemotherapy procedure that did not do the job. Then they came up with another diagnosis—this one less hopeful—and a whole new treatment protocol with ghastly sounding chemicals. All the while they were uncertain and disputing among themselves how to identify the condition. It was leukemia, all right, but what kind? They did the best they could, I suppose, but Bill was the mouse in the maze, getting poked, prodded, and tormented by well-meaning people who were trapped in their own labyrinth of scientific methodology, and nobody could find the thread to get out. Bill was dying, and there was nowhere to turn. The doctors did agree that things were not going well, but we had no way of knowing if this process would continue for weeks, months, or years.

I departed for the retreat center to sit a few weeks before the main event; Shoshana would soon follow in time to begin the two-month retreat with U Pandita, the Burmese master. The plan was to end our retreat if we were needed, or, God forbid, if Bill should die.

During the first week of sitting, all I could think about was death, hospitals, medicine, and suffering. I may have appeared serene, but my monkey mind was chattering along, and I grew weary of the constant thinking. It was not helped by my daily telephone calls to Florida, which broke the rule of silence. This lack of discipline kept me in a state of mental uproar. Then the retreat routine began to settle in, the telephone calls ended, I was assured that I would be contacted if I could help in any way, and only then did

I begin to slide gently into the peaceful inner realms of silence and solitude.

I am standing in a field of golden grain that has grown chest-high; it extends as far as I can see in every direction. Swells ripple toward the horizon of this ocean, heading for shores of unknown lands. A Victorian house stands ahead in a clearing. It has a gray and dingy blue facade as if wrapped in a huge web of grime and dust; many shutters hang askew. It feels sinister, but I am drawn to it.

Through a smoke-darkened window I see a shabby character seated at a rough oak table. Without ever looking up, he beckons to me with crooked, knobby fingers crowned by sharp and jagged nails. I know I should run, but my hand reaches for the greasy doorknob, and as the door slowly opens, its frame shutters and the hinges shriek like terrified mice in their captors' jaws.

The old man's skin hangs on his cheeks and jaws; he sits bent beneath a dark, rough cape—a cowl covers his head. As I enter farther into his sanctuary, he turns his face toward me, and I see for the first time his terrible black eyes hovering in hollows on either side of a beaked nose. His eyelids are rimmed in gleaming crimson, giving the appearance of a flaming cauldron surrounding an emptiness as deep as an abyss.

He never speaks out loud, but his voice echoes in my mind: "Welcome to this humble abode. But be careful where you step, lest you trespass into the future."

I ask his name and he answers, "Death." A shiver accompanies this word as it arises in my mind. Bile burns the back of my throat, and I feel clammy sweat soaking my shirt. In this moment, Death is no longer an abstraction; it is at the center of my consciousness. I know this intimacy is dangerous, but this is not our first encounter.

As the old man turns and begins to walk away slowly, I feel compelled to follow in his footsteps. We walk onward into an oblivion so complete, I wonder for a moment about where I am standing and what I am breathing. I feel the gripping fear that this actually may be the moment of my death; it seems clear that this is the way many people die—Death beckons, and they follow.

After a timeless passage, we enter into a lush garden. It is teeming with life, endless varieties of plants, insects, and small animals. Death approaches the different life-forms, and each greets the hunched phantom like a long-lost friend. As Death's companion, I too am greeted.

Each greeting reveals wondrous secrets: how a seed begins to sprout, the message in a bird's song, the enthusiasm of an ant, and the imagination of a butterfly.

In Death's garden, all the mysteries of life are solved. I now know why souls that visit here are unlikely to return to the confusion and suffering of earthly existence. Everything in this garden soothes and comforts.

Death turns and gazes at me. The thought arises in my mind: "It is not yet your time, but this garden you must know."

So I am not to be staying. But in this moment, looking Death in the face, I see for the first time gentleness rather than harshness, a serenity that accompanies certainty, and indeed a kind of friendliness. I embraced Death in that moment, hugged it close to me, felt its grandeur, and delighted in its affection.

As I write these notes, I know I will feel Death's attraction in the future, especially in difficult times. But that was not the primary message. What was communicated was that life is full of riches beyond description; life offers an opportunity that can never be matched by death. Indeed, the most exciting element of life is to discover its source; we are privileged to use every breath in this pursuit.

In that moment, however, I understood that when life is over, there is nothing to fear. Fear limits the full exploration of life's secrets. Death became my friend, the only friend that will accompany me when I leave this body behind.

The two weeks before Shoshana arrived were filled with many bright, clear hours. There was a women's weekend retreat during this period, and I spent the time in my room, barely moving between a meditation cushion and the bed, encapsulating my life in a space five by eight feet. But physical dimensions are deceptive. Each time I closed my eyes in meditation, there were no limits to my universe; it would not have mattered if I were on top of the Himalayas, on the moon, or in my tiny room.

By the time Shoshana appeared, I did not want to interrupt the flow of my routine, but we had made plans to visit friends in Woodstock to celebrate the Passover *seder*, so we went off for a few days. We returned to the retreat center with our arms full of *matzot* and food that was kosher for Passover, and we set up a little kitchen and cooking area in the back of the dining room. At other times, we had often experienced considerable resistance among many people, particularly Jews, when we adhered to the dietary constraints or other limitations of traditional Jewish practice. But here, it was heartwarming to have our eccentricities genuinely accepted and honored by the Buddhist community. Indeed, a number of the staff people—currently practicing Buddhism, but born Jewish—joined us in eating *matzot* and other Passover food, to evoke memories of special times with their parents or grandparents.

The Burmese monks were scheduled to appear just after the last day of Passover. Tensions began to rise as the arrival day approached; cleaning and preparation was more concentrated, and the atmosphere became electric as participants began to appear, having traveled from all over the world. This retreat had attracted a large number of well-known meditation instructors and spiritual teachers. When the staff began to realize that this was the first time in memory that so many influential Western devotees and leaders in the *Vipassanā* school were coming together for an extended period of practice, they nicknamed the retreat the "Summit."[24]

I was honored at the thought of sitting shoulder to shoulder with many of these meditators. Some of them were monks or nuns, some had been ordained during extensive travels in the Far East. Many had spent years in Thailand, Burma, India, or some other exotic place, committed as spiritual aspirants in numerous practices—and now they followed this particular lineage of *Theravāda* Buddhism.

When the new people began to arrive, it felt to me as though each person was a turbine being hooked into a main power generator, and soon the high tension lines coming out of the retreat center were crackling with an enormous amount of voltage. During this period, I was sitting four or five times a day, in semiretreat, too caught up in the excitement to undertake complete solitude.

I have been feeling on the edge of something about to happen; perhaps a major breakthrough. It is not nervousness, but a sense of something impending, a vague harbinger fluttering just below my consciousness. I've had this sensation in the past, and as I reflect on those other times, nothing earth-shattering ever came of it. One teacher noted a similar experience, saying, "Something always gets in the way." He said this as a joke because it is common for people who practice hard to delude themselves into thinking that a great turning point lies just ahead.

It may be that I am trying to psyche myself up for the coming event and that this is the way I manufacture courage. But I want it to be true, after all; I want to attain some special level—even though I know that this is a self-defeating frame of mind. It is the syndrome called MORE. We are never satisfied; the essence of our nature is desire—wanting, chasing, grasping. But we will surely fail to merge with what we see in the distance, because as long as we have the concept of distance, that which we think we want is constantly moving away from us.

Thus I know that my anticipation is a signal that I am not "here," rather I am looking somewhere over "there." As long as I want "more" than what I have, it will elude me because there will always be more. It is the paradox of this practice that we must find a way to make enormous effort without any expectations. Objectively, of course, we are invariably succeeding in some way, strengthening our concentration, improving our abilities, softening our hearts, expanding our consciousness. But subjectively, if we have any hope of achievement, we will suffer a continuous sense of dissatisfaction because what we want is infinite.

This syndrome of "more"—never enough—is obvious in the material world. The billionaire is not satisfied with success, the artist with the finished canvas, the politician with the acquisition of power, the professional with skills developed over years of training. We always expect more from our spouses, parents, children, friends, and everyone we encounter. But most insidious, we always demand more from ourselves.

It may well be that this is the ultimate lesson I will learn here: Transmute the incessant need for more into the acceptance of what is.

Our teacher, the Venerable U Pandita, finally arrived with his small entourage. Draped in saffron robes, the bald-headed monks were like forest creatures with brilliant plumage. They usually remained close to one another, but the presence of the master was obvious by the respectful distance his subordinates observed. A large host attended this small group, helping them maintain, to the degree possible, the precepts of their ordination. They have many rules—as with all orthodox traditions—that restrict their behavior, like the prohibition against swatting mosquitoes or stepping on ants. They cannot eat things that have growth potential, such as an apple with seeds, without special preparation. They have dietary restrictions, rules of bathing, customs of propriety and behavior, laws concerning the separation of men and women, and constraints regarding a wide variety of daily activities.

I found it interesting that although there are doctrinal differences between *Theravāda* Buddhism and Orthodox Judaism, many practices parallel each other, and the spirit of practice was almost identical. I heard a few critical comments from the people who had to accommodate the unusual requirements of the monks, but their requests were merely a reflection of general principles observed by people around the globe who take their spiritual practices seriously.

World history has recorded all too often the destruction resulting from religious disputes. These usually are the consequence of doctrinal differences, power struggles, or the plain hatred that follows when ignorance mutates into bigotry. But the spiritual and mystical side of traditions have a robust seasoning of universalism.

Thus, when I was asked by a number of people what I would do when meeting the master—as it is a rule in his culture to kneel to his spiritual authority, and everyone knows this kind of bowing is forbidden in the Jewish tradition—I was certain that it would be no problem as long as I was able to communicate to him that this was part of my spiritual practice and not an expression of arrogance. Some fellow retreatants and staff were uncertain that he would understand, but I had not a moment's doubt.

When I had my interview at the beginning of the retreat, rather than drop to my knees, I placed my hand over my heart and nodded respectfully, telling him of my Jewish practice. He looked at the yarmulke I was wearing and asked if I was a rabbi. I said that I was not yet a rabbi, but simply a student of the Jewish tradition. His response: "But, in any case, you are my brother." With that brief acknowledgment it was clearly understood that although the master was far superior in development, his student was no less the Buddha—and each genuinely respected the other's discipline.

The retreat has just begun. It is like no other that I have experienced. The strength and commitment of the participants add enormously to the collective power of concentration. The meditation room is often perfectly still for an entire hour of sitting—not a cough, sigh, or rustle of clothes disturbs the balance of a hundred people sitting side by side. In the rooms used for walking meditation, the subtle sounds of moving clothes can be heard—arms brushing waists, legs against each other—but even here each meditator's focus of attention is quite still despite the body's motion. We walk on a track to nowhere, back and forth, from one wall to another.

Many of these retreatants have published articles and books on meditation, and some have a following of their own. Probably the best known among them is Ram Dass, who continues to inspire thousands of people each year, as he has for over twenty years. I cannot help but notice that spiritual practice is a great equalizer. When Ram Dass is sitting or walking in the same room, I am struck by the fact that we are each making a sincere effort to fulfill the practice requirements, and although he has an enormous depth of experience compared with mine, we are both engaged in a timeless process that has been repeated by hundreds of millions of people over thousands of years.

I have the feeling that all the retreatants, regardless of their individual background, relate to each other as equals. There is a common bond in the inner struggle. The experiences of pain, fear, anxiety, and boredom are thought-threads that we have all known, as well as the moments of bliss, ecstasy, and joyful harmony. Nobody here would claim to be enlightened; yet I am certain that most of the retreatants know that the process is paradoxical, and that we are all enlightened—whatever that means. We are not trying to "get somewhere," but are working hard at "being here."

A wonderful rhythm has developed in these first few days. The schedule is more rigorous than that at most retreats. One hour of sitting is alternated with one hour of walking. Most people are meditating this way fourteen to sixteen hours a day. If people had trouble adjusting, as is the situation for the first three days in most retreats, I did not notice anything. These are athletes trained in stillness, and this their Olympics.

17

A little over a week into the retreat we received news that Bill had died. It happened suddenly, just after he had returned from Florida to the family home in Voorhees, New Jersey. He had gone to the hospital for a transfusion and suddenly passed out of his body as if having abruptly made a decision—once back in the area where he had lived most of his life—not to suffer a minute longer.

We learned that the tradition in Burma at the time of a death is to contribute a meal to monks as compensation and thanksgiving for their efforts and prayers to ease the passage of newly deceased beings. In return for our donation, the monks invited us to their supper, and in their conversation at the table we gained a new perspective of death. Their view of the life cycle, reincarnation, and the transformation of creative substance was essentially optimistic, and someone's passing out of this world is little cause for grieving. One death is simply a link in a long chain of birth and death through thousands of lifetimes until we finally shatter the shackles that bind us to the wheel of karma and thereby succeed in escaping the inevitable suffering of existence—an emancipation we will surely accomplish, according to these monks, because the Buddha has shown us the way.

Shoshana and I departed from the retreat that afternoon and drove to New Jersey. During the long drive, despite the sadness that accompanies a journey to a funeral, we could not avoid appreciating the springtime beauty that abounded alongside the road.

The ten days of concentrated meditation we had just completed had shifted our consciousness; the landscapes were gorgeous, the sky sparkled, and life seemed full, vibrant, almost shimmering. In many ways, each breath was cause for elation; everything seemed to fuse together in perfect symmetry. From that perspective, death took on a cosmic quality, and in this great, spacious expanse everything felt fitting and proper.

A few days later, the family church was filled with hundreds of friends and business associates paying respects. Bill had been an extremely popular, gregarious man, and this death in his mid-sixties came as a blow, especially poignant as he was one of the first among this group to pass on. I felt the true sadness of family and friends, yet could not help being grateful that his dreadful torment during the last few months had finally come to an end.

The Catholic mass was lovely. While I listened to the eulogy, my mind was drawn toward the stained-glass windows high above the church. The organ began to play, and the ceremony swept my soul into holy communion with the Divine. The congregation went forward to receive the wafer symbolic of this communion, but I sat quietly, absorbed in angelic realms, captivated by the prismatic streams of light that bathed his casket. In that moment I was certain that Bill was far better off than those of us who mourned his loss.

After a week, I returned to the retreat center. When I passed through the invisible membrane that separated the active outside world from the pervasive quiet within the meditation halls I felt clumsy—an alien from outer space. At this point I made the common mistake of trying too hard to regain "lost" momentum, as if I could catch up with "something," and I tried to enter the rhythm of the retreat too fast—thereby causing myself a great deal of physical and emotional pain.

Pain! Endless, mind-bending, all-consuming pain. My knees, ankles, lower back, upper back, neck—it seems to be attacking me everywhere. A hasidic teaching says: "Hell is not as bad as getting there!" I used to think that life was one long passage to hell—and now they tell me it is worse than hell itself!

Things seemed to be going so well a few weeks ago, before I left. Now, within minutes after I begin an hourlong sit, I feel the dull ache in my knees that warns me I am not positioned properly. But it is too late to adjust. The whole room is motionless. After only fifteen minutes have passed, my knees begin to throb as if someone were pounding on them with a sledgehammer! And I say to myself, "Oh, God, I'll never make it!"—but somehow, I do.

I crawl into the pain, explore it, describe it to myself in detail. It burns, rips, scrapes, tears; it is hot, white, and then beyond hot, like black ice stuck against helpless flesh. The pain is sometimes the size of a pinhead, at other times it spreads wide and seems to jump from one place to another. The more I try to observe the pain and hold it steady, the more it moves and is enigmatic. It screeches and howls in my mind; tears burn through my eyelids like molten lead, and I think I am going insane.

Pain can kill, they say. How much can I take? Perhaps some part of my body is being damaged permanently; will I ever walk again without a limp? There must be another way; this is too masochistic. "Please, dear God, help me . . . help me . . . help me. . . . "

Then, a moment of peace. The pain stops. How could this be? Within minutes, I am sitting as if there had never been a problem. This respite keeps me from becoming despondent, and I regain my psychic composure. It could continue like this for the rest of the sit, or a number of meditations to come. But sooner or later, a new pain presents itself.

I wonder why it works this way. If there actually is a pleasure principle—and we really have choice—why do we continually pull ourselves into the hell realms? I sit; I sweat; I search for a solution— but I know it is useless to probe my mind, because the answer is in the pain itself.

Why is sitting still, doing nothing, sometimes so painful? When we move about in the course of daily life or when we sit relaxed, we do not normally suffer. But try to sit motionless, no matter how comfortably we arrange the cushions, and within a short time pain will appear. I have experienced these pains many years and know that this is a common experience for meditators. I used to think that the tension of trying to be stationary somehow induced the pain, and I took for granted that this was simply part of the meditation experience.

But as I was struggling with extraordinary pain during this retreat, an intriguing insight arose: Pain is not an occasional guest, it is a steadfast companion. Most of us have learned to avoid it—

or ignore it—by being physically and mentally engaged all of the time. We distract ourselves through constant activity; in essence we do not allow ourselves time and space to experience most pain, except for that which clearly demands our attention.

Thus, without consciously realizing what we are doing, we find ways to blanket the initial pain responses by moving our bodies or minds away from them. Mostly, we move our minds—we think, fantasize, plan, review, obsess, anything to evade the consciousness of pain. This realization, once we really understand its nature, leads to an amazing conclusion—a large percentage of our everyday thought process is nothing more than an attempt to avoid pain!

Consider our normal mental activity. We do not use our minds most of the time to think about things that need to be resolved. Most of our thought process is mental commotion leading nowhere; it could easily be eliminated without impairing our ability to function. Only a tiny percentage of our thought process is necessary; in fact, thought is most often circular and nonproductive.

Why then do we think so much? It may well be that a dramatic portion of the thought process is the result of a subconscious attempt to blunt our experience of pain. Spiritual teachers point out that although we may succeed in avoiding awareness of pain this way, it also cloaks our sense of pleasure and is the major cause of unhappiness, suffering, and the sense of aloneness. As the well-known Zen master Yasutani Roshi said:

> What we term suffering is our evaluation of pain from which we stand apart; that pain when courageously accepted is a means to liberation in that it frees our natural sympathies and compassion even as it enables us to experience pleasure and joy in a new depth and purity.[25]

A hasidic rebbe taught: "My master [the Baal Shem Tov] revealed to me that when a person has pain, whether physical or spiritual, he should meditate that even in this pain, God can be found. He [God] is only concealed in a garment in this pain. When a person realizes this, then he can remove the garment. The pain and all evil decrees can then be nullified."[26]

Despite the fact that I am participating in a Buddhist meditation practice, the pain I am experiencing has no loyalty to any particular religious tradition, so I call on God for help. It does not matter to me that elementary Buddhist principles refute the idea of God because it is viewed as a human invention.

I have begun visualizing myself cradled in God's hands, soothed by God's infinite love. I have also invented a new game for myself, called God's Smile. As my point of concentration, I imagine the presence of God's pleasure; when I am distracted and in my own world, I soon notice the absence of this transcendental smile and quickly sharpen my point of concentration until it has returned. This has been extraordinarily effective.

Of course, this use of imagination of God's presence is a no-no in Vipassanā *practice; I will not be able to discuss it with the monks. It is not that we are really in disagreement; indeed if I substituted the word "Buddha" for "God," and said that I was experiencing the enigmatic smile of Buddha Mind, I suspect they would understand; but I am still not sure that they would approve.* Vipassanā *attempts to avoid any potential dualistic thinking, and this is why it is so effective.*

Still, the apparent distinction of East versus West is not so simple. Western mystics do not relate to God as a concept, and when we scratch the surface of the apparent dualism, more often than not we find Western mysticism in complete agreement with its Eastern kin who refer to the highest level of awareness as the Unconditioned, or the Unborn. For a mystic all language falls short, so the word "God" is merely an approximation. Nor are mystics interested in the attempt to categorize their universalist views as pantheistic or panentheistic, for all of these definitions are limited to an intellectual perspective that is antithetical to complete awareness.

The Western view of God is simply that all creation is a paradox. It is impossible that a perfect God could create a universe filled with deficiency; nor is it possible that this universe could exist without an original source. Even someone who asserts there is no source, and things are and always have been the same, supports a paradoxical position because something apparently arises from nothing. Good and evil are paradoxical, as is the contrast between God's omniscience or omnipotence and the doctrine of free will. All these things have been debated by philosophers and theologians over thousands of years, while a mystic sips tea knowing that paradox reigns supreme and will never be resolved.

Thus, although on a Buddhist retreat, I follow my Jewish practice every morning at sunrise of wrapping tefillin *and huddling under a prayer shawl in my tiny room—I feel no contradiction. I read psalms, meditate on liturgy, and glance at the Bible, profoundly moved by new insights that I discover. It all fits together, somehow, East blends with West; and I never fail to marvel how wonderfully the traditions interweave in the mystical fragrance that is released through silence and solitude.*

Unfortunately, when I intermix the practices of various religious traditions, I alienate many friends who believe not only that the path they have chosen is the best for them, but that all other spiritual practices are second-rate. Traditional Jews are wary of other religions because of the fear that people may be deceived by false gods. Buddhists, on the other hand, generally believe that theirs is the ultimate path of Truth. The sense of superiority and spiritual elitism applies to many religious traditions, each of which thinks it has the answer—the window into ultimate reality.

From a mystical perspective, however, there are no definitive answers; paradox is an underlying principle of existence. It is true that I am fulfilled by the process of searching out my Jewish roots and practicing traditional Judaism to the best of my ability, for I have discovered that this discipline raises me to levels of spiritual maturity that I rarely find in people who do not follow a dedicated practice. Indeed, there is an ancient Indian parable that says that we will be much more successful in quenching our spiritual thirst by digging one deep well than dozens of shallow holes. This remains a lesson still unlearned by many people today who consider themselves universalists. Yet although Judaism is my main orientation, I have found essential elements on other paths that enhance my growth and actually deepen my insights into the Jewish tradition.

This approach of working in a spiritual garden filled with a variety of plants is often confusing for people who are accustomed to single-crop farming. Many people remain fearful of anything not stamped with the correct imprimatur. Others cannot understand why anyone would want to be associated with an archaic religion that is stuck with a vindictive God, one that is filled with primitive beliefs, superstitions, and rituals. Some wonder how a person can learn anything in the presence of godless people, seated in a room with a graven image. Although many are happy to join together in chanting, gospel singing, or the repetition of mantras, they find many combinations of Eastern and Western traditions incompatible.

The great Islamic Sufis confronted this difficulty head-on. The well-known poet Rumi said:

> I am neither Muslim nor Christian, Jew nor Zoroastrian; I am neither earth nor of the heavens, I am neither body nor soul. . . . [27]

Another celebrated Sufi, Ibn Arabi, said:

> My heart has opened unto every form. It is a pasture for gazelles, a cloister for Christian monks, a temple for idols, the Ka'ba of the [Muslim] pilgrim, the tablets of the Torah and the book of the Koran. I practice the religion of Love; in whatsoever directions its caravans advance, the religion of Love shall be my religion and my faith.[28]

In the end, religious traditions over the years have separated themselves on exoteric principles, doctrine, or theology. It is for these external beliefs that people have been imprisoned and wars have been fought. Mystics, however, view things differently. They have a unique vision of how things fit together, and they believe that even paradox has its own perfection. Often these people have paid with their lives; but their teachings continue to illuminate.

An infant cries in its crib. Nobody picks it up. It is sheltered, fed, and changed on occasion, but nobody cradles it in their arms. Soon it stops crying. It merely stares with vacant eyes, never smiling. The food was helpful, but the infant needed another kind of nourishment, something we cannot measure—it needed love. Without love, a human being does not want to exist. If a newborn infant does not receive love and affection through physical contact, it will be seriously retarded, become psychotic, or die.

The soul too needs some kind of nourishment. In most people it is shriveled and dry; for them, life is without taste. In others, the soul whimpers and cries at times, but it is difficult to hear because its soft murmur is blanketed by the busy-ness and noise of daily life.

In silence and solitude, we are able to listen more carefully, and it is easier to hear the soul calling. Once we recognize its impoverishment, we quickly learn how to nourish it. We merely need to stop, commune

*with the unknown, experience the abundance of life, open an inspira-
tional book, feast on the moment, or contemplate a blade of grass.*

I remember not long ago hearing a well-known rabbi speaking
in Jerusalem. He was giving his inspirational talk of the week, and
the theme was that we will be standing before God someday and
will not have any excuses for the way we lived our lives. The rabbi
suggested that the fear of this ultimate confrontation with the
Great Judge should be present in our consciousness in every living
breath.

This did not feel right to me. We need not wait for that awesome
moment of heavenly judgment, it is not something in the future
but an ever-present reality; if only we had the eyes to see, we would
recognize the ramifications of our every thought and act. The
"punishment" we might experience at the end of our lives—standing before God, so to speak—is the realization of lost opportunities
because that is the moment we can actually experience how much
our acts have reverberated throughout the universe.

Hell is the realization—too late—of how much influence each
act has in the ultimate healing of the universe. The wisdom teachings say that the angels are not held as highly as human beings
because angels have no choice, while human beings do. Indeed,
hell is a man-made world; we do not have to wait to experience
it—we are constantly in it. As Rebbe Nachman teaches:

> Everyone says there is This World and the World to Come.
> We believe that the World to Come exists. It could be that This
> World also exists—somewhere. But here? From the suffering ev-
> eryone goes through the whole time, it would appear that this
> is Gehenom [hell].[29]

*It is 5:45 A.M., and I have just completed a two-hour sit. Now I
am wrapped in my prayer shawl and tefillin, and for some reason
my thoughts have turned to enlightenment. Suddenly a new idea: God
is a verb, never a noun. God is misnamed; it should be called "God-
ding" to avoid the error that is implied with a noun form.*

*Also creation is misnamed. Better it should be called "creation-
ing." It is not a thing—not something of the past—but an ongoing
process. And every object is really a process—there are no things! There*

are really no nouns! Everything is in constant motion, nothing is the same as it was just a moment ago. Nor will it be the same a moment from now. This table is "tabling," this cup is "cupping." Or perhaps the table is "wooding," or "treeing." As "table" it is simply in a passing phase.

Enlightenment is also a process, and therefore misnamed. It should be called "enlightening." We cannot become enlightened; enlightenment does not exist—rather, we are constantly enlightening. Moreover, as the process of enlightening is a transition, it is not a something we can possess, it is always in motion.

What does this mean? It means that the enlightening act is not that somebody gives or does something because he or she is at a particular stage of enlightenment; rather it is just the opposite, that a person is in the process of enlightening because he or she gives or does something. Simply said, giving or doing things for others is enlightening. There is no gain of substance because it is only a process. At any moment that giving or doing for others stops, enlightening ceases.

Thus, we need never wait a single moment to develop into enlightened beings, for enlightenment cannot be obtained. However, the moment we begin to perform a generous act by giving or doing things that help others, we enter the realm of enlightening, and are fully "enlightened" throughout the entire process.

Something happened to me when this idea rushed into my thoughts. At first it was like an explosion of synapses gone haywire, and then there was a great calm, a lucid perception that this was not like many other insights that arise in rapture only to melt away when subjected to the heat of critical analysis. Rather, this opened to the center of existence, and there I found—once again—the heart of pure stillness.

I began to cry—and then to laugh—and then to cry again.

How could it be so elementary and so profound? No answer is an answer. Nothing to do, but doing. Nothing to be, but Being. And Being does not mean merely being the recipient of an inflow; rather Being is the dynamic interaction of taking and giving. The process of enlightening has to do with awareness, and awareness flowers through acts of lovingkindness in which not only is the enlightening of the giver enhanced, so too the enlightening of the receiver. Indeed, one cannot happen without the other.

Words become blocks of stone as I contemplate the implications of a new awareness growing within. My attempts to capture the full meaning with language force abstractions that limit and bind ideas, and then these concepts ossify and sink into oblivion. How to say it? More important, why say it? It is too simple, we have all heard it before: Love, share, serve. That's all there is in the enlightening process. Nothing else to do; nothing more to become; nothing higher to attain.

IMS, BARRE, MASSACHUSETTS: JUNE 1989.
THE LAST PART OF A ONE-HUNDRED-DAY
RETREAT.

Today, I am floating on velvet clouds, my body is soft and radiant. Each move is a dance with partners who take the form of wind, trees, and rocks. I also had the good fortune today at noon to explore a different kind of dance with a five-foot black snake coiled on the stairs to my room. It is not always like this. Just last week I had a string of difficult days: monkey mind hanging off the rafters, pain in the depths of the abyss.

The hard days and the good ones are really identical. My mind chooses its heaven or hell. Nothing changes but the mental breezes, at times tropical and warm, while others are gale-force blasts of stinging sleet on black frozen nights. My inner complainer is conditioned to groan whenever I am uncomfortable, but another reality has gained a foothold. They call it equanimity.

The goal of this work is not so much to feel good as it is to let go. Yesterday was tough, today is gorgeous, tomorrow . . . another day. The mind is like a sticky tar baby; whatever happens, it grabs without discretion. Our business on retreat is to learn how to ignore this ever-present glob of tar. Because if we do not ignore it, we get caught by it.

It is simple, really. The tar baby can only stick to something that presents itself. It cannot adhere to us if we do not have a boundary that separates the outer from the inner. We can defeat the tar baby only when we lose the sense of ourselves. Then there is no more "me" to have a good day or a bad day; the days just come and go.

The flowers along the front path have been blooming for weeks, but each day it is as if I see them for the first time. I watch green pods swelling pregnant with flower-life, and then one morning they have burst into complex shapes and unimaginable colors. Their fragrant sensuality is so alluring, all life is drawn to taste the nectar. A hive of bees hums in nearby rafters, protecting this flower bed, drawing nourishment from the blossoms of spring while pollinating the seeds for next season.

There is more for me here than ecological balance. This is the poet's song, the fairy's dance, the supreme creative impulse. In this center of knowing, there is only awareness—some would say God-consciousness—and everything is much more than it seems to be. From this perspective, the exquisiteness of the flowers, their symmetry and interdependence with insect life, and the miracle of my being present in the moment is but one drop in an infinite ocean, permeating every aspect of creation in such a way that there is no difference between the grandeur of the entire universe extending beyond billions of light-years, and the tiny dot marking the end of this sentence.

During the last month, the retreat rhythm became slow and steady, like a giant lizard hardly breathing, watching motionless for its prey; each hour it blinked—a bell rang—and we would shift from one mode of meditation to another. I found myself intimate with subtle details of the surroundings: a rock with its own castle turret and ant farm alongside; an imperfection in the window joinery that was now a spider's haunt; a squeaking plank in one corner of the small walking room; a dripping pipe forming a ministalactite. Thousands of familiar landmarks filled this universe of silence.

Many retreatants had gone through a metamorphosis. Their appearance may have seemed the same to an outside observer—perhaps they walked more slowly, turned more gracefully, were less anxious in the food lines, seemed lighter on their feet, or sat more quietly with soundless breath—yet it was clear that profound changes had occurred. Fellow retreatants do not have to speak with each other to make an acquaintance; something happens on a more essential level than verbal communication. We can sense when things are in balance, and more important, we know that our own struggles are common experiences.

It is not all sweetness and light for retreatants. We go through periods of self-induced torment and then come out the other side. When I feel the presence of suffering nearby, I need not look up to identify the personality; the experience of suffering is universal. I find myself working with the other person's pain, absorbing it, breathing through it, praying for release, and sending all of my love. It is not his pain or hers, it is ours.

During the first weeks after I returned to the retreat, time seemed to expand, the days got increasingly longer. Then the sense of time evaporated and disappeared. The only relevant indicator of movement from one event to another was the Tibetan gong carried by an individual retreatant through the halls, with its sonorous voice that cried OM with each blow of the striker. We slept, ate, walked, and sat according to these announcements.

Shoshana returned for the last month of sitting. Once again, I broke my rhythm the day she arrived. It was our seventh anniversary, and we spent the night in a beautiful suite in a local hotel in Barre. The mix of life and death, pain and joy, the business of the world and the emptiness of silence all combined into multicolor, fragrant bouquets. In my state of consciousness, everything tumbled in slow motion—we reconnected, shared, loved—it seemed not to have a beginning or an ending. I know it happened—I have the receipt for proof—but it occurred in a dream realm, a soft world of billowing clouds and endless sun-drenched dunes; it was another level of profound meditation.

We returned to the retreat center, and in a few days my rhythm was reestablished. The past and future were no longer meaningful—only the experience of this moment, this breath, right now. I began to measure my life not in terms of day and night, or the transition point of meals, but by an internal chronometer that noted my mental states. Periods of tranquillity were punctuated by sequences of fantasy or anxiety; segments of equanimity were interwoven with phases of doubt, frustration, or desire. I soon began to realize that at times I induced various states of mind as a logical consequence to my thought process, and other times these mind states seemed to arise on their own, without being invited. The longer I watched this phenomenon, the clearer the mechanical nature of the mind became. I understood the degree to which it is conditioned by everything leading up to each moment, and the relative ease by which it can be rechanneled into a different mode.

Indeed, the rapidity with which we can transform obsessive or angry thoughts into calm and loving ones, or vice versa, is stunning.

I began experimenting and found that I could treat my thoughts as if they were encased in balloons. When I observed that my mind was in a troubled world of its own, I would pop the balloon by merely deciding to think about something else. Moreover, when I wanted to induce a mind state of lovingkindness, friendliness, or sympathetic awareness, I simply imagined scenes that would manifest these feelings. We all do this, to some extent, in everyday life; but in my altered state of mind I was able to dissect the process and examine it with great precision under a mental electron microscope.

This is when I noticed something that changed my perspective dramatically, for I discovered that although our mental process is highly mechanical and predictable, there is another phenomenon occurring in each moment that—once recognized—is breathtaking.

I slipped into fantasy in the morning meditation and began musing about what it would be like to encounter the ideal guide, someone so perfectly attuned to my essential being that he or she would provide an environment that would maximize my spiritual growth. Where is such a person, anyway?

Suddenly, in an unforgettable instant, the certainty arose that every experience I have ever had, or ever will have, is precisely the gift of an ultimate mentor; each thought, every event down to its most subtle nuance, everything that happens to me is offered precisely as if my teacher had custom-ordered it. This ideal mentor lives within each of us and is constantly whispering advice—sometimes it even screams at us—but usually we are oblivious of its presence.

Even though we are unaware of our mentor, it continues to send us hushed messages. What draws us into spiritual inquiry? What attracts us to the peace and serenity of contemplative experience? What gives us the strength to undertake arduous practices? What compels us to reject the conveniences and comforts of life in the pursuit of inner truth? Even though many people do not have strong motivation along these lines, they are touched, nonetheless, in moments of crises or stress to listen more carefully to this inner voice.

Our mentor often accomplishes its task in unimaginable ways. It sends us on many journeys; it harasses, confuses, and challenges us. It uses the tools of joy and revelation; but also has an arsenal of torture, using pain and suffering to force new levels of realization.

This guide dwells at the source of our being; in fact, it is literally the germ of life. As long as we fail to recognize that life itself is the perfect teacher, we identify with our thoughts or experiences in a way that gives shape to a false image of ourselves—we miss the message and merely suffer. When the realization arises that each moment holds the potential for growth that an ideal mentor could provide, every experience and every thought is approached as if it holds the most important lesson we could learn. We never again complain about the things that happen to us; rather we explore how the inner teacher is helping us transcend our limitations.

So as each thought arises in meditation, the presence of the mentor gives strength to what is sometimes called the "witness," helping us disassociate from the thought, drawing us away from the trap of thought's illusion. As I rest in this pervading emptiness, the vast, black stillness that surrounds pinpoints of thought-embers, my mentor/companion can be felt through its smile and its quiet laughter. Indeed, it is constantly laughing to itself because everything that we believe is real, is not.

When I connected with my mentor, my meditation changed dramatically. I began to see everything through its eyes. I never felt alone again.

In the Brihadaranyaka Upanishad, Prajapati teaches the lesson: "*Da! Da! Da!*—Be self-controlled [*damayata*], Be charitable [*datta*], Be compassionate [*dayadhwam*]."[30] The simple ratio of this lesson is two to one: two parts engaged in others, one part—the first—engaged in the self-control. *Damayata* may be translated as restraint. Through restraint we gain mastery, we subdue our urges and refine our potential. This works hand in hand with reaching out to others. The greater our self-mastery, the more we raise the spirits of those with whom we work.

The nourishing aspects of the self comes through reaching out to touch other souls through compassion and charity. As we feed others, we ourselves are fed; it is like pouring liquid from a cup while standing under a waterfall, the cup is immediately refilled. In the end, of course, it is not one soul giving to another; rather, it is the One, the Great Mentor, using souls as vehicles to nourish each other. This is the message of all great teachers: The potential power of healing and love within each of us is nourished by feeding others.

Shadows danced in a darkened cave, the walls glistened moist. Suddenly, I entered a cavern, black as doom, without walls or ceiling. Floating in emptiness, heart thumping in my throat, I felt death beneath my eyelids. A faint trace of light beckoned in the distance. It rapidly came toward me, filling the empty space with a dazzling radiance. This light poured out of a chalice held by something hidden. A river of phosphorescence gushed over the edges of the cup, revealing hands holding it, but too bright to see beyond. The hands came closer and raised the cup, offering its elixir to me.

I did not hesitate, welcoming this presence with joy and gratefulness. A bridge of light linked the space between us. Now I could see the entity behind the hands. It was very old with long white hair and penetrating eyes. It looked at me for only a moment and then glided toward me along the light-bridge. Without hesitating, this being flowed into me; its radiance glowed within.

Another appeared across the bridge, and it too joined with me. Yet another and another. Names of saints and angels arose like froth on a windy sea. Each presence added brightness to an inner light that soon became dazzling. When I thought that I could not bear more of this exquisite intensity, there was a moment's pause, and then . . .

Two resplendent beings of light appeared across the bridge heralding something wondrous about to appear. It began to form between them and soon blazed incandescent, a presence so powerful, its light penetrated everything. It was the light of transfiguration—the ultimate light of healing—and it saturated everything in its domain. An eternal moment overflowed in this radiance—and, beginning with my outer skin, each cellular layer vaporized until my body disappeared and there was only the iridescence of pure love.

As the retreat approached its conclusion, I reflected upon the events that had changed our original plans. Every retreat has its own lessons. This one was marked by the constant adjustments we encountered because of Bill's illness and death, and now I understood a new level of practice. Yes, sitting in silence enhances the development of awareness; many say it is a crucial element of the spiritual path. Yet, although essential, if it is done exclusively—as with any practice—it can lead to a trap, the sweetness of silence may transform into the bitterness of alienation.

Indeed, we did have a one-hundred-day retreat after all. Part of it was in an accustomed form—sitting quietly—and part of it occurred in a new way, dealing with the experience of family crisis. Serving, helping, loving, sharing, and keeping our hearts open through actual engagement is, in itself, a profound spiritual path. The mentor was obviously teaching that we needed more than one hundred days of quiet and seclusion, we needed to grow through the practice of "compassion in action."

The Middle Path of Buddhism refers to a process that takes place between the excesses of asceticism and self-indulgence. This middle path seems to be evolving in the spiritual efforts of twentieth-century Westerners—it is the balance of effort between individual pursuit and engagement in social causes. If either is done to excess, the result is a psychic or emotional burnout. We can sit for just so long, or we can give just so much, and then we need to attune our lives.

Each era seems to have its own flavor: The spiritual practices of the past may or may not be applicable to the present. The twentieth century may be noted in history as the first to have instant worldwide communication, enormous information flow, and the capability to accumulate and focus vast amounts of resources in short periods of time. This potential has implications for our spiritual development. We may need to take our retreats—just as seekers have done for thousands of years—but we may also need to serve others in a new and more committed way because we know people from around the world more intimately than ever before, we increasingly realize our interdependence, and we are beginning to understand that the human condition is similar in many more ways than it is different.

Just as each individual has an inner mentor, so too is there a teacher in every particle of creation—and in every event. The ancients taught that each blade of grass has its own angel saying, "Grow! Grow!" It follows, then, that every generation has its living spirit, and each has its task to understand the teachings that are being offered.

*   *   *

During the last few days of the retreat, silence was broken so that people could have time to integrate socially. The chatter of human voices in the dining room at first was jarring, but soon it was one great voice overlapping itself, and the sound of talking was no different from that of wind in the trees, rain against the window, or steam clanking in the radiator.

I wandered outside to my favorite spot on the lawn and lay down in the midday sun. A red haze penetrated my eyelids, and the scent of warm, moist, freshly cut grass turned my consciousness green. Someone once said: "No body, no mind—no problem."

I am still lying in the grass. Months have passed—years—I have not moved. After a while my body stood up, brushed itself off, and continued with the business of living. But I am still here. No time, past, or future disturbs me. I could not leave even if I wanted to— there is nowhere to go. But, of course, there is no wanting either. My body visits every so often; it sits quietly in meditation or on retreat, and remembers me. I am always here, always have been. . . .

EPILOGUE

From the ridge of the land we have purchased in Colorado, we can see to the west a broad sweep of mountain peaks that form a section of the Continental Divide, while looking east, we gaze across miles of plains leading to Kansas. I have been sitting on this peak of land often during my Sukkot retreat this year.

The seed of contemplative awareness that sprouted on our forty-day retreat in May of 1988 turned out to be a hardy plant that grew in all kinds of conditions—and was even able to withstand long periods of drought. Time and again, Shoshana and I would reflect on the experience we shared sitting on that bench in the forest behind IMS, at the end of our forty days, when we knew beyond a doubt that the contemplative path was our destiny.

The trauma of leaving Jerusalem—or even thinking about it—was often too much to bear. Quite simply, we loved the inner spirit of the city, its holiness. We were connected to it by an unbreakable bond. The city had nourished our infant souls and—through rituals and customs, through the Sabbaths and the Holy Days that opened the floodgates of inner longing—had given us access to deep running waters of primal love.

The shadow side, however, continued to make its presence known. We needed to balance the intensity with silence, the continuous engagement with solitude, the ongoing social interaction with introspection. Moreover, there was an undertone in the Old City that rubbed like a whetstone, sharpening our levels of anxiety, fear, and even paranoia. The violence of the Palestinian conflict was not merely the subject of news, it was life across the street. A few times a week we heard the rat-ta-tat of Uzi machine guns a few hundred yards away. Usually these weapons were shot in the air as warnings, but sometimes they were pointed at people.

Whole sections of the city were now dangerous territory, and the marketplace that I loved when I first arrived in Jerusalem, where I wandered for hours each day, was now off-limits. This market began a block from our home, and sections of it were still attractive for tourists; but even these safe sectors were uncomfortable for me because they were permeated by the sullen mood of oppression.

Arab children, ages five to eight, had eyes brimming with terror and loathing; older preteen children—nine to twelve—were big enough to be dangerous. I suspect that the few ineffectual firebombs thrown at our Jewish neighbors' homes were done by some of these kids in a kind of corrupted innocence because teenagers have more savvy and quickly learn that gasoline is far more devastating than kerosene in a Molotov cocktail.

We had slowly grown accustomed to this environment of enmity; hatred was a common, everyday experience. When we examined how this had changed our lives, we realized that our hearts had been enclosed in a protective sheath to avoid acknowledging the truth of the situation and our feelings in general had been suppressed. We also discovered that our sense of helplessness had generated in us a feeling of apathy. When we acknowledged this condition and began to speak out, we found that many of our friends were polarized on the other end of the political spectrum, and this added to our growing alienation.

We can only hope and pray that the new initiative for peace in the region will come to fruition. When lifelong enemies like Yitzhak Rabin and Yasir Arafat can shake hands in public at the signing of a peace accord, things seem to be looking up. But it will be a long, rocky road; the animosity runs deep—the children on both sides have learned to hate—and it may require another generation before the violence is ended.

After our one-hundred-day retreat, the impetus to arrange a new home base in the U.S.A. began to build. It gained momentum when we were compelled to reflect on our mortality. Following that retreat, soon after our return to Israel, Shoshana had serious surgery and not long after that I survived a fall that could have easily killed me or crippled me for life. Her recovery of a few months, and the two months I spent on my back, were unplanned retreats in which we each ultimately came to the conclusion that the time was close for us to make our move.

We decided in June 1990, two years after our forty-day retreat, one year after the hundred-day experience. Any ambivalence we may have had in this decision melted away when the clouds of war began to form on the eastern horizon. In August Iraq invaded Kuwait and in September the Israelis began to prepare for a poison gas attack.

We received our gas masks in cardboard cartons two weeks before we were scheduled to leave. It was a pathetic experience standing in line alongside older people whose forearms still bore blue-gray serial numbers tattooed there fifty years earlier in the death camps, and my heart wept when I realized that the cycle of ignorance had not yet been broken. Leaving Israel in a time of crisis was yet another cause for feelings of guilt—but Israel is often in crisis, and the guilt is endless.

Now we live in two worlds—our new home in the mountains of Colorado and our spiritual home in the land of Israel. It is a compromise, a way to counteract the negative aspects of living entirely in one place or the other.

Many people who know of my serious work in Buddhist meditation have asked me about the practice of Judaism, why it attracts me, how it fits in with contemplative work, and why I continue to be observant. More specifically, they ask me which aspects of traditional Judaism are useful for spiritual development. My answer to them is that individual practices—whether Jewish or from any other tradition—do not carry much power on their own; the true benefit for a spiritual aspirant is when practice becomes a way of life. Judaism is not merely a collection of rituals, laws, and customs; it is part of one's consciousness from the first moment of awakening in the morning, when an observant Jew is obliged to offer a prayer of thankfulness for being alive, to the last moment of awareness in bed at night, when the Jewish practice is to ask for the protection of angels while we sleep.

Every spiritual tradition has the potential of being a way of life. Indeed, the major orientation of our spiritual search is to find the tradition most compatible with our rhythms and the nature of our soul. Often our heritage provides an important clue in this search, for no matter what path we ultimately follow, our inner work will always be influenced by the legacy of our parents, families, language, culture, and belief systems.

Despite the fact that I was not raised in a household that identified with its Jewish lineage, I have found myself drawn more to this path than to any other I have explored. Its lunar calendar and pulse of Holy Days afford me a constant awareness of physical time and space in relation to a binding thread that weaves throughout the generations; its weekly Sabbath invites rest from daily thought so that spiritual inquiry is deeply enhanced; its symbols are abundantly imbued with mystical significance; its Torah and Talmud, and all of the commentaries connected with them, provide an enormous wealth of inspirational material that transcends earthly limits; its Kabbalah presents an uninterrupted stream of mystical nectar; its vast set of laws offers a practitioner endless potential for raising consciousness every moment of the day—indeed, traditional Judaism is a practice that is sweet and pleasurable as well as rigorous and demanding.

On many occasions I have compared notes with serious devotees in other traditions—Eastern and Western—and we find that the Orthodox Jewish practice is as engaged in ongoing spiritual discipline as the cloistered practice of most priests, monks, or nuns. My own experience is that I have gone through periods of extremely careful observance and other times of a more relaxed approach. As with all other aspects of life, spiritual practice has its own rhythms; the tradition provides a form, but its substance arises only when the practice has a clear quality of connectedness with the soul. Judaism is a marvelous template for a spiritual seeker, but works well only when it is accomplished with deep meaning. Like all other traditions, if practiced in a rote manner, it tends to be dry, archaic, and incomprehensible.

In addition to being a fertile source for intense inner work, Judaism has the benefit of being relationship- and community-oriented—it encourages family life and community service. In Judaism, the ultimate spiritual practice is not through self-attainment, but how we interrelate with others around us and with the world as a whole. A central focus in Judaism is called *tikkun olam*—fixing the world—the responsibility we have as human beings to constantly work toward a better life, a constant process of

perfecting that ultimately gains messianic consciousness for everyone. Yet, despite all of this—the broad opportunities for meaningful practice and the potential for service—my attraction to Jewish
observance, so clear to me now, was slow in coming.

As I have noted, my early practice of Judaism worked with form
but missed an essential quality of understanding. The quality I
sought became alive for me when I followed a serious meditation
discipline—which Buddhists have developed over thousands of
years. Thus, I continue to balance my practice, using meditative
"technology" from many traditions, while focusing on the Jewish
experience as the baseline of my daily life. I have discovered that
I am not alone in this process; quite a few people who consider
themselves religious in their Jewish observance use meditative techniques to deepen their practice. Some stay in the closet, so to
speak, because the general opinion of the mainstream is that practices used in other traditions—by definition—cannot be Jewish;
others are beginning to express themselves, and the result is that
there is a trend toward greater spirituality in Judaism today.

Recently Reb Zalman decided it was time for me to become a
rabbi. My ordination followed twelve years of study and practice,
eight years living in Jerusalem. We agreed that my job would be
to help people from all backgrounds to use meditation and retreat
in a way that would open inner gateways. There are only a few
places where this is being done in Judaism.

Just as I uncovered a new entry into Judaism through contemplative insight, many Christians with whom I work have had similar
experiences, rediscovering the depth and wonder of their own tradition through the process of silent retreats. The mystical nature
of humankind is not identified with any religion. Indeed, when
people ask whether I am Reform, Reconstructionist, Conservative,
or Orthodox in my Judaism, I find myself using the answer that
Reb Zalman suggests: I am postdenominational. The postdenominational practitioner is more concerned with an intimate and
meaningful relationship with the Divine than with the formulas and
definitions of group identity.

Shoshana has also become more universal in her practice, following a number of paths. She delights in most of the Jewish ritual,
perfects and teaches the wisdom of Japanese Tea Ceremony, works
with seriously ill patients as an oncology nurse, and tends our beautiful land and all its creatures with gentle caring. Together, Sho-

shana and I share in welcoming individuals, small groups, and families from all walks of life to our land to engage in the process of inner work. We are particularly drawn to sharing our time with people who are facing terminal illness—whether they come alone or with their families—to provide an environment of deep contemplation and expanded awareness in a magnificent natural setting of mountains and forest.

Our experience has been that individual practice through contemplation and silent retreat without service to the community ends up being too isolated and exclusive, while community service without taking time for individual growth often results in burnout. The blend of the two seems to suit us perfectly at this point in our development.

Our one-hundred-day retreat taught us more lessons than we could have foreseen. The depths of the meditative experience proved that the human potential for expanded awareness is enormous, and Bill's illness and death opened new gateways of compassion and lovingkindness. In retrospect—three years later—this retreat was another major turning point, just as the first forty-day retreat had been, and our lives once again were uprooted.

We never know which way our spiritual path will continue to weave through the thicket of life, but we try to listen carefully to that hushed voice within in a way that will open our hearts, develop our insight, and constantly raise our awareness.

Seated atop the rocky ridge of our new land, I notice two hawks circling just above. In my hands I hold a lulav *and* etrog, *a palm branch and citron—plus myrtle leaves and willow branches—which I have just waved over the land in the ritual blessing that is part of the prayers during Sukkot.*

Each time I reread my previous retreat notes, I am stunned by the difference in the contemplative world and the experience of daily life. If I could follow my own clear advice when I am in the altered consciousness sparked by intensive inner work, when my mentor's voice is as bright as the morning sun, I would be living much closer to the truth. Now I realize more than ever how difficult it is to maintain constant awareness in the everyday world. Yet, despite the difficulties we face as individuals, I trust that the group process of spiritual development is evolving in a positive direction. If this were not so, I feel that humankind would be doomed.

The hawks continue their slow, gliding arcs, and I notice that a flock of high-flying birds glistening white against an azure sky have interrupted their voyage to cruise a thousand feet above the hawks. There are hundreds of them, but I cannot identify them at such a height. They twist and turn over our land like puffs of cotton in a gentle wind.

A down feather as soft as an infant's curl floats earthward and brushes the granite rock by my side. It feels like a messenger from above, and I wonder what it is telling me. In Jewish folklore, most angels are created to do just one thing, accomplish one task or deliver one message. I pick up this angel-wisp and hold it to my cheek.

When I glance up again, the birds have vanished, but the feather brushing my face is not an illusion. I feel it as a caress, a gentle and loving touch, and I realize that this IS the message—the way the Divine fondles creatures. It is a silent communication that opens new gateways of understanding, a different kind of poetry—one that transcends words, concepts, and thoughts. It touches my heart and a place of inner knowing. In that moment I am complete, thankful, and fully at peace.

> *My beloved has gone down into his garden,*
> *to the beds of spices,*
> *to feed in the gardens,*
> *and to gather lilies.*
> *I am my beloved's and my beloved is mine:*
> *he feeds among the lilies.*
>
> *(Song of Songs 6:2–3)*

NOTES

⋘⟁⟐⟁⟐⟁⋙

SUFISM AND JUDAISM

1. *Sukkah* 51b, *The Soncino Talmud* (London: Soncino Press, 1936).
2. *Kiddushin* 49b, *The Soncino Talmud.*
3. For a more detailed description, see the end of chapter 4.
4. *Encyclopedia Judaica* (Jerusalem: Keter Publishing House Jerusalem Ltd., 1972) vol. 14, p. 1471.
5. Rabbi Gedalia Fleer, Old City, Jerusalem, related this story.
6. David Godman, ed., *Be As You Are: The Teachings of Sri Ramana Maharshi* (London/New York: Arkana, 1985) p. 90.
7. Christopher Isherwood, *Ramakrishna and His Disciples* (Hollywood, California: Vedanta Press, 1965) p. 71.
8. Quoted in Evelyn Underhill, *Mysticism* (New York: Penguin, 1955) p. 235.
9. Pir Vilayat Inayat Khan, *Toward the One* (New York: Harper & Row, 1974) p. 642.
10. J. Krishnamurti, *Think on These Things,* D. Rajagopal, ed. (New York: Harper & Row, 1964) p. 78.
11. P. D. Ouspensky, *The Fourth Way* (New York: Alfred A. Knopf, 1957) pp. 116–17.
12. Sufi Sam died in 1971.
13. *Dhikr,* meaning "remembrance," is a form of mantra, using a divine name or quality, often as a praise. It is done seated, standing, or twirling; vocalized or under the breath; with eyes open or shut. *Dhikr* is a primary practice of Sufism. A description of it will be found in my book *Silence, Simplicity, and Solitude* (New York: Bell Tower,

1992), in the chapter on devotion and prayer, and the one on mantra.

14. William Johnston, trans., *The Cloud of Unknowing* (New York: Doubleday/Image, 1973) pp. 137–39.

15. Quoted in Lex Hixon, *Coming Home* (Garden City, New York: Anchor Books, 1978) pp. 115–20.

16. Quoted in Paramahansa Yogananda, *Autobiography of a Yogi* (Los Angeles: Self-Realization Fellowship, 1946) p. 450.

17. Ramana Maharshi uses the word "Self," with a capital *S,* to mean the essential nature of all creation. This should not be confused with the self, which others often discuss as a synonym for the ego.

18. Godman, *Be As You Are,* p. 26.

19. Aryeh Kaplan, *Meditation and the Bible* (York Beach, Maine: Samuel Weiser, 1981) p. 58.

20. William C. Chittick, *The Sufi Path of Knowledge* (Albany, New York: State University of New York Press, 1989) p. 224.

21. David Steindl-Rast, *Narrow Is the Way,* included in *Speaking of Silence,* Susan Walker, ed. (Mahwah, New Jersey: Paulist Press, 1987) pp. 186–87.

22. *Shema Yisrael* is the quintessential Jewish prayer, said every morning and evening, and at the moment of death: "Hear O Israel, the Lord is our God, the Lord is One."

23. *Shabbos* is the Eastern European (Ashkenazic) pronunciation of the Hebrew word for the Sabbath, which is commonly pronounced *Shabbat* in modern Israel—where the convention of Sephardic pronunciation is used.

24. *Mekilta de-Rabbi Ishmael,* J. Z. Lauterbach, trans. (Philadelphia: Jewish Publication Society of America, 1933) vol. 2, p. 3.

25. See Louis Ginzberg, *The Legends of the Jews* (Philadelphia: Jewish Publication Society of America, 1968) vol. 5, p. 125, n. 134.

26. *The Jerusalem Bible* (Jerusalem: Koren Publishers Jerusalem, Ltd. 1984) p. 402.

27. Aryeh Kaplan, *Inner Space,* Abraham Sutton, ed. (Jerusalem: Moznaim Publishing, 1990) p. 32.

28. Ginzberg, *The Legends of the Jews,* vol. 4, p. 154.

29. *Yoma* 21a, *The Soncino Talmud.*

30. *Berakoth* 17a, *The Soncino Talmud.* (The yeast in the dough is symbolic of the evil impulse, which causes a ferment in the heart.)

31. Rebbe Nachman of Breslov, *Advice,* Avraham Greenbaum, trans. (Jerusalem: Breslov Research Institute, 1983) p. 163.

32. *Omer* literally means "sheath." The Counting of the Omer is a remembrance of ancient times when an offering of sheaths of barley was "waved" in the Temple. The Kabbalists use this forty-nine day

period to "repair" through prayer and contemplation all the component parts of the mystical Tree of Life.

33. Ven. Achaan Chah, *A Still Forest Pool*, J. Kornfield and P. Breiter, eds. (Wheaton, Illinois: Theosophical Publishing House, 1985) p. 162.

34. See *Encyclopedia Judaica*, vol. 2, pp. 956–77.

35. See *Zohar, Pinchas* 240b.

36. Larry Dossey, *Space, Time & Medicine* (Boston and London: Shambhala, 1985) p. 134.

37. *Abraham Isaac Kook*, Ben Zion Bokser, trans. (New York: Paulist Press, 1978) p. 215, from *The Lights of Holiness*, vol. 1, p. 177.

38. William C. Chittick, *The Sufi Path of Love* (Albany, New York: State University of New York Press, 1983) p. 186.

JUDAISM AND BUDDHISM

1. John G. Bennett, *Long Pilgrimage* (Clearlake, California: The Dawn Horse Press, 1983) pp. 81–82.

2. Ibid., pp. 176–77.

3. *Baba Bathra* 75a, *The Soncino Talmud* (London: Soncino Press, 1936)

4. Paul Reps, *Zen Flesh, Zen Bones* (Garden City, New York: Doubleday, 1957) p. 48.

5. J. Krishnamurti, *The Awakening of Intelligence* (New York: Harper & Row, 1973), pp. 101–2.

6. Annemarie Schimmel, *Mystical Dimensions of Islam* (Chapel Hill, North Carolina: The University of North Carolina Press, 1975) p. 133.

7. Chögyam Trungpa, *Cutting Through Spiritual Materialism* (Berkeley: Shambhala, 1973) pp. 98–99.

8. See Yehuda L. Ashlag, *Talmud Esser Sfirot* (Jerusalem: Yeshivat Kol Yehuda) pp. 14–28.

9. Idries Shah, *The Sufis* (New York: Anchor Books, 1964), p. 357.

10. See Ashlag, *Talmud Esser Sfirot*, p. 24.

11. Moses Cordovero, *The Palm Tree of Deborah*, Louis Jacobs, trans. (New York: Sepher-Hermon Press, 1974), pp. 82–83.

12. David Godman, ed., *Be As You Are: The Teachings of Sri Ramana Maharshi* (London/New York: Arkana, 1985), p. 1.

13. Exodus 10:21–23, The Jerusalem Bible (Jerusalem: Koren Publishers Jerusalem, Ltd., 1984.)

14. Louis Ginzberg, *The Legends of the Jews* (Philadelphia: The Jewish Publication Society of America, 1920), vol. II, pp. 359–60.

15. Ginzberg, vol. I, p. 86.
16. Ibid., p. 135.
17. Ibid., p. 132.
18. Exodus 24:16–18, The Jerusalem Bible.
19. Exodus 20:15–16, The Jerusalem Bible.
20. *Shabbath* 88a, *The Soncino Talmud*
21. Ibid.
22. Ginzberg, vol. III, p. 106.
23. Larry Dossey, M.D., *Space, Time & Medicine* (Boston & London: Shambhala, 1988), p. xii. (ital. his)
24. I have referred to the "Summit" retreat in another book: *The Heart of Stillness* (New York: Bell Tower, 1992).
25. Philip Kapleau, *The Three Pillars of Zen* (Garden City, N.Y., Doubleday, 1966), p. 18.
26. *Toldot Yaakov Yosef, Va Yakhel,* p. 67d, quoted by Aryeh Kaplan, *Meditation and Kabbalah* (York Beach, Maine: Samuel Weiser, 1986) p. 294.
27. Huston Smith, *The World's Religions* (New York: HarperCollins Publishers, 1991) p. 264.
28. Ibid.
29. Rebbe Nachman of Breslov, *Likutey Moaran* II:119, Avraham Greenbaum, trans., *Garden of the Souls* (Jerusalem/New York: Breslov Research Institute, 1990), p. 1.
30. Swami Prabhavananda & Fredrick Manchester, trans., *The Upanishads* (New York: New American Library 1948), p. 112.

ACKNOWLEDGMENTS

❦

To my wife, Shoshana, for her constant support and counsel as well as for being my biggest fan.

To my rebbe, Zalman Schachter-Shalomi, for his guidance, trust, and blessing that I should serve as a rabbi.

To my mother, Helene, a woman far ahead of her times and who is assuredly nudging the heavenly realms to quickly resolve the world's problems; and to my father, Sampson, who struggles to maintain his dignity under the weight of relentless aging.

To Bill Irish, who as a practicing Catholic loved the Friday night Jewish Sabbath ritual, and who was the best salesman I have ever known; and to Meg McCormick Irish, my mother-in-law, for her perseverance and devotion to her family.

To my other immediate family members, Ralph and Mark, for their assistance and ever-present advice for their kid brother.

To my associate Alan Secrest, for his honesty, his decency, and his monthly checks.

To my editor, Toinette Lippe, for her skillfulness, her good judgment, and her grace under pressure.

And to the innumerable friends, associates, mentors, and students who have filled my life with love, compassion, insight, and gentleness, and who have been an unending source of inspiration.

Thank you, one and all.

ABOUT THE AUTHOR

David A. Cooper has been a student of mysticism for over thirty years and has practiced spiritual retreat for the last sixteen. Rabbi Cooper is widely traveled and has studied extensively the mystical elements of a variety of traditions, including Buddhism, Christianity, Hinduism, Islam, and Judaism. In the early 1980s, he sold his Washington, D.C., political consulting firm to a partner, and he and his wife, Shoshana—who had been an assistant professor of nursing—moved to the Old City of Jerusalem, where they lived for eight years. There he studied the hasidic and kabbalistic aspects of Judaism. In 1991 the Coopers moved to the mountains of Colorado—near Boulder—where they currently caretake a modest, nondenominational retreat facility for individuals, small groups, and families who wish to gain new awareness through a method that enhances quieting the mind and clarifying the thought process. For information about retreats, please write to Heart of Stillness Hermitage, P.O. Box 106, Jamestown, Colorado 80455.

OTHER BELL TOWER BOOKS

Books that nourish the soul, illuminate the mind, and speak directly to the heart

Valeria Alfeyeva. PILGRIMAGE TO DZHVARI: *A Woman's Journey of Spiritual Awakening.* Hardcover 0-517-59194-4 (1993), paperback 0-517-88389-9 (1995).

Tracy Cochran and Jeff Zaleski. TRANSFORMATIONS: *Awakening to the Sacred in Ourselves.* Hardcover 0-517-70150-2 (1995).

David A. Cooper. THE HEART OF STILLNESS: *The Elements of Spiritual Practice.* Hardcover 0-517-58621-5 (1992), paperback 0-517-88187-X (1994).

——SILENCE, SIMPLICITY, AND SOLITUDE: *A Guide for Spiritual Retreat.* Hardcover 0-517-58620-7 (1992), paperback 0-517-88186-1 (1994).

James G. Cowan. LETTERS FROM A WILD STATE: *Rediscovering Our True Relationship to Nature.* Hardcover 0-517-58770-X (1992).

——MESSENGERS OF THE GODS: *Tribal Elders Reveal the Ancient Wisdom of the Earth.* Paperback 0-517-88078-4 (1993).

Marc David. NOURISHING WISDOM: *A Mind/Body Approach to Nutrition and Well-Being.* Hardcover 0-517-57636-8 (1991), paperback 0-517-88129-2 (1994).

Kat Duff. THE ALCHEMY OF ILLNESS. Paperback 0-517-88097-0 (1993).

Noela N. Evans. MEDITATIONS FOR THE PASSAGES AND CELE-BRATIONS OF LIFE: *A Book of Vigils.* Hardcover 0-517-59341-6 (1994), paperback 0-517-88299-X (1995).

Burghild Nina Holzer. A WALK BETWEEN HEAVEN AND EARTH: *A Personal Journal on Writing and the Creative Process.* Paperback 0-517-88096-2 (1994).

Greg Johanson and Ron Kurtz. GRACE UNFOLDING: *Psychotherapy in the Spirit of the Tao-te ching.* Hardcover 0-517-58449-2 (1991), paperback 0-517-88130-6 (1994).

Marcia and Jack Kelly. SANCTUARIES—THE NORTHEAST:
A Guide to Lodgings in Monasteries, Abbeys, and Retreats of the United States. Paperback 0-517-57727-5 (1991).
——SANCTUARIES—THE WEST COAST AND SOUTHWEST.
Paperback 0-517-88007-5 (1993).
——ONE HUNDRED GRACES: *Mealtime Blessings*, eds., with calligraphy by Christopher Gausby. Hardcover 0-517-58567-7 (1992),
paperback 0-517-88230-2 (1995).
Barbara Lachman. THE JOURNAL OF HILDEGARD OF BINGEN.
Hardcover 0-517-59169-3 (1993), paperback 0-517-88390-2 (1995).
Katharine Le Mée. CHANT: *The Origins, Form, Practice, and Healing Power of Gregorian Chant.* Hardcover 0-517-70037-9 (1994).
Gunilla Norris. BEING HOME: *A Book of Meditations.* Hardcover
0-517-58159-0 (1991).
——BECOMING BREAD: *Meditations on Loving and Transformation.*
Hardcover 0-517-59168-5 (1993).
——SHARING SILENCE: *Meditation Practice and Mindful Living.*
Hardcover 0-517-59506-0 (1993).
——JOURNEYING IN PLACE: *Reflections from a Country Garden.*
Hardcover 0-517-59762-4 (1994).
Ram Dass and Mirabai Bush. COMPASSION IN ACTION:
Setting Out on the Path of Service. Paperback 0-517-88500-X (1992).
Rabbi Rami M. Shapiro. WISDOM OF THE JEWISH SAGES:
A Modern Reading of Pirke Avot. Hardcover 0-517-79966-9 (1995).
Richard Whelan, ed. SELF-RELIANCE: *The Wisdom of Ralph Waldo Emerson as Inspiration for Daily Living.* Paperback 0-517-58512-X
(1991).